teach yourself®

ethics

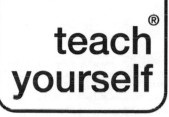

ethics
mel thompson

For UK order enquiries: please contact Bookpoint Ltd, 130 Milton Park, Abingdon, Oxon, OX14 4SB. Telephone: +44 (0) 1235 827720. Fax: +44 (0) 1235 400454. Lines are open 09.00–17.00, Monday to Saturday, with a 24-hour message answering service. Details about our titles and how to order are available at www.teachyourself.co.uk

For USA order enquiries: please contact McGraw-Hill Customer Services, PO Box 545, Blacklick, OH 43004-0545, USA. Telephone: 1-800-722-4726. Fax: 1-614-755-5645.

For Canada order enquiries: please contact McGraw-Hill Ryerson Ltd, 300 Water St, Whitby, Ontario, L1N 9B6, Canada. Telephone: 905 430 5000. Fax: 905 430 5020.

Long renowned as the authoritative source for self-guided learning – with more than 50 million copies sold worldwide – the **teach yourself** series includes over 500 titles in the fields of languages, crafts, hobbies, business, computing and education.

British Library Cataloguing in Publication Data: a catalogue record for this title is available from the British Library.

Library of Congress Catalog Card Number: on file.

First published in UK 1994 by Hodder Education, 338 Euston Road, London, NW1 3BH.

First published in US 1994 by The McGraw-Hill Companies, Inc.

This edition published 2006.

The **teach yourself** name is a registered trade mark of Hodder Headline.

Copyright © 1994, 2000, 2003, 2006 Mel Thompson

Typeset by Transet Limited, Coventry, England.
Printed in Great Britain for Hodder Education, a division of Hodder Headline, 338 Euston Road, London, NW1 3BH, by Cox & Wyman Ltd, Reading, Berkshire.

The publisher has used its best endeavours to ensure that the URLs for external websites referred to in this book are correct and active at the time of going to press. However, the publisher and the author have no responsibility for the websites and can make no guarantee that a site will remain live or that the content will remain relevant, decent or appropriate.

Hodder Headline's policy is to use papers that are natural, renewable and recyclable products and made from wood grown in sustainable forests. The logging and manufacturing processes are expected to conform to the environmental regulations of the country of origin.

Impression number   10 9 8 7 6 5 4 3 2 1
Year   2010 2009 2008 2007 2006

contents

'What should I do?'

'How do I know what is right?'

These basic questions are the starting point for ethical debate, for ethics is about moral choices. It is about the values that lie behind them, the reasons people give for them and the language they use to describe them. It is about innocence and guilt, right and wrong, and what it means to live a good or bad life. It is about the dilemmas of life, death, sex, violence and money. It explores human virtues and vices, rights and duties.

To be interested in ethics is to be interested in life! Each day we are bombarded with news of personal choices and their consequences, from the sexual proclivities of the famous to the violence and tragedy of war, and from the sight of those who are starving in an otherwise prosperous world to the casual vandalism and petty crime of inner city streets. The explanations given for these things may vary, from elaborate justifications in terms of a political or economic ideology, to the general complaint that traditional values have vanished. We cannot escape from moral issues, even if our own lives are untouched by painful decisions or tinges of guilt.

One day ...

Wondering whether ethics is relevant to your life? Let us take a look at one newspaper, on one day, and see what moral issues are to be found in it. The paper to hand as this present edition is being updated happens to be *The Independent*; the date, 6 January 2006.

A personal problem, a political crisis

The headline on the front page deals with the admission by Charles Kennedy, leader of the Liberal Democrats, that he is being treated for alcoholism. This raises questions about the degree to which the personal lives of those in public life should be open to scrutiny. Do different rules apply to politicians, compared with private individuals? Does everything depend upon their ability to do their job effectively? If someone is doing their job, should it matter if they are alcoholic, or divorced or gay? Isn't that just a personal matter? What responsibility do the media have in dealing with such issues?

Binge-drinking blamed for increase in liver cirrhosis across Britain

Should the government try to curb the drinking habits of private citizens? Do you take action on the basis of the needs of society as a whole, even if that appears to deprive individuals of the right to live as they choose? But when does a personal choice become a moral issue? Should society be expected to pay for medical care for those who, by their own choice, ruin their health? We shall see later that there is often a difficult balance to be struck between the rights of individuals and the overall benefit of society.

Clarke may reverse cannabis liberalization after health fears

As with the previous issue, there is a balance here between giving maximum freedom to individuals to behave as they wish, and taking into account the needs and resources available within society. Does government have a responsibility to protect people from the effects of their freely chosen actions?

Carpenter who posed as priest for 25 years is finally defrocked

Exposed as a fraud because he was not ordained, this raises questions about whether actions are right or wrong in themselves, or whether they depend upon who does them. After all, many people may have been helped by this man. Does the fact that he was not ordained as a priest change the quality or effectiveness of that help? A spokesperson for the Church said 'There are conmen in every profession. Why should priesthood be any different?' What is the difference between a conman who performs well, and an authorized practitioner? Of course, if he had posed as a brain surgeon, he might have been found out earlier!

Is God the root of all evil?

In a double-page spread, Professor Richard Dawkins argues that religion is a form of abuse, and that God is man's most destructive invention. The complaint that religion can harm humankind has a long history, including criticisms made by Nietzsche, Marx and Freud. We shall need to look at how religion and religious ethics relate to secular ethics – is it simply a matter of reason versus superstition, or is it more complex? And if Dawkins judges 'God', by what absolute standards does he do so? Some might argue that a universal sense of justice or of 'the good' is the secular equivalent of god; an ultimate point of reference. But – to use traditional language – is 'God' to blame or are we, when things go wrong? And can reason alone explain some of the horrors of human behaviour, including those for which religion has been responsible? We need to explore the interface between morality, beliefs and values.

An individual tragedy, but spare us the pictures

Photographs of a woman balancing on a narrow fourth-floor ledge and then leaping to her death were published in a number of newspapers. Although it makes a dramatic story, there is a question about the morality of publishing pictures that could be distressing to her family and friends, as well as offensive to other people. The Press Complaints Commission has no specific advice to give on reporting suicide, but it is generally agreed that editors have a moral responsibility to consider the implication of all that they publish, including the possibility that images of suicide may encourage copycat behaviour. When does the right to know become the right to become a voyeur?

Women lead the fight-back against 'honour killings'

An article estimates that each year at least 5,000 women are killed by their relatives because they are said to have brought shame on their families. Such killings are deliberate and carried out with the full knowledge of the rest of the family and society. Often it is a matter of young women behaving in a way that is unacceptable to their own social group, but considered normal by the rest of society, e.g. anything from talking to a male neighbour to getting pregnant, demanding a divorce or rejecting the partner chosen for an arranged marriage. In a multi-faith and multi-ethnic society, who decides what is morally acceptable?

An elegy for lovesick cowboys

This is the headline for a review of the film *Brokeback Mountain*, which depicts the relationship between two cowboys and explores questions about the acceptability of homosexuality in American society in the 1960s. The film itself has been controversial, but – by a sensitive portrayal of the relationship – it helps to get beyond the stylized image of gay as opposed to straight relationships, drawing out the complexity of feelings. Do all good film producers have a moral slant to explore? Is it possible to draw attention to the moral dimension of human experience without appearing to 'moralize' about them?

The broken hearts of men

A review of *Oedipus Revisited* by Shere Hite, examines gender roles. Gender and sexuality have always been central to ethical debate. A key suggestion in this book, which raises a number of ethical questions, is the idea that boys who grow up with their mothers are better at relationships with women later in life than those who grow up with both parents, challenging the assumption that single parents place their children at a disadvantage.

In the age of Armageddon

A review of a book about the Cold War raises the many ethical issues about the threat to use nuclear weapons. Can such weapons ever be justified? Is it wrong to *threaten* to use overwhelming force, even if (by threatening to do so) you may avoid actually having to use that force? If a balance of power, guaranteed by the ability of superpowers to mutually self-destruct, achieves peace, does that make it morally right?

Morgan Stanley fires strip club bankers

Four employees were fired for going to a strip club while entertaining clients at a conference in Arizona. Although they went in their own free time, the bank has a rule that clients are not to be entertained in this way. This is part of its attempt to eliminate sexist behaviour, following a legal action taken against it by a female employee who claimed discrimination, and received a 54,000 dollar settlement. What limits, if any, should be placed on sexist behaviour? If all concerned freely and willingly choose to go to a strip club, and if the dancers and those who run the club freely and willingly make their living in that way, on what grounds should those who participate be sanctioned?

'Our duty to uphold the law admits no exceptions in wartime'

This quote, from a speech by Dick Cheyney, is in connection with the approval by President Bush of international communication intercepts (e.g. phone and e-mail tapping) of those thought to be involved with terrorism. There is an ongoing debate about the right of government to gather information by tapping phones and using other methods of data collection that would normally be considered illegal, in tracking the activities of individuals who are thought to be acting illegally or have connections with terrorist organizations. As with many similar ethical discussions, the issue is about finding a balance between the needs of national security and the rights of the individual to privacy.

Chocolate makers eat their words on king-size snacks

This is part of the debate about one-third of all children being obese, and the agreement with sweets manufacturers to cut down on the larger size bars. Should manufacturers be required to take the overall needs of society into account? If so, would cigarette manufacture be outlawed? Should people be free to choose what they consume, whatever the consequences?

Muslim Council leader steps into the ring with gay rivals

This short news item featured comments by Sir Iqbal Sacranie, who said that homosexuality was not acceptable, both on health grounds and with regard to the moral issues with which society is faced. These views were opposed by a gay rights campaigner, who found it strange that such comments should come from someone who had accepted a knighthood, since many of his fellow knights were gay. This not only raises issues concerning the difference between a traditionally Muslim attitude and that of the secular West, but also the assumption that you should be expected to agree on moral issues with others in your same station in life.

Work rest & play

A supplement under this title offers '20 ways to improve your life', but above the headline, in smaller type, it says 'Advertisement Promotion'. Much of the advice is general, but it is surrounded by references to the bank that has paid for the promotion, and one of the recommendations is to bank online. It does not actually say which bank you should go with, but the appearance on the page of the logo of a well-known Internet bank gives a broad hint, and the final page of the supplement shows a bulging wallet and the suggestion that readers should quit their existing bank. To what extent is it right to give general advice as the means of attracting customers? Does it suggest that the supplement offers more objectivity about what might be to the readers' benefit than is actually the case?

Sharon

Another supplement features the life of the Israeli Prime Minister, Ariel Sharon, following his sudden illness. It notes that he is regarded by President Bush as a 'man of peace' and yet links him with what is regarded by some as a Zionist war crime – the killing of Palestinian refugees in the Sabra and Chatila camps in Beirut in 1982. It is a reminder of the complex issues of war and political power, and of the responsibilities of political leaders.

These are the issues presented on that one day. A different newspaper would probably have included different ones, or taken a different angle on those included here. Notice, however, that there are fundamental ethical questions in all of them. To study ethics is to grapple with those questions and to examine the validity of the arguments used.

Not everyone is aware of ethics or subject to ethical scrutiny; in that respect, babies are lucky. They feel hungry, or dirty, or wet, and just scream until someone figures out what is wrong and gives them what they need. They do not have the intellectual ability to question how they got into their particular mess, or the steps they need to take to get out of it. They are not morally responsible. One essential difference between a baby and a mature adult is that the adult recognizes when there is a problem to be overcome, or a difficult choice to be made, takes action and then accepts responsibility. **Ethics is the rational discussion of that process.**

In this book we shall be looking at a variety of ethical arguments, from Aquinas to Nietzsche, Machiavelli to Hobbes and Bentham to Kant, testing them out as we apply them to a whole range of moral issues. But first we need to explore just what it is that makes something moral or immoral.

What makes something moral?

Many choices are a straightforward matter of personal preference, and the actions that spring from them are neither moral nor immoral. They only become the subject of moral debate because of the intentions behind them, their results, and the values – of society or of the individual – that they reflect.

Example

Someone asks you 'Shall I wear red or blue?' This is not a moral question and, unless they are going to a political rally, your answer will reflect no more than a preference for one colour rather than another.

BUT – What if the person who asks you is about to take a walk that will lead him or her across a field in which you know there is a particularly unfriendly bull? (Assuming that the bull is not colour blind and hates red!)

The answer now becomes a matter of moral choice. Shall I, out of hatred or mischief, suggest red? If the person is injured or killed, am I to blame? Is the bull guilty, or am I?

If the bull cannot help but charge when it sees red, can it be blamed for doing what comes naturally? On the other hand, if I have a compulsion to cause mischief, which makes it emotionally impossible for me to suggest the safer colour, can I use the same argument to claim my own innocence? If not, then what degree of freedom (psychological, emotional, physical) renders me morally responsible? And are we free, anyway, if every factor is fully taken into account? A close friend, seeing the glint in my eye as my lips frame the word 'red', might comment 'I just knew you'd say that!'

What if I know the bull is in the field, but refuse to suggest which colour the person should wear? Do I bear any moral responsibility for the consequences of withholding that information? Does it make any difference if I secretly hope that they will be hurt, or if I am indifferent? Am I less guilty by taking a passive rather than an active part in the decision?

This example shows that a central question for ethics is that of freedom. If we are not free to choose what we do, we cannot be held morally responsible for our actions.

But our freedom to choose is often limited by the choices of others, and our moral responsibility is therefore proportional to the degree to which our choice is significant. In this case, I take greater responsibility, because the bull was not free to choose whether or not to charge. Where freedom is shared more equally, a person's contribution can be seen positively ('aiding and abetting') or negatively ('contributory negligence').

Actions can be divided into three categories:

1 **Moral** – if they reflect a person's values and those of society.
2 **Immoral** – if they go against a person's (or society's) values.
3 **Amoral** – if they do not reflect choices based on values or social norms.

Of course, an individual may think that something is moral, even if the rest of society thinks it immoral. Doing something immoral is not the same thing as breaking the law. Actions can be moral but illegal, or immoral but legal.

Whether you think an action is moral or immoral will depend on your values and the ethical arguments you use to decide what is right. How many actions or choices are moral and how many relegated to the general 'amoral' category will depend on your moral sensitivity, the range of values to which you consciously subscribe, and whether you belong to a society which operates by definite rules and values.

Example

When faced with a restaurant menu, a newly convinced vegetarian with a residual passion for meat will have a greater moral dilemma than a cheerful omnivore. A hungry Jew or Muslim will have added problems if faced with nothing but pork, and for some Buddhists, Hindus and Jains, eating meat may go against their most basic principle of not harming other creatures.

- A crucial moral question for one person may be of negligible significance to another.

Issues that are morally significant usually have to do with relationships, agreements between parties, intentions and possible outcomes. The moral status of an action may therefore depend less on what actually happens than on the intention of the person who performs it and the appropriateness of what is done.

Example

A masked stranger makes you lie on a table, drugs you into unconsciousness, takes out a sharp knife and slices into your naked body. Is the action moral, immoral or amoral?

At this point you might well want to know if the person with the knife is a competent surgeon or a student of the Marquis de Sade! A description of the action itself is not necessarily the best guide to its moral consequences. You might therefore ask:

- Is this a qualified surgeon?
- Have I consented to this operation?
- Is it likely to benefit me?
- Have the implications of it been explained to me?
- If the person is not a surgeon, do I want him or her to continue? (It might, after all, be an emergency, and an unqualified surgeon might be better than none.)
- What are his or her motives for doing this operation? (Money? Genuine altruism?)
- If for motives other than these (e.g. sexual gratification) would I still want him or her to continue, if I believed that it would benefit me?

Facts alone do not decide whether something is right or wrong: 'People are dying of starvation' is not a moral statement. But if you add '... and you are doing nothing to help', then it becomes a moral issue, if the person addressed is in a position to help but does not do so.

Nuclear Power ...

A headline, highlighting a report published in March 2006 into the future of nuclear power generation in Britain, read:

'Nuclear Power is dangerous, expensive and unwanted.'

This may look like a moral statement, but it is not. It simply records an interpretation of facts that have been investigated. In order to turn it into an ethical argument about whether it is 'right' to go ahead with a new generation of nuclear reactors, one would need to say whether, and on what grounds, the danger and cost were worthwhile – a life-saving operation can be dangerous and costly, but people do not say that it is therefore wrong to carry it out! Whether it is wanted or not depends on the views of those consulted and the alternatives available – and that, in itself, does not make an ethical argument.

In other words, for an issue or an action to be described as moral, it needs to take into consideration human choice and intention. Simply presenting facts, however important they may be, is not the same thing as framing an ethical argument.

What is the point of ethics?

In practical terms, the study of ethics can offer two things. First of all, it helps one appreciate the choices that others make, and evaluate the justification they give for those choices. But secondly, it involves a reflective sharpening of one's own moral awareness – a conscious examination of values and choices, of how these have shaped one's life so far, and (more importantly) of how they can be used to shape the future.

You already know far more about ethics than you might realize, for although 'Ethics' is a branch of philosophy with a long history of debates, its own special terminology and standard arguments, it is based on principles which, consciously or unconsciously, people use all the time in deciding what to do. You do not have to know the term 'utilitarian' in order to see the sense in wanting to choose what promises to give the greatest benefit to the greatest number of people. Therefore, although this book will outline ethical theories and the terms used in ethical debate, they will be examined in the context of actual dilemmas. Some moral choices are clear-cut; others are more problematic. It is by looking at the problematic ones that we start to appreciate the issues involved in ethical debate.

A situation

In November 1999, the former pop star Gary Glitter pleaded guilty to charges of making indecent photographs of children, when it was found that he had downloaded more than 4,000 obscene photographs from the Internet. This had been done privately, and only came to light when he took his computer to be repaired, and the images were discovered on its hard drive.

At the same time, he was accused of having had under-age sex with a girl of 14, who had been 'besotted' with him 20 years earlier, and with whom he had gone on to have a long-term relationship. She had sold her story to a tabloid newspaper for £10,000, but had been promised £25,000 by the newspaper if Glitter was convicted. Glitter was acquitted, once it emerged that she had been paid for her story. The judge said that, because of this 'highly reprehensible' deal, the jury had to regard her evidence with 'the very greatest care'.

This illustrates some general ethical considerations:

• Should you be held legally or morally responsible for an activity carried out in private (e.g. downloading obscene material from the Internet)?

• Who is morally responsible for pornographic material, the person who has produced it, the person who sells it, or the person who views or reads it?

• Should accepting money for a story alter the moral or legal status of the events described?

• Should there be a time limit on the lodging of complaints? In other words, quite apart from any legal considerations, is it morally right to decide, 10 or 20 years later, to raise a matter about which one has previously remained silent?

In the autumn of 2005, however, Glitter was arrested in Vietnam, accused of having sex with two under age girls, to whom he claimed to have been giving English lessons. In Vietnam, sex with a child under the age of 13 counts as statutory rape (i.e. rape, even if the young person is a willing participant), and carries the death sentence. However, Glitter was charged with the lesser crime of having molested the girls.

• Newspaper reports in 2005 tended to relate the earlier charges brought against him in 1999. Is it possible to assess a person's actions fairly if one either does or does not know their history?

Although protesting his innocence, and having paid compensation to the girls' families, as a result of which they wrote to the court asking for charges to be dropped, Glitter was sentenced to three years in gaol (the minimum sentence available for this crime) in February 2006.

• If compensation is paid, and the 'victim' asks for charges to be dropped, is it right to continue with a trial?

• However, if financial compensation is deemed sufficient, might this not allow those who can afford it to avoid responsibility for their actions?

In practice, ethics tends to start by observing the moral choices people make and the reasons they give for them. From these it produces theories about what is, or should be, the basis for moral choice. It then returns to actual situations, to see whether the theories help to make sense of the moral issues and to come to conclusions about matters of right and wrong. In doing this, ethics follows scientific method, for scientific hypotheses are framed as a result of observations, but are then tested out against subsequent evidence to see if they are adequate.

What price integrity?

Maturity is about taking responsibility for your own life and taking rational decisions that reflect personal values. In one sense, the whole of ethics is about maturity: what it is to think and act in a way that reflects the full stature and integrity of a rational human being.

But the touchstone of maturity is personal integrity – applying basic values to the decision-making process, and therefore living in a way that allows your personality to be expressed in what you do. But what price integrity? One of the hazards of taking ethics seriously, and of trying to live up to personal values, is that one may have to take the consequences. Think about those people who are determined to live with integrity; do they necessarily have the most comfortable or hassle-free life? Those who risk their own lives in order to save others? Those who publicly expose corruption? Those who campaign for human rights in a country where they are systematically denied?

There is always a temptation to compromise principles for the sake of an easy life, but often it is a matter of scale. If a moderately well-off person is offered a quick, risk-free way of making £10 through some morally dubious scheme, he or she might well refuse. But what if the same scheme involved millions of pounds? If it promised to benefit not just that person but many other people as well? When the stakes are very high, integrity (and the morality that it entails) becomes expensive!

Example
Let us look at an example connected with the two great motivators, sex and money. If you were to be offered £50 to have sex with someone you do not particularly like, you could well afford to take a moral line (e.g. that, as a matter of principle, you will only have sex with someone you like, and that you will certainly not set aside that principle, and therefore your integrity, for the sum of £50). You therefore decline the offer.

But what if you were desperate and hungry? What if you were on the streets (literally) with no means of support? Compared with the need for food, shelter and £50, sex might be regarded as an inconvenient necessity of survival. You could argue that your integrity requires that your own survival, and perhaps that of other people who depend on you, should take precedence over your sexual preferences. There are many places where prostitution is undertaken for just such reasons. How does that change the moral nature of the act?

Or change the scale of rewards on offer:

There is someone who has fallen in love with you, but you do not find him or her attractive. On the other hand, he or she is wealthy. This relationship will provide you with all that you have ever dreamed of. Might it not be worth a little pretence? Might you not feel that you really could 'fake it' – for years if necessary – for the sake of all that? Might it not be possible, you argue, justifying your decision, that you will eventually get to like this wealthy partner?

The crucial test, however, is the choice between integrity and survival; to choose death rather than loss of integrity is the basic question behind every martyrdom, from Socrates, through centuries of religious persecution, to those who agree to give testimony against criminals or terrorists, knowing that they risk their lives doing so.

Rights and responsibilities

So far we have been looking at individual moral choices, but there is another side to ethics. Much discussion in ethics is about the rights that a person should have – in other words, what they can reasonably expect society to do for them, and what they are expected to contribute to society in return. These are embodied in, for example, the United Nations Universal Declaration of Human Rights. We assume that, in a civilized society, people will be treated in a way that respects their basic needs (as in the American Constitution) for life, liberty and the pursuit of happiness. Where there are gross violations of these basic rights, we may recoil in horror. We say, 'It should not be allowed!' but are then forced to recognize that there may be nobody able to enforce those standards – that torture, execution or genocide is allowed in that place. Innocent people are allowed to be killed. Society does not act to impose a moral standard, either because it cannot, or because it will not.

Looking at society as a whole we can ask:

- What rights should you have?
- What responsibilities should you accept?
- Do you have a duty to fulfil a certain role in society?

In other words, what can we expect of other people, and what can they expect of us? What is it that makes a society 'civilized'?

Not all rules imposed by society are necessarily moral. In Britain a person is required drive on the left-hand side of the road. In the United States, the same person is required to drive on the right. That is a social convention, so obeying it is not a matter of morality. Social etiquette and convenience are not the same thing as social morality, even though they can influence behaviour. They only become the subject of moral debate when they concern matters of value, and imply general views about the purpose and nature of human life.

For reflection

In Kigali, Rwanda, on 24 April 1998, 22 people found guilty of genocide in the 1994 civil war were executed. Tied to posts in a football field, hoods were placed over their heads and 'targets' tied around their chests. Masked police ran from one to the next, pumping bullets into the targets, followed by another policeman with a pistol who gave the coups de grace at point blank range. This was watched by a crowd of many thousands, including women and children, who cheered as justice was seen to be done. Many of those watching had suffered and been bereaved as a result of the earlier civil war.

This took place in spite of calls for clemency, and was condemned by the United Nations, the European Union, the Vatican and human rights groups.

- Issues are never simple. How do you deal with the aftermath of genocide? Is there a place for retribution? What responsibility does the international community have to attempt to prevent the atrocities of civil war in the first place? How, in the confusion of a bloodbath, do you establish the sort of evidence needed for a fair trial? Exactly how do these executions differ legally or morally from those carried out on convicted criminals in the United States and elsewhere?
- Faced with the horror of what human beings can do to one another, instant or emotionally charged responses are seldom adequate. We need to assess the whole situation and look logically at the moral principles involved.

But genocide continues in Africa. In the Darfur region of Sudan, 300,000 people have been killed and 2 million have been displaced in a wave of ethnic cleansing. The rest of the world condemns what is happening, and provides aid for those who are still living in camps because they fear to return home and anyway have nothing to return to. But it cannot provide the protection they need.

In asking these questions, we have already started the process of ethical debate; we have asked about laws and rights and about the expected consequences of actions; we may sense instinctively that certain things are wrong, no matter what the circumstances, and seek to justify that conviction.

The art of living

A work of art is something created, by inspiration, by intuition, by a sense of balance, by a thoughtful use of the materials available. It offers more than a simple view of canvas, paint, stone or whatever else has been used. It may be minimalist, saying something through its very simplicity. It may be rich in symbolism or colour or form, complex and challenging. But whatever it is, a work of art is the deliberate product of a mind. It is an attempt to 'say something', to express meaning, or value, or hope. It is an attempt to probe beneath the banal and the superficial.

'Ethics' can be limited to a study of the meaning of moral language, but more broadly it is what used to be called 'moral philosophy': the study of moral choices and the arguments that spring from them. It is with this broader sense of 'ethics' that this book is mainly concerned. We can therefore say that ethics is about the art of living – seeing our life as the material out of which, through the choices we make, we are gradually constructing a work of art. We are more than flesh, bones and mortgages. We cannot be defined by our financial, work, social or political status. We are not simply consumers, nor unthinking slaves in society. We are not automata, programmed by genetic, environmental and social factors. We have feelings, intuitions, dreams, ambitions.

Our lives are continually being shaped by the choices we make, and by the convictions and values that underlie them. In this way, our lives are like works of art: they are what we make of them, and they 'say' what we are.

But what has this to do with a more usual list of moral issues?

- Should I have an abortion?
- Should I help these people to die if they are in pain?
- Should I join the army or be a pacifist?
- Should I take advantage of someone else's financial miscalculation?

You may choose to think through all these things (and this book will encourage you to do just that), but if you are faced with one of these choices, especially if the stakes are very high, your choice may not be based on rational thought alone. It will be based, in all probability, on the cumulative effect of many other choices that you have made over the years. Fundamentally, it will be based on what your life is actually trying to 'say'. It will be based on the image you have of yourself and your (perhaps unconscious) convictions about life.

As thinking beings, we have a choice. We can take what life throws at us and either react to it in a passive way, always remaining life's victim and refusing to take responsibility, or we can use it creatively.

01

free to choose?

In this chapter you will learn:
- to explore how much freedom we need to make sense of morality
- how reductionism challenges moral arguments
- how philosophers have tackled the issue of freedom and determinism.

What kind of freedom?

Nobody is completely free to do anything that he or she may wish. Freedom is limited in different ways:

- I may decide that I would like to launch myself into the air, spread my arms and fly. I may have dreamed of doing so. I may have a passion for Superman films, and feel certain that in some way it should be possible. But my physical body is, and will always be, incapable of unaided flight. To overcome that limitation, I must resort to technology.

- I may wish to be a famous and highly talented artist, musician or gymnast, but my freedom is again limited. It may not be physically impossible for me to achieve these things, but it requires such a level of experience, training and natural ability, that my chances of achieving what I want are severely restricted.

- I may wish to go to London and parade myself naked before Buckingham Palace. There is no physical limitation to inhibit me and no great skill required, but I am likely to be arrested if I do so.

These are examples of limitation to actual freedom. Whether by physical laws, natural abilities, or legal or social restraints, we are all limited in what we can do.

If I am to make a moral choice, I must be free to do, or not to do, the thing in question. It cannot be morally wrong of me not to fly, because I am unable to do so. On the other hand, walking about naked in public could become a moral issue – if it were argued that I gave offence by doing so – because it is a matter of free choice.

Determinism

Science is based on the observation of cause and effect, and the formulation of theories by which events may be predicted.

You look up and say 'I think it is going to rain'. You do not thereby imply that the weather has a personality, and that you guess that it has decided to enjoy a little precipitation. Rather, you make a comment based on the clouds, wind, dampness in the air, and on your observation of similar things leading to rain on previous occasions.

- The falling of rain is determined absolutely by certain atmospheric conditions.

- The fact that you may be inaccurate in predicting those conditions, and therefore the coming of rain, does not detract from the fundamentally determined nature of that event.

- Given certain conditions, it will rain; without them, it will not: the weather is determined. Its absolute prediction is theoretically possible, even if practically difficult.

The prediction of rain is possible because it is recognized that all physical phenomena are causally connected. Everything from the weather to the electrical impulses within human brains can be explained in terms of physical laws.

From the rise of modern science in the seventeenth century to the early part of the twentieth century, it could be said with some certainty that science was mechanistic. The whole world was seen as a machine, knowledge of which would enable mankind to predict and control the action of individual things. Even the process of evolution, as set out by Darwin, had a mechanistic and determinist basis. With the theory of natural selection, we have a clear example of the way in which change is forced forward through the operation of an impersonal law; that only those who survive to adulthood are able to breed, and it is they, rather than others of the species, who pass on their characteristics to future generations.

Although, in the general run of things, science still appears to be largely deterministic, some philosophers have made much of the fact that in quantum mechanics, for example, things at a sub-atomic level happen in a random way. Overall trends can be seen, but the action of individual particles cannot be predicted. At that sub-atomic level, the very act of observing some phenomena causes them to change, so it is not possible to formulate and test out physical laws with quite the crude certainty that prevailed in the nineteenth century.

Nevertheless, overall, including the spheres of sociology and psychology (which explore issues that are morally significant) science has retained a largely determinist viewpoint. There is a general acceptance that all events (including human action) may be explained in terms of prior events, which are considered to have caused them. And in the case of human action, this may be explained to a significant extent at least, in terms of the effect of environment or upbringing on the individual.

Example

A car swerves across the road and collides with a tree, killing the driver.

Why did the car swerve? Did a tyre burst? If so, how worn was it? Was there a fault in its manufacture? Was there a steering fault in the car? If so, was there a design fault? (Accidents in which the harm done is made worse through a design fault can lead to the manufacturer being prosecuted, as having contributed to that overall harm.)

What if you trace everything back, from the skill of the driver, to the food that he or she has been eating (was the driver faint? sick? drunk?), to whether the tree should have been planted so close to the road? The driver may have had control over some of these things, but not over others. Yet everything that has ever happened contributes in some way to each event. Is anyone to blame? What if the road had not been built? What if cars had not been invented?

If we had total knowledge, everything would be seen to fit a seamless pattern of cause and effect. But the experience of that event (for the driver before dying and for those who know him, or witness the crash) will be different. People may wish that other decisions had been made. They may feel guilty. There is an inescapable sense that events are influenced by human choice. Without that, there would be no morality.

We may be socially or psychologically predisposed to act in a certain way, as a result of upbringing or environment. Our genetic make-up may give a predisposition to violence, depression, schizophrenia or our particular sexual orientation. Does that imply that we take no responsibility for these things?

If a direct causal link could be shown, then the case for determinism in these areas of life would be strengthened. On the other hand, whereas physical traits (e.g. the colour of one's eyes) are 100 per cent due to heredity, studies of twins have suggested that behavioural factors, such as homosexuality, can have a heredity factor as low as 31 per cent. This illustrates what common sense would suggest, that there are other factors as well as our genes that influence our behaviour. This does not, however, disprove a claim that everything is determined. It merely shows that *no one factor alone* can be shown to determine the final result, but *taken together* they do so, each contributing something to the determinist equation.

Example

With advances in genetics, it has become widely recognized that many features of life, from sexual orientation to the predisposition to certain illnesses, could be detected via one's DNA. Thus, for example, insurance companies or mortgage lenders could require a genetic test to assess a person's likely future health. But what are the implications of such information?

Take homosexuality as an example:

- If homosexuality is genetically determined, would that imply that one's sexual preferences are not a matter for moral debate?

- For those who are anxious about their sexual orientation, it may alleviate a sense of guilt, instilled by social or religious opposition to homosexuality, for it is difficult to see how a person can be blamed for his or her genetic constitution.

- If a simple blood test could show homosexual orientation, and if that test could be carried out on a foetus early in pregnancy, would that be a sufficient reason for abortion, if the parents felt that they did not want homosexual offspring? If so, on what moral grounds?

- If varieties of behaviour (whether sexual or otherwise) are due to genes, should all forms of behaviour be accepted as of equal value? If not, then on what basis do you hold that some forms of behaviour are right and others wrong?

Even if genetic determinism were proved, that would not in itself remove all these moral issues.

These things may influence our freedom, but not necessarily *the freedom of our will*. We may *believe* we are free to choose, even if the psychologist, sociologist or behavioural geneticist claims to know better.

Reductionism

Reductionism is a philosophical rather than an ethical problem, but it is relevant because it claims to render moral language, and the whole idea of personal freedom, meaningless.

I raise my arm, reaching out to pick up a pen. What is actually happening?

- The muscles contract due to a chemical change.

- That chemical change is brought about through stimuli passing through nerve cells.
- The tiny electrical impulses in the nerves originate in the brain.
- The brain contains many millions of tiny circuits. For every movement of the body and thought passing through the mind, there is the corresponding electrical impulse in the brain.

If you pass an electric charge across my brain, I will twitch my muscles involuntarily. If the blood supply to part of the brain is cut off, those brain cells will die, and as a result parts of my body will cease to operate normally (as happens when someone has a cerebral thrombosis). I may not be aware that the damage is in my brain; all I will know is that my leg will not work.

Now this leads a reductionist to claim that the thoughts we have are 'nothing but' electrical impulses. Freedom of the will is therefore an illusion in two ways – firstly, it is theoretically possible to predict any choice, and secondly, that choice is actually nothing more than a set of electrical impulses that follow the laws of physics. Against this one could argue that such reductionism is like saying that a book is nothing other than a collection of letters printed on paper, or that a painting is nothing but spots of pigment on canvas. Whatever physical analysis a reductionist may offer, my experience of the book or of the painting is of something *more than* their material bases.

For moral choice (and therefore ethics) to make any sense, I have to believe that a person is *more than* determined electrical impulses. Yet there is nothing I can do that does not also involve the operation of my brain and, however many life-support systems I may be plugged into, once my brain is dead I am, in a physical sense at least, no more.

If a person accepts that all physical processes are causally determined, and that all personal choices and moral decisions can be reduced to electrical impulses in the brain, then ethics is meaningless. Our apparent freedom is an illusion caused by our failure to perceive the significance of brain activity.

A reductionist view also drains moral language of any valid meaning. A philosophical movement called **logical positivism**, which was influential in the early part of the twentieth century, took the view that statements had a valid meaning only if they were true by definition, or if they could be shown to be true by observation. 'Two plus two equals four' would make sense, because it is a matter of mathematical definition. 'There is a tree in the garden' would also mean something; that, if you were to look out into the garden, you would see a tree. But the statement 'It is wrong to kill' is neither a definition, nor could you find anything in the world 'out there' corresponding to the word 'wrong'. On this test, morality is meaningless, because it deals with choices and values, rather than with simple facts.

Therefore the *only* valid form of ethics for a reductionist is descriptive ethics – saying what in fact happens in different societies. To say that any such things are right or wrong, remains meaningless.

Notice why it is important to think clearly about reductionist and determinist claims:

- A determinist says that all decisions are the result of prior factors. If determinism is true, we are not free to choose what to do. We therefore deserve neither praise nor blame for our actions. We do not have to know all the causes to take a determinist view – we just have to believe that there are sufficient causes.
- A reductionist claims that all talk about moral choice is really about electrical impulses in the brain. A reductionist therefore has little to say in moral debates.
- We cannot be told that we ought to do something, unless we can do it. Freedom is the basis of all moral argument.

Freedom and the State

In the discussion so far, we have been looking in a rather abstract way at whether or not a person is free to decide how to act. But in practical terms, even if we feel that we are free, we are actually constrained by the legal and social rules of the society within which we live.

If we are caught breaking a law, we are punished. If we are not caught, we may still feel guilty. Freedom is not simply a matter of biology, but of social and political life. If a person joins in a demonstration in favour of greater freedom, he or she is unlikely to be concerned about whether there can be a scientific explanation for each muscular action as he or she walks forward, but more likely to be campaigning for social or political freedom and restoration to the individual of choices presently prohibited by some authority.

But should every individual be free to choose exactly how he or she should live? In a particular country people need to decide whether they will all drive on the right or the left: otherwise there will be chaos on the roads. Common sense dictates that an individual should not have the freedom to drive on the other side. But should everyone automatically have a right to take part in the democratic process to select a government? The answer to this is not so clear, because the results are less obvious.

Plato, for example, (in *The Republic* book IX) argued that most ordinary people did not have a strongly rational nature, and therefore needed to be constrained in what they did by being ruled by those who were naturally more rational. Philosophers alone, he thought, would have sufficient detachment to be able to legislate for the good of society as a whole. In that book, Plato presents the different arguments in the form of a debate between individuals. One of these, Thrasymachus, argues that laws are always made in the interests of the ruling class, and Glaucon comments that basically everyone would like to act from purely selfish motives, although all would suffer as a result of the ensuing chaos. Both of these views of human and social motives find echoes throughout the history of ethics. If most people live selfishly, social anarchy may result – therefore, some argue, you must have some established principles of right and wrong, to which people are required to give their allegiance.

Google and China

Google, the Internet search engine, announced in January 2006 that it had reached agreement to launch in China with a self-censored search engine, which would not permit Chinese users to look up information that the Chinese government considered sensitive.

Clearly, China is a huge market. It therefore makes sense for Google to want to operate there. However, it raises something of a moral dilemma. On the one hand, Google aims to give people information, so launching a self-censored search engine appears to go against its basic purpose. On the other, accepting censorship imposed by the political regime in China seemed the only way to become established in that country. Hence, it can be argued, some additional information via a censored search engine is better than none at all.

Giving people unrestricted access to information is to give them power, to encourage criticism and free thought. Many governments are threatened by that, and seek to determine what is 'good' for their people.

How much freedom does morality need?

Notice what moral language is not claiming:

- It does not claim that we are absolutely free.
- It does not claim that we are free to choose without any influence upon that choice (indeed, the more sensitive a person is, the more he or she is aware of such influences). It would be difficult to make sense of moral dilemmas unless there were some external constraints upon us – I struggle to know what is the right thing to do just because there are conflicting rules, loyalties or values, and I have to choose between them.

However, it claims that:

- Whatever may happen in terms of the mechanical side of life, we experience ourselves as free agents who can made genuine choices.
- Even if I admit the existence of external moral pressure to conform to some rule, I am acting morally only if I am in a position to think about and either conform to or reject the pressures upon me.
- Other people, observing my behaviour, may come to conclusions about my personality and general attitude towards life. Having done so, they may predict accurately what I will do in any given circumstance. That element of prediction, however accurate, does not in itself prevent me from making a free choice.

Free will

It is important to make the distinction between freedom in general and freedom of the will. I may look at various options, and think that I am free to choose between them. Someone who knows me well may, on hearing my decision, say 'I just knew you would choose to do that!' Is it possible for my will to be free, for it to be possible for me to weigh up all the factors involved and come to a genuinely free choice, and yet for someone else to be able to predict accurately what I will do? (And it will not be any use changing my mind at the last minute, or acting out of character, because those things too could be predicted.)

There is something intensely irritating about people saying that they know exactly what you will freely choose to do. This is because, in the moment of choice, we experience freedom.

Robots and computers may be totally predictable, but most humans are convinced that they themselves are not.

Consider the following cases of murder:

1 A thief shoots and kills a bank clerk in the course of a raid.
2 A husband or wife kills his or her partner after years of provocation and unhappiness.
3 A young man rapes and kills a girl whom he has not met before, on account of his particularly violent sexual urges.
4 A psychopath, unwisely released from a secure hospital to live in the community, kills someone for no apparent reason, does not attempt to conceal the crime, and shows no remorse when apprehended and charged with murder.

All four have killed another human being. But are they all equally guilty in a moral sense? Do any of them have genuine grounds for having the charge of murder reduced to that of manslaughter, for example?

1 It is assumed that the bank robber freely chooses to carry a weapon. Even if the actual shot were the result of being startled by a sudden movement, for example, that does not detract significantly from the general view that his act was murder, because he exercised freedom of the will in deciding to carry a loaded weapon.
2 With domestic murder, there may be a significant element of provocation. In that case, especially if the murder takes place in the course of a heated argument, it might be argued that the victim contributed to the situation that brought about the crime, or that (if sufficiently provoked) the murder took place while the person concerned was temporarily deranged. He or she might be charged with manslaughter on the grounds of diminished responsibility.
3 The issue in the case of the sexual murder is one of the freedom of the murderer to decide whether or not to act on his sexual impulses. If it can be shown that the condition is such that the person is not in control of himself or herself in certain situations, then psychiatric reports would be relevant evidence to bring before the court.
4 The psychopath is not in control of his or her actions, and does not respond to the normal inhibitions and rational constraints that apply to those who are sane.

Two situations

A woman suffering from schizophrenia stabbed and killed a worker in the hostel into which she had moved on discharge from hospital. She was found not guilty of murder on grounds of insanity. She claimed to believe that her victim was the antichrist.

In another case, a plea of manslaughter was accepted because 'his responsibility at the time of the killing was substantially impaired as a result of schizophrenic illness and/or psychopathic personality disorder' but that 'that mental state was likely to have been compounded by abuse of crack cocaine and alcohol.'

In the first of these, the plea for insanity seems straightforward, but in the second, there is the additional factor of having taken drugs.

- Does this mean that the person is morally responsible, because taking drugs (as opposed to his illness) was a freely chosen act?
- Is it reasonable to argue that someone with that degree of mental disturbance is able to take responsibility for choosing whether or not to take drugs?

In each case, the law accepted a charge of manslaughter. But is there any moral responsibility here? Does it lie with the killer, or with the society that allows killers to be in a situation where their lack of normal restraint can lead to such harm? In what sense was either of them free?

The issue here is one of freedom of the will. The psychopath is certainly not free to choose how to act. But is the man with the uncontrollable sexual urge free? Or the provoked wife? In each case we have to examine personal, psychological and social factors.

- In November 1999, the UK government unveiled plans to compel mental patients, cared for in the community, to submit to treatment. In one sense they were thereby removing a freedom, but it was actually a recognition that a person with mental illness may be controlled by that illness, and may therefore need an element of external compulsion. Research published in May 1999 had revealed that three murders and 80 suicides were committed each month in the UK by the mentally ill.

Suppose it is shown that there is more vandalism in areas of high unemployment. Does that imply that those who are unemployed are less able to choose freely what they do? Are social pressures enough to justify actions that can be regarded by other people are morally wrong?

In extreme situations, the pressure on a person is so great, that he or she feels that all freedom to choose what to do has been taken away. Unlike the psychopath, he or she is fully aware of the implications of what is done, but the need to act in that particularly way is overwhelming. This is loss of freedom, but not of freedom of the will. An extreme example of this is where death is the only alternative to a particular course of action.

Examples

Survivors of a plane crash in the Andes realize that they will die unless they get food. The only possibility is to eat the flesh of those of their number who have already died. Some refuse, and die. Others, reluctantly, eat the flesh, and many of them survive. The fact that some of them are able to make the choice not to eat, shows that the survivors can still exercise freedom of the will.

- But if the only option is death, freedom is severely limited.
- In these circumstances, can cannibalism be regarded as a morally acceptable choice?

In 2004 photographs were published showing the abuse of Iraqi prisoners by their American guards in Abu Grahib prison. One feature of the abuse was forcing men to perform actions of which they would feel ashamed. In such cases, the prisoner loses his freedom to act as he wishes, but not his free will. The fact that he can feel humiliation and guilt shows that he is acting against his will, and yet feels responsible for what he has actually done. In other words, the person feels guilty at having been forced to behave in a particular way, even if the only alternative was to accept whatever was threatened if he did not obey.

Interestingly, in such situations there may be a mismatch between what is observed and what is experienced. From the external point of view, the humiliated prisoner is innocent and a victim, since he was forced to act against his will. From the point of view of the person experiencing it, however, there may be a sense of guilt at having given in to the pressure to obey.

One particularly interesting example of the way in which freedom can be limited is that of blackmail or hostage taking.

In the case of blackmail, there may well be three different moral situations involved:

1 The blackmailer is trying to limited the freedom of his or her victim, which, in itself, is a moral (most would say 'immoral') act.

2 The person blackmailed may be required to do something that he or she regards as morally wrong.

3 But the person blackmailed may also act out of fear that some other action from his or her past will be exposed if he or she does not comply with the blackmailer's demands – the acceptance of responsibility for this creates the third moral dilemma.

Hence, the blackmail victim has three choices:

1 To admit to whatever past action the blackmailer is threatening to expose.

2 Go public on the blackmail, which may also involve an admission of the action for which he or she is being blackmailed.

3 Do what the blackmailer says.

Where hostage taking or blackmail affect the lives of others, the pressure to conform to the blackmailer's demands may be even greater, as in the following situation:

A situation

The manager of a supermarket is attacked in his home by thieves who demand that he takes money from his own supermarket and deliver it to them. His wife and two children are held. He is told that they will be harmed if he fails to carry out the orders he has been given.

- As he drives to the supermarket that morning, is he free to choose what he will do?

- Should he be morally blamed for taking the money and handing it over?

- If he informs the police and his wife or children are harmed as a result, who is to blame for that harm? Does he share the blame with the thieves who actually carried it out, on the grounds that he could have prevented it by following their instructions?

In February 2006, a robbery at the Securitas Depot in Kent, in which thieves made off with over £50 million in banknotes, posed exactly the same moral dilemma for the security manager, who was threatened at gunpoint and told that his wife and son, who were being held by the thieves, would be at risk if he did not co-operate. In the end, the robbery went ahead and no one was harmed physically. No blame of any sort attached to the manager, as it was recognized that, with his wife and son held, he was not free to do other than as ordered. A Securitas spokesman said, 'Clearly our thoughts go out to everyone who has been affected by this. It is a terrible thing for anyone to have to go through. We are particularly pleased … that no one has been hurt.'

Blackmail, whether of an emotional or physical variety, is the attempt to take from a person the freedom of his or her will. In fact, however, this does not happen. A person who is being blackmailed is still free to choose whether or not to conform to the blackmailer's demands. The difference is that the values expressed in and the likely consequences of whatever it is that the blackmailer is demanding, provides a person with a new set of criteria for deciding what to do.

In the case given above, if there had been no threat, the supermarket manager would have been in a position to balance the benefit of having a large sum of money against the likelihood of being caught stealing from his shop, and his sense of honesty and loyalty to his company. In such circumstances, he would probably choose not to steal, which is what happened on every other day as he went to work. On the other hand, if the choice is between the death of wife and children on the one hand, and stealing from the company on the other, then – even if he were to be caught, blamed and given a long prison sentence – he might judge it the right thing to do.

What is being taken away from him is the freedom to act without duress – not free will as such. The choice for the supermarket manager is therefore still a moral one.

A situation

After years of what was described in court as 'constant abuse, withdrawal of sexual relations and suggestions that he was not a real man and could not provide a proper home' a Cambridgeshire man battered his wife to death and buried her body in the garden. During his trial in December 1998, it was pointed out that her abuse and ridicule had destroyed his self-esteem, affected his health, and caused him to attempt suicide twice. On the night before the murder, he was said to have suffered a 'torrent of abuse'. He pleaded manslaughter on grounds of diminished responsibility, and was sentenced to six years imprisonment.

- In such a situation, to what extent can the husband be considered 'free' at the point at which he killed his wife?

Overall, we need to be aware that nobody is completely free, for we all act within physical, emotional, social, legal or political constraints. On the other hand, such constraints still leave scope for freedom of the will; if we make choices, if we decide whether or not to obey a rule, we are exercising what feels like personal freedom. The key question is whether that experience of freedom is real or illusory. And if it is illusory – if it can be shown that everything is determined and explicable – does that take away all personal responsibility?

02 what do we mean?

In this chapter you will learn:
- about the three different kinds of ethical language
- some key terms used in ethical language
- four basic theories about ethical language.

Three kinds of language

To make moral statements, or to argue about them in ethical debate, we have to use language, and much of ethical debate in the twentieth century ethics was concerned with the meaning of moral statements, and whether it is possible to show that they are either true or false. So once we have decided that we are free to make moral choices and to talk about them, we need to address the problem of the sort of language that we will be using to do so.

In ethics, three different kinds of language are used. We need to distinguish them carefully, and know which we are using at any one time, if we are not to become confused.

Descriptive ethics

This is the most straightforward form of ethics. It consists of descriptions of the way in which people live, and the moral choices they make. It simply presents facts. Here are some simple examples of descriptive ethics:

Most car crime is carried out by young men in areas of high unemployment.

The actual information may be correct or incorrect. It can be checked by referring to police records and employment statistics. But notice that the statement does not make any moral claim about youth and crime, nor does it say whether unemployment is a good or bad thing. It does not even make (although it may be taken to imply) a connection between crime and unemployment.

Muslim men may marry up to four wives, provided that they are able to provide for them and treat them equally.

Again, this makes no moral judgement, nor does it enquire whether it is possible to treat wives equally. It simply states the fact about what is permitted within a certain religious and cultural setting.

The danger with descriptive ethics is that it may imply moral judgements by the way in which information is presented, without actually explaining the basis on which those judgements are made.

Normative ethics

Ethics is concerned with ideas about what is right, about justice, about how people should live. It examines the choices people make and the values and reasoning that lie behind them. This is sometimes called 'substantive' or 'normative' ethics. Almost all moral argument, when it is concerned with the rights or wrongs of particular issues, is of this kind.

It is always wrong to steal.

This is a normative statement. It can be challenged by using another normative statement, e.g. 'No, I think it is right to steal on some occasions.' What you cannot do is challenge a normative statement by using a descriptive one. So a person who responds by saying 'but everyone around here steals if they get a chance' is not actually countering the claim that it is wrong to steal. Everyone may do something, but that does not make it right.

Descriptive ethics is about facts, normative ethics is about values. Both are needed, but it is essential to realize that you cannot argue directly from the one to the other: **you cannot get an 'ought' from an 'is'.** The attempt to do so was termed the 'naturalistic fallacy' by G. E. Moore in his influential *Principia Ethica* (1903).

Meta-ethics

It is also possible to stand back from moral statements and ask:

- What does it mean to say that something is right or wrong?
- Are there any objective criteria by which I can assess moral statements?
- What is moral language? Is it a statement about facts of any kind?
- Does a moral statement simply express a person's wishes or hopes about what should happen?
- In what sense can a moral statement be said to be either true or false?

Questions like these are not concerned with the content of moral discourse, but with its meaning. Now this fits in very closely with much twentieth century philosophy, which has explored the nature of language and the way in which statements can be shown to be true or false. Looking at moral statements in this way is called **meta-ethics**.

For a person coming to a study of ethics primarily in order to examine moral issues (rather than treating it as a branch of philosophy), there are two questions that might be asked of meta-ethical theories:

1 Does this theory ring true to my experience of making moral statements?
2 Does it actually help me to decide if something is right or wrong?

In other words, it may be correct in terms of linguistic analysis, but is it plausible and is it usable?

In this chapter we shall be looking at the meaning of some important moral words – some definitions of which were given by the ancient Greek philosophers, and which have been part of ethics ever since. But we shall also be looking at a number of meta-ethical theories. Although meta-ethics is a recent arrival on the philosophical scene, it is worth considering it now so that, as we look at ethical theories of the past, we may assess them in terms of meaning, as well as in terms of their moral conclusions.

Notice that each kind of ethical language has its dangers:

• The danger of descriptive ethics is that facts will be mistaken for values.
• The danger of normative ethics is that, in arguing that something is right or wrong, one may end up preaching rather than informing, recommending one particular course of action rather than setting out all the possibilities, consequences and values, and then allowing a person to make an informed and thoughtful choice.
• The danger of meta-ethics is that one may become so obsessed with the issue of meaning that it becomes impossible to offer any practical guidance for the difficult choices that people have to make.

Defining key terms

Moral language uses certain words, without which normative ethics would not make sense. One of these is the word **ought** – expressing a sense of moral obligation. We shall see in Chapter 05 that this is fundamental to the experience of moral choice. Another is **justice** – examining the rights of individuals in society and the way in which they 'ought' to treat one another. Justice has been an important concept in social ethics since the ancient

Greeks, and we shall look at it in Chapter 07, as part of our consideration of law and order.

The most basic word, however, is **good**. An action is judged 'right' or 'wrong' depending upon whether or not it is a 'good' or 'bad' thing to do. Before we can talk about moral values we need to know what we mean by this term. Actions cannot be right or wrong unless we know what we mean by goodness. But can it be defined?

You could try to define 'good' in absolute terms (that something is good in itself) or in relative terms (that it is good in its particular context). You can also define it in terms of what it can achieve – so an action is 'good' (and right) if the results of that action are 'good'. This would be a utilitarian assessment, as we shall see later. But we are still using the word 'good' and are therefore no nearer a definition.

Aristotle argued that something was 'good' if it fulfilled its purpose. On this theory, a good knife is one that cuts well; a good plant is one that grows strong and healthy. This formed the basis of what is called the Natural Law approach to ethics. According to this, everything has a natural purpose in life, and actions are right or wrong depending on whether or not they contribute to the fulfilling of that purpose.

A religious believer may say that 'good' is what God approves, and take a particular revelation (e.g. the Bible) as the norm for understanding goodness. Another may take a particular experience, or the life of a religious leader, as the starting point for understanding the 'good' life. The meaning of the word good will therefore depend, in part, on the source of the values that are called 'good', and that is not something on which everyone will automatically agree. It is a key feature of the intuitionist theory of ethics that 'good' cannot be defined (see below).

There are two important distinctions to be made when defining key words. Your definition can be **subjective** or **objective** (based on your own personal preferences, or based on external facts). It can also be **relative** or **absolute** (depending on individual circumstances, or something that should apply to all people at all times). Generally speaking, claims that are based on subjective preferences tend to be relative, and those that claim objectivity will also claim to be absolute.

Some theories

Ethics is concerned with what moral language means, what it does, and how it may be verified. We shall therefore look briefly at some theories about moral language. But first, before we can say anything about goodness, we have to decide whether or not we can actually know what goodness is:

Intuiting what is good

In 1903, G. E. Moore published *Principia Ethica*. In it he argued that goodness could not be defined, because it was unlike any other quality. In other words, if you try to say 'Something is good if ...' you will never find a definition that does not reduce and limit the idea of goodness, and therefore make it inapplicable to other things.

He therefore came to the view that to say something is 'good' is rather like saying that it is 'yellow'. You cannot define a colour, you simply point to it and say 'That is what I mean by yellow.' Try defining yellow for the benefit of someone who has never seen that colour – it cannot be done!

We know that something is 'good' by intuition – it is self-evident. We can define an action as being 'right' if it leads to a 'good' result. We can argue rationally about many moral problems – deciding which of various options will lead to the 'good' – but we cannot define that basic idea in itself.

> Everyone does in fact understand the question 'Is this good?' When he thinks of it, his state of mind is different from what it would be, were he asked 'Is this pleasant, or desired, or approved?' It has a distinct meaning for him, even though he may not recognize in what respect it is distinct. Whenever he thinks of 'intrinsic value' or 'intrinsic worth', or says that a thing 'ought to exist', he has before his mind the unique object – the unique property of things – which I mean by 'good'.
>
> (from *Principia Ethica*, chapter 1)

Although Moore himself did not use the term, this approach became known as **intuitionism** and was later developed particularly by W. D. Ross (in *The Right and the Good*, 1930, and *Foundations of Ethics*, 1939) and by H. A. Prichard (*Moral Obligation*, 1937). Prichard argued, for example, that the idea of 'duty' was not definable. Our obligations to other people are self-evident.

Now there would seem to be a major objection to the claim that we all intuit what is good. If what is good, and my duty, are self-evident, how is it that I can find myself in a quandary? Life is seldom straightforward, and I may find myself at a loss to know what I should do. Indeed, if people were never uncertain about what they should do, there would be no ethical debate at all! Ross overcome this difficulty by suggesting that I know what my duty is, but that sometimes that one duty conflicts with another, and a choice therefore has to be made. Ethical dilemmas are therefore the result of such conflicting duties. Even so, it would seem that there are times when people do not know what is right, and in a multi-cultural environment, where there is no single ethical tradition, people may not have clear intuitions about such matters.

A situation

Children have to be taught how to behave. A baby simply screams until it gets satisfaction; a growing child learns what is socially acceptable, and curbs its needs. Later in life, the adult appears to have an innate sense of right and wrong.

- If this is so, at what point does a person develop that innate sense?
- And how can you tell if that sense of right and wrong is not just the product of early training, now permanently enshrined in the unconscious?

Moore accepted that, in practical terms, one might judge an action according to its predicted results – trying to do what maximizes good in the world – but he differs from utilitarianism (see Chapter 04) in that **he will not allow that this assessment of results *defines* what is meant by 'good'.**

Emotivism

In the early part of the twentieth century there developed an approach to language that is generally known as logical positivism. It was an attempt to break down language into its simplest components and examine their meaning. This movement, inspired by the early work of Wittgenstein (as seen in his *Tractatus Logico Philosophicus*), is represented by the Vienna Circle of philosophers (including, for example, Carnap and Schlick) and became widely known through the publication in 1936 of A. J. Ayer's controversial book *Language Truth and Logic*.

The details of this approach need not detain us, except to say that it held that all meaningful propositions could be divided into two categories – **tautologies** (statements that are true by definition, e.g. all bachelors are unmarried) and **empirical statements of fact**, verified by observation. If a statement was not a tautology, and could not be shown to relate to externally perceived facts, then it was said to be meaningless. Now, on that basis, moral statements are meaningless, as they are neither statements of fact nor definitions. If my saying that you 'should' do something is neither a statement of fact nor a tautology, what is it? Ayer suggested that it is more like a command:

> The exhortations to moral virtue are not propositions at all, but ejaculations or commands which are designed to provoke the reader to action of a certain sort. Accordingly, they do not belong to any branch of philosophy or science.

For Ayer, moral judgements expressed the feelings of the speaker. Carnap (a member of the Vienna Circle) also thought that moral statements were commands (If I say 'This is the right thing to do, I really mean 'do this!') while Schlick thought that they were rules. Bertrand Russell argued that differences in values (and therefore differences in the moral statements that are based on them) are not a matter of facts, but of taste.

One response to the challenge of this approach is emotivism, represented by C. L. Stevenson's *Ethics and Language*, 1947. Once you strip the supposed facts away from moral statements, they are revealed for what they really are: expressions of a person's own preferences and emotions. **To say that something is right is really just another way of saying that I approve of it.** Stevenson therefore argued that 'good' was a **persuasive definition**. He was less concerned with what moral statements meant in themselves, and more with what they were for. **A statement has an emotive meaning if it is intended to produce a response in the person who hears it.**

There are two main criticisms of this approach:

1 A moral argument is not really judged according to the response it evokes, but on whether its claims are valid. Morality is not just about emotions, but may be discussed rationally.

2 To claim something is right or wrong is to make a policy statement. If I claim my moral judgements are universal (they should apply to everyone) they cannot be based on feelings, for I cannot say what others should feel, nor can I know what I will feel on other occasions.

To put it crudely, the emotive theory reduces morality to a set of cheers or boos, sounded off in response to experiences that are liked or disliked. Some people may indeed make moral statements on that basis, but it does not do justice to the rational character of moral arguments.

Prescriptivism

Whereas the emotivist asks what sort of effect a moral statement aims to have, a prescriptivist is more concerned about what is happening when someone actually makes a moral statement. R. M. Hare (in *The Language of Morals*, 1952, and *Freedom and Reason*, 1963) is the best-known representative of this approach. He asks about what a moral statement is meant to do, and concludes that a moral statement is 'prescribing' a course of action – recommending that something should be done, rather than just expressing the feelings of the speaker.

This may sound similar in practice to a command, but there is a difference. If I see someone about to steal a car and I shout out 'Stop that!' I am referring to that single incident. I am not suggesting that stopping doing things is a general principle on which I expect the person to base his life! On the other hand, if I say 'It is wrong to steal!' I am giving a piece of advice that can apply to future situations as well.

Nevertheless, prescribing and giving commands have something important in common: they both relate the content of what is said to the response that saying it is intended to evoke. Now this is certainly true of all commands, but is it true of all moral statements? I may discuss moral issues related to something that happened in the past. I may say, for example, that I believe the extermination of millions of Jews and others under the Nazi regime was absolutely wrong. That is a moral statement. But it is not directly suggesting that anyone with whom I am discussing that issue is actually in a position to respond to it in practical terms. I am not recommending a course of action. I am merely commenting on the way in which a certain action conforms to or goes against fundamental values that I hold.

An important point made by Hare is that moral statements should be **universalizable**. We shall consider this again in Chapter 05, when we look at the philosopher Kant. For now we need note only that this underlines the distinction between a command and a prescriptive statement. The prescriptive statement is making a general point; one that could be applied to situations in the past and the future, and to other people, as well as to the person to whom it is addressed.

A situation – the Bentley case

In 1952, Christopher Craig and Derek Bentley, following a break-in at a confectionery warehouse in South London, were cornered on the roof of the building by police. Bentley, having already been caught, called out to Craig (who was carrying a gun and being pursued by a police officer) 'Let him have it, Chris.' Craig shot and killed the officer.

The words used by Bentley were ambiguous. They could have been taken to mean that Craig should hand over the weapon, or that he should shoot. The court decided the latter, and Bentley was therefore found guilty of murder along with Craig. Craig, being only 16 at the time, was given a prison sentence. Bentley, who was 19 but had a mental age of only 11, was hanged in January 1953.

In July 1998, after a long campaign by his family, the Lord Chief Justice Bingham ruled that Bentley had not received 'that fair trial which is the birthright of every British citizen', and he was officially cleared of murder.

Quite apart from the issue of capital punishment, the Bentley case raises many ethical points:

- To what extent should someone be responsible for the actions of another, if it is judged that he or she incited that person to act?
- Should a person with a mental age of 11 be deemed responsible under the law? But, if so, of what could an 11-year-old be held responsible?
- In the heat of the moment, many things might be said or done that, on reflection, are unwise. Should Bentley's shout be considered something he freely chose to do, or simply a reaction to the situation he found himself in?

But notice that Bentley was considered to have 'prescribed' a course of action in saying 'let him have it'. He was therefore deemed responsible for what followed. The problem with the case lay in the ambiguity of what was prescribed. If that is so, we may ask:

- Is a person who makes a moral statement responsible for actions taken by those who accept it as something 'prescribed' for them to do?

This issue was raised again during a court case in London in early 2006 in which a radical Muslim cleric was accused of inciting acts of terrorism, and in legislation proposed by the UK government to limit criticism of religious groups that could be taken to incite hatred or violence. But notice:

- In such situations we have to distinguish between what is said and the intention of the speaker to 'prescribe' a course of action.
- The problem is that intention is subjective. If a speaker, whose words have provoked violence, claims that it was not his or her intention to do so, on what grounds can that claim to contradicted?

Naturalism and metaphysical ethics

Reading Plato's *Republic*, or Aristotle's *Nicomachean Ethics*, we get the very definite idea that, in spite of the various views that are put forward and examined, there is ultimately a rational basis for the idea of goodness and justice – arising from the nature of human life, or the needs of a society to organize itself in a harmonious way.

The implication of this is that there is an objective basis for ethics. On the other hand, some of the theories put forward in this chapter may suggest that there is no objective truth in ethics, but that everything centres on the wishes or feelings of the person who makes the moral statement. This 'ethical subjectivism' may seem appropriate for a society that has no single religious, social, political or cultural base, for people differ from one another so greatly that it is unlikely that they would share the same values, or choose to act in the same way.

However, when it comes to moral issues, people try to persuade others about how they should behave. They argue as though there were some objective truth about which different people could in principle agree. Indeed, if every moral choice is only right or wrong depending on personal and individual tastes, there would seem little point in discussing moral issues at all.

This situation gives rise to two other theories about ethical language. **Naturalistic ethics** is the term used for the attempt to explain a set of moral terms from the facts of human life. It is the positive side of what G. E. Moore criticized as the 'naturalistic fallacy' – the attempt to derive an 'ought' from an 'is'. To be fair, those who propose a modern naturalistic ethic (e.g. Richard Norman in *The Moral Philosophers*, 1983) do so on the basis of observed social relationships and in a way that gets round the simple application of Moore's criticism. But naturalistic ethics still seems to 'reduce' moral language to the task of giving pieces of social information'.

By contrast, **metaphysical ethics** insists that morality should be valued in itself, and should be related to our understanding of the world and of our place within it. It points out that moral choices are related to our general understanding of life, and the value that we find in it: in other words, to our 'metaphysics'.

An interesting exposition of this approach was given by Iris Murdoch in her book *Metaphysics and a Guide to Morals* (Penguin, 1994), where she points out that the moral choices people make in times of crisis are based on the values that they gradually build up in their habitual way of dealing with the world. Hence, we should not separate off the moment of moral choice from the rest of our experience of life and our interpretation of it. We make ourselves what we are, and our choices follow from that.

Summary of theories

- Intuitionism – one just instinctively knows when something is right!
- Emotivism – one uses moral statements to express feelings, and influence the feelings of others.
- Prescriptivism – one uses moral statements to 'prescribe' a general course of action.
- Naturalism – relating moral statements to particular features of the world and of social relationships.
- Metaphysical ethics – relating moral statements to a general understanding of the world, its meaning and its values.

Now it is clear that, when we use moral language, we may be doing a combination of some or all of these things. We may speak about something being good without knowing how to define what we mean by that word. We may speak out because we want to express our emotions. We may want to recommend a course of action. We may also feel convinced that there are objective grounds for saying that something is right or wrong.

It is important to be aware of these meta-ethical theories so that we recognize the basis upon which we are using moral language

– and hopefully save a great deal of misunderstanding and arguing at cross-purposes.

These theories suggest that we can take either a subjective approach to ethics (it expresses my feelings, my intuitions about what is right, or my prescribed course of action), or an objective approach (there are features of the world and of human beings that make this particular action right and that one wrong). In general, the more subjective approaches will produce criteria that are personal and individual. The more objective ones will produce criteria that are able to be applied universally.

'Is' and 'ought'

We have already mentioned G. E. Moore's 'naturalistic fallacy' argument that you cannot get an 'ought' from an 'is'. This reflected a position taken much earlier by the eighteenth-century philosopher David Hume. He pointed out that those who write on religion or morality tend to slip from matters of fact to matters of value:

> In every system of morality, which I have hitherto met with, I have always remarked, that the author proceeds for some time in the ordinary way of reasoning, and establishes the being of a God, or makes observations concerning human affairs; when of a sudden I am surprised to find, that instead of the usual copulations of propositions, **is** and **is not**, I meet with no proposition that is not connected with an **ought**, or an **ought not**. This change is imperceptible; but is, however of the last consequence. For as this **ought**, or **ought not**, expresses some new relation or affirmation, it is necessary that is should be observed and explained; and at the same time that a reason should be given, for what seems altogether inconceivable, how this new relation can be a deduction from others, which are entirely different from it.

A Treatise on Human Nature, 1738

Hume, here as elsewhere, delights in debunking traditional religious and moral arguments. But he highlights a feature of moral argument that is absolutely crucial, and which links with our discussion of the nature of religious language.

The logical positivists argued that, since they were neither tautologies nor matters that could be proved true or false with reference to evidence, moral statements were meaningless. We looked at the reactions to this claim – principally in pointing to the emotive and prescriptive approaches to understanding what moral language was about. In effect, the logical positivists were restating Hume's point. Although based on facts, moral language goes beyond them. In the crudest sense this is simply the 'just because everyone else does it, does not make it right' argument.

To what extent, then, can moral judgements be based on facts? If facts have to be interpreted, or if something more is needed before we can move from saying 'is' to saying 'ought', then we need to make clear what that extra is. This issue is illustrated most clearly by the 'natural law' approach to ethics, to which we now turn.

03

is it natural?

In this chapter you will learn:
- about the origins and basis of natural law
- about challenges to the natural law approach
- to consider whether people are naturally good or bad.

So far we have looked at whether or not we are free to decide how to act, and what it means to make a moral statement. But moral statements, even if they are expressing a personal preference or recommending a course of action, make claims about 'right' and 'wrong'. If moral issues cannot be settled simply by checking facts, what other rational or objective basis can there be to argue that something is 'right' or 'wrong'?

In the chapters that follow we shall be looking at some attempts to find a basis for moral judgements: to justify them in terms of the expected results of an action, or the experience of a sense of 'ought', or the desire for personal growth, or the needs of society. But first we shall examine a theory which claims that everything is created to a particular design and for a particular purpose, and that fulfilling that purpose is the 'good' to which everything aims. It is called the theory of **natural law**.

The natural law approach was developed by Thomas Aquinas in the thirteenth century, and became a central feature of Catholic moral thinking. To find its roots, however, we need to go back to the fourth century BCE and the philosophy of Aristotle.

Does it have a 'final cause'?

Aristotle distinguished between 'efficient causes' and 'final causes': an efficient cause is what gets things done, a final cause is the end product. A child grows up to be an adult. Aristotle would say that an 'efficient cause' of the child's growth is food and drink, but the 'final cause' is the adult into which the child is growing. Similarly, if I take a piece of wood and carve it into a statue, the efficient cause is the knife that I use, but the final cause is the image that I seek to create.

On this theory, everything (both every object and every action) has some final meaning and purpose (its 'final cause') and this is what determines its 'good'. If we understand what that final cause is, we will know what we need to do in order to achieve it. There are other important themes in Aristotle's ethics, including the idea of achieving a balance between the extremes of excess and deficiency, but the 'natural law' theory is based on this idea of final causes.

Aquinas used Aristotle's ideas to argue that the world was created by God, and that everything should therefore have God's ultimate purpose as its final 'end' or 'good'. To understand God's will for it, and therefore what is 'right' for it, you only have to look at the purpose for which it has been made. A good knife is one that cuts well: that is what it is designed to do. But how do you decide what is a good human life?

Aquinas argued that everything had its proper 'end', as part of God's providential ordering of the world, but humankind was special in that it was also given reason and freedom. Humans could therefore understand and choose whether or not to follow their proper 'end'. This he called 'natural law' – the rational understanding and following of God's final purpose.

Let us take an example that has been important within Catholic moral thought:

Example

Consider the act of heterosexual intercourse. (Sadly, we need to consider its 'final cause', although its 'efficient causes' tend to be more entertaining.)

- Its natural purpose is to fertilize an egg, which in turn will be nurtured within a womb to produce another human being. This process helps to maintain the human species.
- Given the physical contortions involved, it is difficult to imagine how copulation could occur by random chance in the course of normal social life! Sexual attraction and arousal is therefore the means that nature has supplied for achieving this particular end.
- Sexual arousal and the act of penetration are therefore the 'efficient cause', while the production of a new human being is the 'final cause' of the sexual act.

However, if it is only the final cause that determines right and wrong, then strictly speaking, in terms of sex:

- intercourse between members of the same sex is wrong (because it cannot result in conception)
- intercourse with those who are outside the age range for childbearing is wrong (for the same reason)
- anal and oral intercourse and masturbation are wrong (for the same reason)
- any attempt to frustrate the process of conception is wrong, because it tries to separate off the sexual act from its natural purpose.

In traditional Catholic teaching it is therefore wrong to practise contraception. Each sexual act should include the possibility of conception. Pope Paul VI's encyclical letter *Humanae Vitae* (1968) expressed it in this way:

'The Church ... in urging men to the observance of the precepts of the natural law, which it interprets by its constant doctrine, teaches as absolutely required that any use whatsoever of marriage must retain its natural potential to procreate human life.'

Sex within the 'safe period' of the woman's ovulatory cycle is generally permitted in Catholic moral teaching because the failure to conceive at that time is part of nature's limitation, rather than the result of a direct attempt to do something unnatural. The same applies to those who are past childbearing age, on the grounds that, by a miracle, conception might take place.

This example shows that 'natural law', unlike most other theories we shall be considering, gives the possibility of producing a clearly defined rule that can then be applied universally. An action is right or wrong in itself, without reference to all its possible consequences (e.g. an act of sex might result in the birth of a child who grows up to be a mass murderer; but that does not make the sexual act morally wrong, only regrettable!).

You may not always know what the results of your actions will be. You are therefore only responsible for the immediate consequences of your action, not for any secondary and unintended effects. This is sometimes called **the law of double effect**. It can be a surprisingly useful theory for those who wish to practise contraception without going against 'natural law', because if a woman suffers from painful or irregular periods, a doctor may prescribe 'contraceptive' pills in order to regulate her cycle. The fact that the hormone in the pills acts as a contraceptive is a secondary effect, and is not the intention of the original prescription. 'Natural law' morality is maintained: the doctor is right in his prescription, because it has the intended effect of regulating the cycle and relieving discomfort; the woman is right in having sex while taking the pill, because the pill is not a deliberate attempt to frustrate conception.

This example is not offered as a cynical attempt to undermine natural law, but to illustrate the problem of trying to find a single objective rule to cover a situation that may have many complex layers of meaning and intention. Natural law requires an 'act analysis' approach to moral argument – it breaks the situation down into the various acts involved and tries to establish the moral significance of each. In practice, a couple may have sex for many different physical and emotional reasons, but the natural law approach does not generally allow for these to be taken into account.

By contrast, the approach to the issue of contraception taken by other religious groups – along with most secular moral thinkers – is based on the expected results. It takes into account factors like the ability of the couple to provide for any children they may conceive. Globally, contraception may be promoted because of population problems in areas of poverty – again, an argument based on results. Because there are many factors to be weighed, the decision about contraception is generally left to the conscience of the individuals concerned.

Example

It was reported in 2005 that a rumour had been spread in parts of Africa to the effect that condoms did not prevent the spread of AIDS, and it was alleged that the rumour had been put about by those who were opposed to the use of contraception.

Two separate issues are raised by this:

1 There is a 'double effect' problem here. Is the condom used to prevent the spread of AIDS, but with a secondary and unintentional effect of preventing conception?

2 There can be few clearer examples of the difference between judging an action according to expected results (contracting or preventing the spread of AIDS), and as an act in itself (the frustration of the 'natural' purpose of sex).

However, the matter is never straightforward. It could be argued, for example, that the availability of condoms encourages promiscuity and thereby – on the assumption that they will not always be used properly or responsibly – the spread of AIDS. But to take that line is already to have accepted the principle that morality is determined by results, exactly what those in favour of the use of condoms are arguing.

Some features of 'natural law'

- The term 'natural law' should not be used simply to refer to the laws of nature, which form the basis of science. It is the result of applying **reason** to what happens in nature.

- As traditionally presented, the 'natural law' theory of ethics is based on the idea that God creates everything with a particular purpose in mind, and that people are therefore required to understand it and act accordingly. Hence, its authority tends to be religious.
- 'Natural law' can be examined quite apart from its religions interpretation, as a rational theory relating behaviour to the basic features of human life, its place within the world, and the basic requirements for its survival.
- It has the advantage that, once a 'final cause' is established, it may be applied to all people at all times. A natural law theory need take little account of prevailing social attitudes.
- It is not based on personal preferences, nor of guessing what the results of an action might be in terms of the happiness or otherwise of those involved – it is simply based on an examination of rational purpose. Potentially, it is a very 'clear cut' ethical theory.

Natural law supports other general views of moral behaviour. Aquinas (in *Summa Theologiae*) presented the four cardinal virtues – prudence, justice, fortitude and temperance (which had been used as a basis for morality by the Stoics) – as fundamental qualities of the moral life. The opposite of these virtues are the seven capital vices (often called the 'seven deadly sins'), which are pride, avarice, lust, envy, gluttony, anger and sloth. From a traditional standpoint of belief in God, one might say that the former allow a human being to fulfil his or her potential as a human being as intended by God, whereas the latter frustrate that intention.

But the issue of what is 'natural' is wider than Aquinas' theory, for 'natural law' is essentially about finding the rational principles upon which the world is made and which may therefore guide action. But many actions that may be described as natural are irrational and destructive, so further questions to be asked.

How do you decide what is 'natural'?

Science builds up laws based on observation. If something is observed that does not fit in with an established law, then either the observation is inaccurate, or another (as yet unknown) law has unexpectedly come into operation. Our understanding of the way in which nature works is therefore constantly being modified.

If this also applies to 'natural law' as an ethical theory, then we cannot establish fixed criteria for right and wrong – which was the aim of Aquinas and others who followed this line of thought – because our concept of what is natural, and therefore of 'final causes', will always be open to modification.

Natural law is about what life should be like, given a rational and purposeful creation, but that may not be what life is actually like.

Examples

It is natural for someone who is seriously ill to die. Does that mean that one should not interfere with the natural course of a disease by giving medicine?

In the natural world, the strongest animals often mate with as many sexual partners as they can, fighting off weaker rivals. Should there be selective breeding amongst humans? Is monogamy unnatural?

These examples suggest that there is no easy way to establish the 'final cause' that will enable us to say with certainty that we know exactly what every thing or action is for, or what part it has to play in an overall purposeful scheme of the universe.

The idea that the universe as a whole has a purpose and direction, and that it (and everything in it) has been created for a specific reason, is not a matter for scientific examination, but for religious belief. Those without such belief will not necessarily see a rationally justified 'final cause'. Indeed, one of the main arguments against belief in God has been the apparent pointlessness of suffering. Once pointlessness replaces purpose as a general view of the natural world, then the 'natural law' argument starts to break down.

Moral statements cannot be established by the observation of facts; you cannot argue from what 'is' to what 'ought to be' the case. When you record facts, you do just that; facts are neutral in terms of ethics. Once you make a moral statement, however, you bring in values and wishes, you recommend that something should be done, or you express feelings. These things are over and above the facts to which they are applied.

At first sight, the 'natural law' argument seems to argue from something that 'is' (the nature of the world) to what 'ought' to be done. It does this on the basis of belief in a creator God who guarantees that things have a purpose which suits their nature, and to which they can freely respond in a positive and creative way.

There are other ways of trying to link 'ought' and 'is'. In Eastern philosophy, the idea of **karma** – that actions have consequences that cumulatively influence the future – relates the state of the world to moral choices. But this gives only a 'hypothetical' command (in other words, one that says 'If you want to achieve X, then you must do Y') not an absolute moral command. To get an absolute command (or 'categorical imperative', as we shall see later) you have to presuppose someone who gives the command. Within the natural law theory, that 'someone' is God.

Applying 'natural law'

It is one thing to have universal principles, another to apply them to individual cases. This is often referred to as a 'deductive' method of moral argument – one that starts with general rules and then deduces the morality of a particular situation from them. This process may also be called 'casuistry'. Often regarded as a pejorative term (implying that the principle is applied in an unfeeling, contrived, or irrelevant way), the process is part of a common-sense approach to ethics. We have already looked at the 'natural law' approach to matters of sex and contraception, so let us continue that theme:

A situation

Two adults of the same sex are attracted to one another. They wish to express that attraction physically, to live together with the same legal and social support that they would receive as a heterosexual couple, to adopt children, and to bring them up in a family home. Is what they wish to do morally right?

- Until the 1967 Sexual Offences Act, homosexual acts between consenting male adults were regarded as crimes in Britain. They were then made legal for those who had reached the age of 21 (as opposed to heterosexual acts, which are legal from the age of 16). In some Muslim countries, following strict Shari'ah laws, homosexuality is punishable by death. By contrast, in Classical Greece, homosexual love was widely practised, and socially acceptable. There is therefore no universally held view about homosexuality and its place in society.

- Since homosexuality involves what used to be called 'unnatural acts', it is a particularly suitable situation against which to test 'natural law' as an ethical theory.

This is how a 'natural law' argument might view that homosexual partnership:

- According to natural law, the purpose of sex is procreation. Since homosexual acts cannot lead to conception, they are 'unnatural' and therefore wrong.
- On this basis, heterosexual acts within a stable relationship (i.e. one that will enable children to be nurtured) or celibacy are the only morally acceptable sexual choices.
- Because of this, there is no moral objection, according to natural law principles, to the couple living together, or feeling attracted towards one another. The only objection is to any physical sexual acts that may take place between them.
- Because they cannot form a 'natural' family group, a natural law argument would suggest that homosexual couples should not be allowed to adopt children, who 'naturally' thrive only with the benefit of both mother and father role models.

Against this line of argument:

- One might argue that the presence of sexual organs in a human being implies that he or she is designed for sexual activity and the conception of children – in which case, celibacy is as unnatural as homosexuality, since it is a denial of the complete natural function of procreation. If this is established, then it is illogical to accept a celibate partnership between those who are sexually attracted.
- Some people are naturally attracted by members of the same sex. They experience their feelings as completely natural. Any difficulties that arise are the result of social conditioning, not nature.
- Sexuality can be said to achieve three ends:
  1 physical pleasure
  2 the deepening of a relationship
  3 the conception of children

  of which only the third is precluded by homosexual relationships. But is not the search for pleasure and for deep relationships as natural as the conception of children? If a marriage is known to be infertile, are heterosexual acts between its partners therefore immoral simply because conception is impossible?

- Marriage is a social function, and promiscuity can be practised equally by homosexuals and heterosexuals. The fact that homosexual couples cannot marry does not preclude deep and permanent relationships.
- If a homosexual couple form a stable relationship, they may be able to offer children a home that is, at the very least, as valuable to their upbringing as one in which there is either a single parent, or a heterosexual couple with a bad relationship. Hence, it would seem illogical to discriminate in this matter.

The introduction of civil partnerships in Britain, in December 2005, was recognition that stable homosexual relationships deserved the same legal and financial protection enjoyed by heterosexual couples who marry.

In pointing out some of the ways in which the 'natural law' view of the homosexual couple's situation might be challenged, it is not intended to undermine the principle of natural law as such, but to show that there are some areas of morality – particularly where relationships are concerned – where it is difficult to consider morality mainly in terms of specific actions.

Example

In October 1999 a male homosexual couple from Britain were granted the right by an American court to be named as the legal parents of twin babies due to be born of a surrogate mother. Both men's sperm were used in the laboratory fertilization of a donor egg, but DNA testing was used later to determine which was the genetic father. The couple spent a total of £250,000 to arrange the birth, recruiting the surrogate mother through an agency in California. One lobby group representing the interests of 'the family' argued that to deprive a child of one of its natural sexual role models (i.e. a mother) should be considered a crime.

One of the partners said, 'The nuclear family as we know it is evolving. The emphasis should not be on it being a mother and a father, but on loving, nurturing parents, whether that is a single mother or a gay couple living in a committed relationship.'

Are we naturally good or bad?

The philosopher Thomas Hobbes (1588–1679), in his book *Leviathan*, saw the life of man in a natural state as 'solitary, poor, nasty, brutish and short'. He took the view that, left to their own devices, people are naturally greedy. They want freedom, but also power (which included riches, reputation, success, nobility and eloquence – all that might give one person an advantage over others), and the inevitable result of this is that they would struggle against one another in order to gain it. In such a society, everyone is judged by his or her power:

> The *value*, or WORTH of a man, is as of all other things, his price; that is to say, so much as would be given for the use of his power: and therefore is not absolute, but a thing dependent on the need and judgement of another.

Unbridled competition, allied to seeing everyone in terms of his or her power, may lead to social anarchy. Hobbes therefore argued that it was in the self-interest of all for people to set aside their claim to total power in order that they might live peacefully with others, for otherwise there will be constant danger of losing everything. In effect, he came down to a form of the 'golden rule' – do as you would be done to. He applied reason to human society, pointing out what was needed for society to function – but recognized that, without reason, people would be in a state of self-destructive greed and anarchy.

Such anarchy would not have been tolerated for long by Niccolo Machiavelli (1469–1527), who (in *The Prince*) argues that a ruler must know how to use his power and needs to be feared as well as respected by his people. His views on political power, and the measures that a person should be prepared to employ in order to gain and maintain it, suggest that in a natural state humankind is ruthless and competitive. Both Hobbes and Machiavelli see natural life as essentially a struggle for power and survival.

By contrast, Jean-Jacques Rousseau (1712–78) thought that people were born essentially good – as was everything that came directly from nature. He argued that, if the conditions are right, people will flourish and be morally good. Human nature is fine in itself; the trouble is with the way in which society is organized. If temptation is put in people's way, a certain number of them are going to fall for it. This way of thinking led many twentieth-century socialists to assume that, once the dictatorship of the proletariat arrived, a just society would be established and all would be well. It also finds expression in the caricature of the social worker who, defending a criminal, lays all the blame on the circumstances of his or her upbringing, thereby diminishing moral responsibility.

Another example of this positive attitude to the natural is Henry David Thoreau (1817–62). In *Walden, or Life in the Woods*, he saw God within all nature and everything as therefore inherently good. He argued that people spent too much time worrying about earning a living, and seeking for things they do not really need – leading lives of 'quiet desperation'. By contrast, he sought a far simpler and more natural way of living.

We shall be looking at some of these thinkers again later. For now we need only recognize that human life is complex, and that it is seldom possible to see what it would be like without the constraints of society. Opinion is divided:

• Are human beings fundamentally ruthless and savage, restrained and tamed by society, but liable at times to revert to their 'natural' behaviour?

• Or are human beings fundamentally good and caring, made antisocial and brutalized by society, but, given the right environment, capable of reverting to their gentler nature?

Points for reflection

• Looking at the items in any newspaper, consider whether you believe humankind to be more 'Hobbes' or more 'Rousseau' (to use an extreme form: more 'savages tamed by society' or more 'angels corrupted by society').

• What do these views suggest about punishment and reform?

• Should society have more rules or fewer?

• Should morality be left to the conscience of the individual, or imposed by society?

• Aristotle saw reason as the distinctive human quality. Was he right?

• John Stuart Mill (whose ethics we will look at in Chapter 04) pointed out that most of the things people are punished for doing (e.g. murder, rape) are common occurrences in nature. Should ethics be seen therefore as a distinctively human step away from the natural order?

• Watch a cat 'play' with a mouse.

So far in this chapter we have moved from a formal and rational view of nature – the 'natural law' argument of Aquinas and others – to a brief look at the more general question of 'naturalism' in ethics. But in modern times such questions have acquired a new context, for it is impossible to consider human nature – or nature in general – without taking evolution into account. We no longer think of fixed entities, but of directions of change.

Evolution, change and the natural law

If the whole world is in a state of constant change; if galaxies are moving outwards towards an unknown future; if stars are born and die, and planets spinning around them are vulnerable to their death and many other cosmic accidents; if life on planet Earth is a recent phenomenon and subject to a process of evolution – how can the purpose or goal of anything be fixed?

Darwin's theory of natural selection is not part of ethics. It is a scientific theory, based on the observation of species. It argues that those best adapted to their environment will prosper and multiply. Species that fail to adapt will eventually decline and vanish. It does not say that this *ought* to happen; it just observes what *actually* happens, and then seeks to provide a theory to explain it.

It is tempting, however, to create a morality based on evolution. Henri Bergson (1859–1941), in his book *Creative Evolution*, felt that you should act in a way that enables you to follow the stream of evolutionary life in the direction of the future, that you should do nothing to impede the progress of evolution. Herbert Spencer (1820–1903), in *The Principles of Ethics*, came to the view that the good is what gives pleasure. But he also considered 'the survival of the fittest' and was prepared to say that misfits, weaklings or those who are stupid should be left to their fate, and should not be allowed to impede the rise and progress of those who are more able.

In a way (although he did not link it specifically with evolution) this reflects the attitude of Friedrich Nietzsche (see Chapter 06), who spoke of slave morality and master morality, and felt that Christianity and democracy were holding back human progress by allowing too much consideration to be given to the weak at the expense of the strong, encouraging the attitude of 'slaves' rather than that of 'masters'.

Notice how very different this approach, which considers the development of individuals and species as a 'good' to be achieved, is from that of 'natural law'. In the latter, you look at particular actions and judge if they are right or wrong in themselves. Any theory of personal or global development – of evolution, in other words – looks at each decision and action in the light of the direction of evolution and change. What will this action allow me to become? What effect will this action have on the future of humankind? Such ethics is dynamic and forward looking – and it is based on results, not on the intrinsic value. The natural law approach was based on the idea of a permanent self, essence and therefore value. How does that square with a world in evolution, where humankind can look towards its future and choose what it wishes to become?

For reflection

Is morality the result of deliberately going against our basic instincts, as suggested by Richard Dawkins at the end of *The Selfish Gene* – 'We alone on earth can rebel against the tyranny of the selfish replicators'? Or is some sense of morality genetically programmed into us? Research on the behaviour of apes suggests that there may be the basics of morality – in the attitude of groups to individuals, and the support given by one individual ape to another. So, for example, animals that fight can 'make up' afterwards. Is this programmed into them in order to help the species survive in a competitive environment?

Looking at the development and survival of species in the wild, one important factor is communication and co-operation – hunting in packs, for example, or warning others of approaching danger. This at least opens up the possibility that morality, in more complex animals, is a survival mechanism and therefore perfectly 'natural'.

04

looking for results

Egoistic hedonism

Egoism

Egoism is the theory that, whatever we may claim, we actually do only those things that we believe will benefit ourselves. There are two ways of looking at egoism.

One could claim that – whether they accept it or not – people in fact act in their own best interests. A psychologist could argue, for example, that even those who appear to do things for the sake of others are in fact pleasing themselves in doing so. They may enjoy helping others, or they may delight in being thought of as kind and unselfish. Deep down they have a need to give themselves to others, a need to bolster their own sense of goodness by doing so, perhaps to cover some unacknowledged guilt. One could, therefore, be utterly unselfish for utterly selfish motives.

The jibe that the unselfish person is a 'do-gooder' may imply this form of egoism. If I say of someone that they are 'too good to be true' it may imply the sense that, at some level, people naturally display selfish tendencies, and the apparent absence of them is suspicious.

On the other hand, we need to keep in mind that the aim of religion is often given as the breaking down of fundamental human selfishness; that people in their natural state are selfish, but that, through spiritual practices, they can genuinely overcome this. St Augustine (354–430) believed that all people had an evil impulse, as a direct result of the Fall of Adam, and that they could be restrained only by the coercive power of the state and the laws of the Church.

Hobbes (in *Leviathan*) argued that people are motivated by the desire for gain, for security and for their own glory. But others (e.g. Rousseau) have seen a natural state as one in which there is a desire to co-operate and feel pity towards others. In either case, this is in general a statement about what 'is' rather than about what 'ought' to be – and is therefore more a comment on the background or starting point for ethics than a conclusion about how people should act.

Whether people are naturally selfish, and whether – through religion, therapy, rehabilitation programmes or the like – this selfishness can be overcome, is a matter for personal judgement. From an ethical point of view, the second view of egoism is more important:

An **ethical egoist** is someone who claims that everybody should pursue his or her own best interest. Here, selfishness is a policy, not a fact to be regretted. Few thinkers have argued in favour of selfishness as an ideal, but argue that, as it is what actually motivates people, it should be taken into account. Perhaps the most obvious example of this is Machiavelli (1469–1527), who claimed that people will do what is right only under compulsion and that generally, given the chance, they will do what is in their own interest. Ambition, and the desire to gain power, is what really motivate people. But Machiavelli was not strictly an ethical egoist, for he did not say that one could define what was right or wrong by reference to self-interest – only that, in the practical business of politics, in order to maintain the integrity and success of the state, a prince must be prepared to do what appears to be evil. He says, for example, that you should not keep promises if that goes against your own self-interest, or if the reason for making the promise in the first place has now changed. This, of course, leads to a sceptical view about the possibility of any objectively established moral values (and we shall therefore need to look at Machiavelli again in Chapter 09, where we will be considering scepticism and relativism).

According to an egoist ethic, the one obligation on an individual is to do that which benefits himself or herself. There is no moral responsibility to help others; you do so only if it pleases you to do so, and therefore you do it for your own benefit. On this basis, personal success in life is the basic motivation for actions and can therefore be used as their justification.

Example

If you are a genuine egoist and recommend that attitude to others, they are likely to develop themselves in a way that threatens you. Egoism is a benefit to you as long as others do not adopt it.

A manager, interviewing two candidates for the post of his immediate subordinate, recognizes that one of them will do the job adequately, and the other is likely to be brilliant at it. Which should he appoint?

If he is an egoist, the manager will certainly appoint the less able candidate, on the grounds that the brilliant one will progress to the point that he will take over the manager's own job. The task of an egoist is to restrain the development of those whose rise will threaten him, and utilize the powers of those who will not.

Hedonism

Hedonism is the term used to describe an attitude that makes happiness the goal of life. Epicurus founded the school of philosophy in Athens in 307/6 BCE that was named after him. He held that the judgements we make are based on our feeling of pleasure or pain. But this is not simple sensuality, for Epicureans held that intellectual enjoyment was a pleasure worth seeking. Nor did the Epicureans indulge themselves, but lived quite simply. They held that mental pleasure was better than physical, and that fulfilment of the mind was superior to the pleasures of the body. The main goal for Epicureans was to have peace of mind.

So hedonism is not always a matter of crude or immediate enjoyment. An athlete may take up training to run a race, and may suffer in doing so, but overall the experience of the training and the race may be positive, something worthwhile, in spite of the work involved.

It is difficult to be a radically honest egoistic hedonist. You are not free to be unselfish, for you cannot argue against the claim of unconscious motivation – that all human responses, however apparently altruistic, are ultimately based on selfishness. You also have to suffer the conviction that every apparently helpful person, who is apparently trying to do something for you, is in fact doing something for himself or herself; you are simply being made the occasion of that person's happiness.

> ## Example
> *I'll carry it myself and hope you feel guilty!*
>
> I shall feel pleased to have denied you the opportunity of helping. I am acting in my own best interest, and an aching back is a small price to pay for the satisfaction of having cheated a do-gooder out of selfishly doing good!

Maximizing happiness may require a consideration of the long-term effects of actions. So, for example, if I come across a vulnerable old person in a dark alley with a bulging handbag that is spilling over with banknotes, the prospect of a quick snatch might, in the short term, give me considerable pleasure. In the long term, it has to be weighed against the likelihood of being caught and punished by law for the action, or by my own conscience at having caused another person to suffer – or even, if I live to be old, the fear of walking down dark alleys while carrying all the wealth I have accumulated by such actions in the past.

We could argue, therefore, that there is short-term selfishness – 'I want that now!' – as well as long-term selfishness – 'I will enjoy life more if I follow these principles.' But in the latter case selfishness may actually be something that benefits others. In this case 'selfishness' does not refer so much to the expected outcome but to the motivation. Thus a person may be selfish by intention, but actually end up with unhappiness, because what is sought may bring only illusory happiness.

Example

- That extra drink before you drive may taste good, and may supply the happiness and sense of global harmony and universal insight that comes with mild intoxication. In the longer term, however, it may be a very short-lived happiness that is soon to be regretted.

- The sexual urge can be hard to resist – it promises intense happiness of regrettably short duration. That condomless moment of passion needs to be weighed against the risk of HIV infection or pregnancy. Refusing to have unprotected sex is not a rejection of happiness but a deferment of happiness; preferring the security of health (with the prospect of future sexual encounters) over immediate gratification.

If our duty is to pursue our own greatest pleasure (which is basic to the hedonistic position), then what follows is largely decided by how we define pleasure, and whether we take a short or long view. Do you only refrain from doing something for fear of being caught and punished? (That would be a radically hedonistic position.) There is a sense in which egoistic hedonism is often self-defeating, as in the old joke where a masochist encounters a sadist. Thinking that this could be the start of a really useful relationship, the masochist cries 'Hurt me!', but the sadist (being a sadist) replies 'No!' – an example of deferred pleasure!

Both Plato and Aristotle held the view that it is in a person's own best interest to act rightly. In this case, pleasure comes from doing good. But this is rather different from saying that pleasure is the same thing as goodness. They both argued for an objective idea of goodness, and then showed that following it would be beneficial.

However much it may be used to illustrate the way in which people sometimes act, egoistic hedonism is very difficult to sustain as an ethic to be shared with others, or to account for the experience of moral choice, conscience and the like. Nevertheless, in making a moral choice, it is natural that a person should hope that happiness, or benefit of some sort, will come from making the right decision. Consequences or results cannot be ignored – but the assessment of them generally takes other people (or the situation as a whole) into account, and not just the benefit of the person making the choice. This therefore leads naturally into the ethical theory called **utilitarianism**.

Utilitarianism

Jeremy Bentham (1748–1832) argued for the **Principle of Utility**, by which he meant that an action should be judged according to the results it achieved. This approach to ethics is called utilitarianism. It has been one of the most influential of ethical theories, and the one most widely used in ordinary 'common-sense' decisions.

Bentham argued that an action should be judged according to its ability to offer happiness or benefit to everyone involved, or to avoid unhappiness and pain. He thought that all should be treated equally, and did not consider one form of happiness to be more important than another although he took such things as the intensity and duration of happiness into account.

In his book *Utilitarianism*, John Stuart Mill (1806–73) further developed this theory, allowing that the effect of rules should also be taken into account, where their observance would benefit society as a whole. He also denied that all forms of happiness were of equal status, distinguishing higher and lower pleasures.

In its simplest form, utilitarianism states that, in any situation where there is a moral choice, **the right thing to do is that which is likely to produce the greatest happiness for the greatest number of people** – a formula that had been proposed in 1725 by Francis Hutcheson (1694–1746) as a way of assessing political regimes, the best nation being that which produced the most happiness for the most people.

This seems a very straightforward approach to ethical decisions. But it raises two important points:

1 How do you evaluate the results of an action?

- Is 'happiness' to be judged by a person's feelings alone, or is there some more objective way of assessing it?
- What are your criteria for saying that a result is 'good'?
- Should you consider only the immediate happiness that an action brings, or should you rather look to its long-term consequences?

Example

In November 1999, the head of the UK government's Rough Sleepers Unit caused some astonishment and anger among charities working for the homeless of London by saying:

'With soup runs and other kinds of charity help, well-meaning people are spending money servicing the problem on the streets and keeping it there.'

In other words, those charities which provided emergency help for people sleeping outdoors might have solved their immediate need, but at the expense of longer-term solutions to the problem. The director of the charity Shelter responded by saying: 'I believe that the voluntary sector as a whole, including Shelter, has sometimes got the balance wrong, but that does not mean that there does not need to be emergency help on the streets.' The argument on both sides is clearly utilitarian, but the assessment of results is not clear.

The same issue faces those who give aid to the developing world. The aim is generally to lift people out of poverty and starvation and to allow them to maintain themselves. The danger is that some forms of aid (e.g. agriculture that depends on machinery or chemicals) may create a situation where they depend entirely on the donor country for their livelihood. Equally, those who switch from subsistence farming to producing cash crops are then dependent upon the market – and if that fails, they have nothing to fall back on.

The aim may indeed be to produce the greatest benefit for the greatest number, but there can be many different routes to that end.

---

2 The actual results of an action are themselves often ambiguous

- How do you balance the unhappiness caused to one person against the happiness of many?

- Is immediate happiness the criterion, or is it the longer-term benefit?

For example, some would recommend that young offenders should be given a prison sentence, in the hope that it would encourage them to reform and thus not re-offend. This could imply that – although it is not experienced as such – the punishment may be regarded as increasing the happiness of the offender in the long term, as well as offering added happiness to those in society that he or she will not be able to offend against.

- By what criteria do you judge what leads to happiness in this case? If you act against someone's wishes, claiming that it is 'really' for their greater happiness, you presumably do so on the basis of *your* idea of what constitutes the good life. On what is that idea based?

The smiling headmaster of old who brandished a cane saying 'It's for your own good!' may have believed just that. But could it be proved? More and more evidence could be brought, and yet there would never be certainty. Some would point to occasions of genuine reform, others to establishing a cult of brutality.

The assumption here is twofold:

1 That a person is reformed through punishment and will, as a result of that reformation, enjoy greater happiness in the future.
2 That society as a whole will experience greater happiness through freedom from the threat of the unreformed person.

But how far can you go with the assessment of what is good for society as a whole? Can a utilitarian assessment be used to justify resorting to warfare to settle disputes between nations?

The Falklands War

In 1982, the UK went to war with Argentina over the invasion by the latter of the Falkland Islands in the South Atlantic. The war was costly, both in terms of the men killed on both sides, and in terms of the weapons and ships destroyed, and the resulting cost of maintaining troops on the islands. As a result of it the Argentine invasion was repelled, and the Islands returned to British rule.

From a straightforward utilitarian position one might argue that it would be better to allow the Falklands to be taken over, rather than suffer such loss of life.

On the other hand, Margaret Thatcher, the British Prime Minister at the time, made clear that the decision to go to war was based on the absolute right to defend British sovereignty. This was a principle itself worth defending, apparently regardless of the cost involved.

Yet underlying this principle was another argument, this time a utilitarian one – if Britain decided that, because of the small numbers of islanders affected, it was not worth defending the Falklands, then all other small dependencies would feel insecure.

Notice that what we have here is a utilitarian backing for the imposition of a general principle – not a utilitarian assessment of a particular situation in isolation. This is important because it points towards a variation of the utilitarian argument – 'rule utilitarianism' – to which we shall turn in a moment.

Similar questions could be asked of the war on Iraq in 2003. Both sides in the debate that took place before the war, and which continues up to the time of writing, use what amount to basically utilitarian arguments. On the one hand there are those who point to the number of those killed in the war and its chaotic aftermath, others who point to the number who may well have died under the rule of Saddam, had he remained in power.

Even, the argument about weapons of mass destruction was fundamentally utilitarian, namely that there was a threat being posed which suggested a future harm that outweighed the damage that a war would inflict. Those criticizing the war in retrospect might point to an increase in violence, suicide bombings and so on. Again, this argument is utilitarian. The fact that assessments of the result of the war were so far wide of the mark, compared with what actually happened, illustrates once again just how difficult it is to get a decisive moral argument based on anticipated results.

Forms of utilitarianism

Act utilitarianism

This is the form of the argument that we have been considering to date. It looks for the results of an individual act in order to assess whether that act is right or wrong. In this form, utilitarianism accepts no general rules except the rule that one should seek the greatest happiness (or benefit – remember this is not a matter of emotions but of welfare) of the greatest number.

This offers no way of deciding between conflicting views as to what constitutes the greatest benefit. It also comes up against many of the problems of assessing results that we have outlined and illustrated above.

Act utilitarianism requires an assessment about pain or happiness that is related to each individual action. But the perceived results of an action may be explicable only in terms of social convention, not in terms of actual pain inflicted. People may choose to suffer – it is their happiness – but this may not be perceived by the external observer.

Example

You observe a scene of extreme suffering. A crowd of people hobbling, shuffling and obviously in pain run between lines of onlookers. You observe their exhaustion, and learn that they have run 26 miles and, in doing so, have suffered blisters, cramp and other aches and pains. Suppose you see one of them, at the limit of his or her endurance, slow to a walking pace, but the crowd of onlookers shouts that he or she should continue running.

Such action could be regarded as cruelty on a mass scale, yet thousands of people the world over will choose to go through just such an ordeal, pushing themselves to the limit. Voluntary suffering may be idiotic, but it is not immoral unless, by accepting it, genuine harm is done to others. A person who is determined to run a marathon in spite of medical warnings to the contrary, risks his or her life and all the suffering that their death could cause their family, so that might be regarded as immoral. Otherwise, running a marathon is an example of the acceptance of pain for no obvious result (other than that of personal satisfaction).

Pleasure and pain are therefore to be set in a social context, and may be misunderstood. It might be possible, for example, by arguing that it inspires others to get fit, to justify a marathon in strictly utilitarian terms, but it is by no means the straightforward assessment of pain or pleasure that act utilitarianism assumes.

Rule utilitarianism

This rather more sophisticated approach to utilitarianism was put forward by John Stuart Mill. He argued that:

• intellectual pleasures should be preferred to immediate physical pleasures, and that one should assess the quality of the pleasure anticipated as well as the quantity. (In this he followed the Epicurean tradition.)

- people may sacrifice themselves (e.g. losing their life in the attempt to save others), but that such sacrifice is not of value in itself, only in terms of what it achieved.

He took an important step in allowing respect for those rules that were formed for the benefit of the whole of society. The rule not to kill, for example, is framed for the benefit of society as a whole. Thus the utilitarian can use general rules and principles, on the grounds that those principles have themselves been framed on utilitarian grounds.

This is the basis (given in the example of the Falklands War) for saying that one should uphold the right of national sovereignty because this principle, applied universally, would benefit humanity as a whole.

As it has developed, those who take this line of argument have divided between:

- **strong rule utilitarians,** who hold that one should not break one of these general rules to fit individual situations, and
- **weak rule utilitarians,** who would allow the particular pleasure or pain involved in a particular situation to take precedence over the general rule, whilst still allowing the general rule and its benefits to be taken into consideration.

Fluoride in water

Fluoride, a substance found naturally in water supplies in some places, is good for teeth. Hence it would seem that a utilitarian argument should be in favour of introducing fluoride into water everywhere, so that all may benefit. However, fluorides (compounds of fluorine) are toxic if taken in sufficient quantity. There might be some straightforward balancing of benefit over risk, therefore.

However, it can also be argued that people should be free to decide whether or not they accept treatment, and that it is generally wrong to impose a remedy, even if it is known to be of benefit. It would follow that a strong rule utilitarian argument would oppose the universal introduction of fluoride, whereas a weak rule utilitarian argument would try to achieve a balance between known benefits and personal freedom of choice.

Preference utilitarianism

This form of the argument says that you should take into account the preferences of the person concerned in each case, unless those preferences are outweighed by the preferences of other people. In other words, this form allows the people concerned to say what for them constitutes pleasure or pain. It does not allow one person to impose his or her own criterion of pleasure on others, nor to make a utilitarian assessment on that basis.

Preference utilitarianism has become probably the most widely used ethical theory in areas of applied and professional ethics, largely due to the work of Peter Singer, whose books (especially *Practical Ethics*, published in 1979) have been immensely influential. On the other hand, Singer's work has been widely criticized by those seeking a traditional and absolutist approach. His basic principle is that one should seek an 'equal consideration of interests'. That does not mean that all have equal rights or should be treated equally, but that each should be treated in a way that is appropriate. Consideration will be given to the interests of animals, for example, but not by treating them as though they were persons. Equally, someone who has been brain damaged and is in a persistent vegetative state does not have interests identical to those of someone who is conscious.

Starting with the situation ...

Utilitarianism works in a way that is the opposite to that of natural law: natural law starts with theories about the nature of the world and the purpose in life. From those general theories, it looks at each and every action and object and asks about its purpose. Once that is known, it claims that the right thing to do is that which fulfils the natural purpose, and the wrong thing is that which frustrates it. You start from principles, and apply them to individual situations.

With utilitarianism, the opposite is the case. You start with the pain or pleasure involved in individual situations and then take into account the wider pain or pleasure involved by the application of general rules, or the preferences of the people involved. The starting point, however, is with the immediate situation.

What the two approaches have in common is their desire to find some external, objective criterion (whether the pleasure or pain involved, or the purpose to be fulfilled) by which to show that an action is right or wrong.

In theory, using either of these approaches, it should be possible to present a case for morality which is convincing to other people, for it can be set out and demonstrated.

The limitation of the utilitarian approach, as we have seen, is that there is never enough evidence to provide certainty. It is always possible that the future will not turn out as we expect, and that our intention to maximize benefit will actually increase harm. A utilitarian has to take a guess on the future, based on the best evidence available. But like any scientist, he or she must always be aware that predicting the future can never offer certainty.

General criticisms of utilitarianism

Society is complex. It does not consist of uniform people, all wanting the same things or expressing the same preferences. There will always be conflict of interests, divergence of views. Utilitarianism has taken this into account to a certain extent by allowing for 'preferences' to be expressed rather than imposing on others what we consider to be for their greatest happiness. Nevertheless, the final decision is made in the interests of the majority, thus making it difficult to justify action on behalf of an individual or minority group. Any sense of social justice seems to demand that there should be cases where the majority freely give up something to their benefit for the sake of a minority or an individual.

> **Example**
> Sometimes, as a result of an appeal on television, the attention of a whole nation is focused on the plight of an individual. This is made especially poignant if the individual is a child desperate for a life-saving operation, or some local hero who is injured in the course of helping others. In these circumstances, offers of help are given that are out of all proportion to what would be allocated on a strictly utilitarian assessment of need.
>
> • Are these the result of emotional indulgence rather than rational assessment of need?
> • If so, is it wrong to have given help to an individual in these circumstances?

A narrowly utilitarian assessment may preclude action being taken on behalf of an individual, on the grounds that it is not in the interests of the majority that so much relief should be expended on a single person. On the other hand, if the majority are presented with the facts in a way that engages them emotionally, they may well freely give up something (generally money, offered to the needy cause) in order that the individual may benefit. In this case, although the end result is an unequal sharing of resources, the preference of a majority of those involved – that they wish to give money – is satisfied. On strictly utilitarian terms, it would be wrong only if the preferences of the donors were outweighed by the preferences of those opposed to the donations being given. As always, the utilitarian assessment remains inconclusive.

Utilitarianism deflects our attention from the personal convictions and values that lie at the heart of moral choices, and makes the decision one that requires external assessment and calculation. As far as moral agency goes, it turns the creative artist into a bureaucrat! Moral responses are not always a matter of conforming to what is reasonable, but of acting out of convictions that may well require choices that may not obviously seem to bring happiness, but that are nevertheless felt to be 'right'.

Often, when a moral choice has to be made, there is no time to calculate who will benefit and by how much. One has to act without knowing all the consequences. In such situations, my choice of action, often spontaneous, is based on convictions, not calculations.

A situation

A father, walking along a river bank, hears a shout from behind him and sees his child topple off a bicycle into the raging torrent. He plunges into the water, but is swept to his death, along with his child.

A utilitarian, confronted with information about the man's remaining five, now fatherless, children, and his work as a surgeon, saving the lives of many, might say that he should not, on balance, have plunged into the water.

But is it possible, in all honesty, to say that he was not acting morally in attempting that hopeless rescue? And who, listening to the oration at such a person's funeral, would not wish, if put to a similar test, to have similar courage?

I am not arguing that a person who did not attempt the rescue could not perfectly well have justified his or her decision to stand by and watch the child drown. Indeed, it might take great courage to do that. But is it the only morally correct option?

Perhaps a situation that illustrates this in its starkest form is given in William Styron's novel *Sophie's Choice*. It explores the guilt of a woman, living in the USA, who had survived a Nazi concentration camp. Gradually the source of her terrible sense of guilt is revealed: she was held in the camp with her two children and was told that one could be saved but the other would be sent to die. But she must choose which: if not, both would die. She made the choice – knowing that, by doing so, she has condemned the other. She is haunted by that choice.

- From a utilitarian point of view, she did the right thing. To have refused to make a choice would have made it certain that both children would die.

- Equally, she is not to blame, because she did not actually choose that either child should die – she was not directly the agent of their deaths.

- But is it possible to live with such a choice? Does a utilitarian justification make the decision any more bearable?

There would seem to be two major limitations to the utilitarian standpoint:

1 Utilitarianism, because it focuses on results, which are external to the person making the moral choice, does not adequately take into account the motive for making a choice – and yet it is motivation which would seem to be important in the assessment of whether a person was behaving in a moral way.

2 Utilitarianism does not explain why people sometimes feel that there are moral rules that should not be broken, irrespective of the consequences. This is a feature of moral dilemmas, and it is one to which we shall turn in the next chapter.

There is one final thing to be said about utilitarianism. It is a popular approach, which appears to offer clear-cut ways of assessing what is right. The problem is that life is seldom so straightforward. Few would argue that utilitarianism is not a valuable rule of thumb for assessing what a reasonable person might choose to do. The question is whether, taken in isolation from all the other reasons why people choose to do one thing rather than another, it is adequate as an ethical theory. Human motivation is subtle, and people may justify their actions by reference to ideology, religion, ambition, personal need and so on. It is seldom simply a matter of weighing up the likely results and then making a choice – although such assessment may be a useful tool for a subsequent justification of a choice made instinctively, or from confused motivation.

Hence, however valuable and straightforward to apply, utilitarianism does not always have the last word when it comes to moral decision making, even if it provides a health-check on other moral theories, by forcing people to face the consequences of their actions.

05
the experience of moral choice

In this chapter you will learn:
- about conscience
- about arguing from the experience of moral choice
- about the Kantian approach to ethics.

In Chapters 03 and 04 we examined two ways in which it is possible to justify moral claims – the first with reference to 'natural law', and the second based on the expected results. Both of these seek an external, objective basis for moral claims, examined rationally.

But there can be quite a different approach: to start not with reason but with experience. What does it mean for us to experience a sense of right and wrong, to have a conscience, or a conviction that one particular line of action is the right thing to do, quite apart from any expected consequences it may have?

Conscience

Conscience is an inner conviction that something is right or wrong, and in ethical debate people sometimes ask whether they should obey moral rules, or whether they should rather obey their conscience. But conscience itself is a strange phenomenon. Clearly, it is not the result of a logical argument, and in some ways it is more like an emotion. A person's conscience may be troubled even if they have tried to follow ethical guidelines, or have fulfilled the expectations of other people or society. So what part can and does conscience play within ethics?

In a religious discussion, conscience may be thought of as the 'voice of God', speaking within the individual. If so, then it is a personal and internalized version of 'natural law', relating moral choice to fundamental features of the world (seen in religious terms as God's creation).

In a secular discussion, conscience is likely to be seen as the natural sensitivity to ethical issues – perhaps even as an unconscious way in which people apply moral principles to the particular situations they face. It is also possible to argue that there is a biological basis for conscience; in other words, that we are genetically programmed by emotions that promote the survival of our tribe or species.

The difficulty with both religious and secular approaches is that conscience, simply because it is experienced rather than being the result of a logic process, is not open to debate or rational challenge. You are unlikely to be argued into or out of having a conscience about something. Hence, conscience seems to have its own authority, and as such it cuts across other ethical principles and arguments.

Logical requirements for conscience

For the experience of conscience to make any sense, it seems to require two things:

- freedom
- knowledge of the good.

If you are not free to decide what to do, then you cannot be blamed for what happens. Morality implies freedom and a mind capable of understanding the significance of that freedom. That is logical, but it applies equally to conscience, for conscience is only experienced in the context of the experience of free moral choice. Of course, nobody is completely free – as we saw in Chapter 01 – but for conscience to operate, we need at least to experience a measure of freedom and choice.

Conscience also implies some innate knowledge of what is 'good'. Without that, it is difficult to make any sense of conscience, since having a conscience about something implies an unqualified 'should'.

Three different approaches

Three thinkers are particularly interesting as a starting point for considering the nature of conscience: Aquinas, Butler and Freud.

Aquinas, dovetailing philosophy and Christian doctrine, considered conscience to be the requirements of God's law written within the heart. Thus, even those who do not understand Christian teaching have a natural sense of right and wrong, given directly by God. Naturally enough, Aquinas recognized that a person might have their moral judgement clouded by passion, ignorance or habits, and he noted that different societies had different views of what was right or wrong. Hence, although he says that you should always follow your conscience, he accepts that you might not understand the relevant moral principle, or appreciate that it applies to your particular situation. Hence your conscience is fallible and may lead you astray.

For reflection

If it is possible for your conscience to lead you astray, is it ever wise to follow conscience rather than reason, where they suggest different courses of action?

Joseph Butler (1692–1752) recognized that people were influenced by the need for self-preservation as well as a natural benevolence towards others. In fact, rather like Plato, he saw the human self as something of a hierarchy. Whereas for Plato, reason was to control the active passions as well as the baser needs, for Butler, priority was given to the conscience, which had the function of sorting out the conflicting claims of self-love and benevolence, thus promoting virtue by ensuring the right balance between the needs of the self and the good of others. Butler echoes what is known as the 'moral sense' tradition – associated with philosophers like Francis Hutcheson and David Hume, and part of the background for the development of utilitarianism – that human nature has a built-in moral sense, and that it is only natural to feel concern for the sufferings of others. Conscience, for Butler, is the experience of that built-in morality, setting other human concerns and needs in balance.

A very different approach to conscience can be found in the psychological explanations given by Freud. He associated conscience with a sense of guilt, arguing that, through our early upbringing, we learn values that continue to influence our moral awareness and conscience later in life. Thus conscience is an aspect of what he called the *super-ego*. Since it is based on early experiences, it becomes an unconscious expression of the wishes of parents or other adults in that early period. As such, it may be very powerful is shaping one's personal choices, but it is difficult to accept it as a significant factor in a rational ethical discussion, for it is not based on any inherent sense of right or wrong, nor is it logical.

Innate or acquired?

A key question for conscience is whether it is innate or acquired. We may experience it as innate, but if Freud is right about its origins, then it is really acquired from our parents in our early years, and its authority is one that they continue to impose upon us. If Aquinas is right, however, conscience is an essential part of being human – deeply innate and linked to the idea of a creator God and a rationally comprehensible creation.

Notice however that, even if Freud is right, it is the *moral principles* that are acquired, not the conscience itself. Conscience appears more like a *skill or faculty* than a set of rules. It is the unconscious ability to recognize moral significance. As a skill, then, it may well be innate and this is suggested by the fact that those who appear to have absolutely no conscience at all are regarded as psychopaths: there is something 'wrong' with them, they are not normal. It is normal to have a conscience. That leaves open the question of why conscience is more developed in some people that in others, and upbringing may have a part to play in this.

The categorical imperative

Whether through conscience or through thinking about right and wrong, the experience of moral choice comes in the form of a sense that there is something I 'ought' to do regardless of the consequences. This is sometimes called a 'categorical imperative'. Notice this distinction:

- A **hypothetical imperative** takes the form 'If you want to achieve X then do Y.'
- A **categorical imperative** takes the form 'You should do Y.' It is absolute, having no conditions attached to it.

The thinker most associated with this 'categorical imperative' is Immanuel Kant (1724–1804). Being an eighteenth-century German Protestant, he was very much concerned with the sense of duty. You do your duty (what you understand to be right) without regard to consequences. His main work on this is *Fundamental Principles of the Metaphysics of Morals* (1785).

Kant held that the categories we use to understand the world – categories like space, time and causality – are not to be found in the data of our experience but are imposed on our experience by our own minds. We cannot prove that everything has a cause, but our minds automatically look for causes. **The mind plays an active part in shaping and ordering experience; it is not merely a passive recipient of what is 'out there'.** This is sometimes referred to as Kant's 'Copernican Revolution': just as Copernicus showed that the Earth revolved round the Sun, and not vice versa, so Kant showed that our minds determine the way in which we experience things.

In the same way, Kant argued that we would never be able to show conclusively that a certain action was right or wrong by reference to its expected results, because we would never have enough evidence, and might disagree about how to interpret it. The starting point for morals cannot therefore be something 'out there' among the data interpreted by our senses, but should be the actual experience of moral obligation – the feeling that there is something we 'ought' to do. In other words, you do not find out first what is 'right' and then decide that you ought to do it; rather, that which you feel you ought to do is what you mean by 'right'.

Kant argued that to do your duty you have to exclude two other considerations: effects (or results) and inclinations. If you decide to do something, expecting that you will benefit by it, that is not a moral choice. Equally, if you decide to do something because you enjoy doing it, that is not a moral choice either. Kant also rejected external moral authority where it conflicted with personal moral conviction. Unthinking obedience is not a valid moral position – **one should act out of a personal sense of what is right.**

Kant therefore sought to develop a universal principle of morality – *the categorical imperative*. There are three main forms of this categorical imperative:

1 Act only on that maxim (or principle) which you can – at the same time – will to become a universal law.
2 Act in such a way as to treat people as ends and never as means.
3 Act as though a legislating member of the kingdom of ends.

The implication of the first, and major, form is that I should only do something if I am prepared for everyone else to be free to act according to that same moral principle. This does not mean that I can only do something if I imagine everyone else doing it as well (that might well cause practical chaos), but I must be prepared for everyone else to follow the same logical principle. I should not consider myself to be a unique or special case.

Notice what this does not tell you. It does not tell you what the content of your moral decision should be; it does not say that this or that action is always right or wrong. Rather it provides a general principle – our willingness to see the basis of our action become a universal law.

There is a general question to ask of a theory such as Kant's: is it possible to give a general rule that can be applied to each and every particular act, or is it essential to know the particular purpose and context of that act, before deciding on its moral status?

Examples
Suicide
A crude version of Kant's argument might be presented like this: What if everyone chose to commit suicide? That would be the end of the human species, and therefore, following Kant's theory that something is only moral if I could wish it to become a universal law, suicide would seem to be wrong.

But is that necessarily the case?

- If I were suffering from a serious and incurable illness, I might wish that everyone, if they were ever in this situation, should be morally justified in choosing to end their life. It might be quite possible to hold the view that no healthy person should commit suicide, but that someone in terminal pain should be allowed to do so. So, following Kant's theory, it is not necessary to rule out suicide in all situations.

- Perhaps an important distinction is between what is compulsory and what is voluntary. If compulsory euthanasia on a universal scale is unacceptable, then it is morally wrong in each particular case. But to say that everyone should be free to choose this option is not to make it a universal law – just a universal option, which is a very different thing.

Breaking a promise

Is it ever morally right to break a promise? If I consider, at the moment when I make a promise, that I shall be free to break it, then – according to Kant – I should be willing everyone else to be free to make promises on the same basis. But Kant argues that this would make nonsense of the whole idea of making a promise, and it is therefore illogical to say that it is right to make a promise that one does not intend to keep.

In the case of suicide, no two people are exactly the same, and nobody can know exactly the scale and quality of another person's suffering. Is it realistic to offer a general guideline for suicide? Should a person who chooses to take his or her own life be able to say 'I would wish that everyone suffering as I am at this moment, be allowed to end his or her life'? If so, then, on Kant's criterion of universalizability, that should be a morally correct thing to do.

The example Kant gives is of a person who borrows money, knowing that he cannot repay it as he promises to do. If he is not prepared to universalize his situation, then he is not justified in promising falsely to repay the money, unless he takes into account some extra circumstances.

A situation

You are held by a terrorist gang, who demand to know the whereabouts of a close friend or relative whom they clearly wish to kill. You know that the person concerned is in hiding. Do you tell the truth and admit that you know where they are, or do you

tell a lie, either by giving the wrong location, or by saying that you
do not know where they are?

Here the dilemma is between anticipating the harm that will be
done if you tell the truth and your friend is killed, and the general
moral principle that you should tell the truth.

You might want to argue that anyone, confronted similarly by the
prospect of the death of an innocent person, should lie. In this
case, although the rule about telling the truth could be
universalized, so also could the rule about doing anything
necessary in order to prevent innocent suffering.

The second form of the categorical imperative follows from the
first. If you are prepared to universalize the principles upon
which you act, it implies that you are prepared to consider
everyone else as an autonomous moral agent, also free to act
upon their freely chosen maxims. And that, of course, implies
that they should be treated as ends in themselves, never as
means to your own end. This aspect of Kant meets with almost
universal approval. Most people would see any treatment of
people as though they were 'things', disposable or merely there
for our own personal convenience, as fundamentally wrong.
Relationships in which one person exploits another are
generally regarded as morally wrong, whatever the particular
circumstances. Recognition of the right of each person to be
treated as a full, autonomous human agent is fundamental to
Kant, but is also implied by the other ethical arguments we are
considering in this book.

The third form follows from the second. Kant argues that you
should always imagine yourself as being in the position of
someone who is responsible for legislating for a society in which
everyone is to be treated as an 'end', an autonomous individual.
What is the right thing to do in such a society?

Notice that Kant sees the important touchstones as rationality
(can you justify it in a rational way?) and universality (can you
apply it to everyone?). The implication of this is that each
individual constructs, and takes responsibility for, his or her
own set of moral values, based on **duty** and the sense of the
highest good, where virtue and happiness come together, is an
idea implied by experience of a moral demand. Notice that this
is very different from the natural law or utilitarian approaches.
But notice also that it is a matter of *intention*. The maxim of my
action is the principle that lies behind my intention to act in a

certain way. That maxim does not depend upon anticipated results, but it does imply certain things about a person's view of the world. Kant argued that, if you respond to an 'ought', you presuppose three things:

1 **God** – because, unless there is some guarantee that ultimately doing the right thing will yield the right results, you will not feel committed to behaving in a moral way.
2 **Freedom** – because, unless you experience yourself as free, you will have no sense of being able to make a moral choice.
3 **Immortality** – because you know that you might not see the results of all that you do in this life, and therefore presuppose that there is some future in which the present imbalance of actions and rewards will be rectified.

Kant does not mean that you have to believe in these three things in order to respond to an 'ought' but that, once you do acknowledge the unconditional nature of that 'ought', it implies that you believe in them.

Not everyone would accept this, for it is based on the idea that there is a rational structure to our thought that underlies our instinctive reactions. This may not be so. We may feel an obligation for the worst of motives, or from unconscious needs. The presuppositions are not necessary – at least not in a conscious sense.

The creative response

There is a further point to note here – one to which we will return in the next chapter. For the natural law and utilitarian approaches, we look out at the world and analyse either its structure (if you are looking for purpose) or the likely results of action (if you are a utilitarian). But when a person makes a moral choice, he or she is not merely responding to an external situation but creating something new – taking an active step to change the world, not merely to respond to the way it is.

This active side of moral choice shapes both external circumstances and the personality of the person who acts. Character is shown and developed through such choices. Morality, including the categorical imperative, is therefore a category by which we interpret and change the world. We do not find a 'categorical imperative' out there; it is not a piece of data in the world. To a person who says it does not exist, there is no objective proof to offer. It is not part of the world, but a feature of the way in which a person responds to the world.

Morality is therefore about creative response, about interpreting the world in such a way that we give it value. Things have value for us, and we are sometimes required to express those values, or choose between conflicting values, but those values do not inhere in external objects, but in the relationship that we have with them.

If morality depends upon awareness of values, which do not inhere in objects, but in the relationship people have with them or with one another, then morality is a far more flexible thing than a straight utilitarian or a follower of 'natural law' might imagine.

Example

A stamp collector comes across a perfect specimen of a Penny Black: its Maltese cross cancellation is clear and bright crimson; it is a printing from a late plate, making it extra rare for a red cancellation; it has perfectly even and large margins; the cancellation has left the profile clear. In short, to the collector, it is a treasure! To me, it is really just a rather drab bit of paper. It serves no useful purpose. I take it between my fingers, tear it in half and throw it on the fire. It flares up for a moment, but gives little warmth – a thing of no value.

Value is not inherent in the Penny Black. The collector has created a web of values; the stamp is part of that web. It receives the value that it is given.

But values and commitments are not decided on rational grounds alone. Individuals and groups develop their own criteria for value and therefore for moral judgement. What one group regards as morally acceptable, even praiseworthy, another condemns. This is a feature of the 'moral relativism' debate, but it can be applied to each moral theory, including Kant's. If people cannot agree on what is 'good', then they are never going to agree on the means of evaluating actions as right or wrong. This stark fact was brought home to the world with terrible force one bright morning in September 2001.

Example

On the morning of 11 September 2001, passenger aircraft were deliberately flown into the North and South towers of the World Trade Centre in New York, resulting in the collapse of those buildings and terrible loss of life. It was an event that no one who watched it on television around the world will ever forget. It was an act of terrorism on a scale never before witnessed, and it provoked outrage, a surge of American patriotism and a determination to hunt down those responsible and the countries and networks that had trained and supported them. It launched the 'War on Terrorism'.

Elsewhere in the world, however, the attack was celebrated by Islamic militants as a triumph. To some young Muslims, Osama bin Laden, leader of the al-Qa'ida organization (which was believed to have been behind the attack), was seen as a hero, and those who carried it out were seen as martyrs, rather than terrorists.

Here, in its starkest form, is the dilemma for ethics. A universally accepted ethic is only possible if all agree on the values and principles upon which it can be based. Both natural law and utilitarianism tried to find that basis, but both have presuppositions that may be challenged. The categorical imperative of Kant (particularly in its first form) assumes that an action is morally right if the person performing it can will, at that time, that it should become a universal law. But that too requires the acceptance of a set of values that are deemed to be 'good'.

What an American citizen and a member of al-Qa'ida would seek to make a universal law are two utterly different things. Each sees the rightness of his or her own cause; each feels the force of the categorical imperative, that there is an unconditional moral demand.

One aspect that does not come under question is Kant's second formulation of the categorical imperative – that people should never be used only as means, but always also as ends. Clearly, terrorism of any sort uses people as a means to an ideological end.

Kant seeks an ethics based on the pure practical reason. It should therefore provide universal guidance, acceptable to all reasonable people. In practice, that simply is not the case. These matters are not based on reason alone, but on deeply held convictions.

Determined and yet free?

Before leaving Kant, let us refer back to the issue with which we were concerned in Chapter 01. Kant held that our minds impose space, time and causality on the phenomena that they encounter. From an external point of view, everything is conditioned. When I observe someone else making a choice, my mind naturally seeks out the causes that led to that particular choice. In the world of phenomena, there can be no freedom. But Kant held that all we know about are the phenomena that come through our senses. We know things as they appear to us, not things as they are in themselves. (Things-in-themselves Kant calls **noumena**, our perception of them **phenomena**.)

On this basis, Kant is able to say that we are *at one and the same time* phenomenally conditioned (perceived from the outside, I have no freedom), and noumenally free (I experience my freedom to act – something that I know, but nobody else can observe). There are therefore two ways of understanding the moral act:

- from the standpoint of one who observes the choices that are made, with their consequences and the implications they have for an understanding of humankind
- from the standpoint of the person who is actually confronted with a choice and who, in a moment of creative action, actually responds on the basis of his or her values and convictions.

This distinction is of crucial importance for ethics. When the logical positivists argued that the meaning of a statement was its method of verification, they dismissed ethics as meaningless, because it could not be verified by experience, in other words, by *phenomena*. And yet – as we saw in the reaction against that position – people continue to find moral statements meaningful. This highlights the division of perspective between a person who observes and analyses the phenomenon of human activity, and the experienced actions of a noumenal agent. As we are in ourselves, we can act morally, and no amount of analysis and observation is going to be able to remove either the experience of freedom and choice, or its moral significance.

06

personal development and virtue

In this chapter you will learn:
- about Hume on benevolence
- about Nietzsche's challenge
- to explore the moral and existential implications of personal development.

Before the sixteenth century, moral thinking was dominated by the influence of Aristotle and mediated through Christian theologians, of whom Aquinas was the most influential. It was heavily dependent upon the authority of religion and of the Church. With the Reformation and the intellectual upheavals that followed, that authoritarian structure was replaced by the desire to find a rational basis for action. From the seventeenth and eighteenth centuries we find the development of two lines of approach to ethics. One is utilitarianism; the other is represented particularly by Kant and the categorical imperative.

Both were dependent, in one way or another, on the values of the older 'natural law' view of the universe. Utilitarianism falls back on values – as it seeks to say what constitutes happiness, or the good of the greatest number. Kant, on the other hand, having come to the conclusion that you could not prove God, freedom or immortality by examining the phenomena of the world, decided that he should reinstate them as *postulates* or *presuppositions* of the practical reason.

So both of these approaches require the acceptance of certain values and qualities, without which we would have no reason to seek the greatest good for the greatest number, or recognize a sense of absolute moral obligation.

But what if we set this tradition aside and explore values that are not found 'out there' in a general understanding of the world, but are ones we create for ourselves as we act and make choices? Can we create values as an artist creates an abstract picture, rather than discover them, as a photographer might record a beautiful but external scene? Can we, as individuals, stop *asking* what is right, and start *deciding what will be* right?

This will be an important question as we look at moral choice from the standpoint of the human individual and his or her personal development. But first of all, it is important to recognize that such development takes place in a social context. So how does personal development relate to the way in which we treat other people?

Altruism?

Can human beings act genuinely for the benefit of others?

Thomas Hobbes, in *Leviathan* (1651), argued that, if people voluntarily give up their rights for the benefit of others, they do so in order to achieve something good for themselves. Indeed, he claimed that every voluntary act had as its aim some good to be obtained for the person performing it. On this basis, although the benefit done to oneself may be less tangible than the benefit offered to the other person (e.g. feeling good for having been charitable), nevertheless in some way, even if we appear to be helping others, we are actually acting in a way that benefits ourselves.

By contrast, Hume's *Enquiry Concerning the Principles of Morals* (1751) takes the view that people do actually experience 'sympathy' – that is, they respond when they see the suffering or the joy of others. He makes this experience basic to his ethics, in that if there were no sympathy there would be no development of altruistic qualities.

This does not mean that people respond to the sufferings of others in a generous way all the time, rather that everyone can experience some degree of sympathy. A psychopath, for example, is someone who has no sense of right or wrong, and who is not going to be persuaded by reason, but who has urges (to kill, for example) that are totally devoid of any sense of sympathy for his or her victim. In other words, for the psychopath, other people are 'things', not fellow human beings who have feelings and to whom one might want to relate in a personal way. In this case, the exception illustrates the general rule – that people are capable of responding to the sufferings of others.

Hume also holds that people can exhibit qualities that give happiness to themselves as well as being useful to others. These 'virtues' include justice, faithfulness and politeness, which are not directly related to self-development or happiness, but to the interests of others. In fact, Hume regards *benevolence* as the highest quality of which human nature is capable.

Such virtues are qualities that a person can develop. In this sense, altruism is a sign of personal development. But this is very different from personal development that is pursued for selfish reasons, or at the expense of other people.

In section 9 of the *Enquiry* ... Hume seems to step back from saying that sympathy is always its own justification. He points out that, even if someone appears to lose out personally because of some action for the benefit of others, he or she will feel inner peace of mind and satisfaction – which lead to personal happiness. Notice that Hume is not saying that one should show sympathy *because* it leads to peace of mind, but that peace of mind happens to be a result of the genuine response of sympathy (unlike Hobbes, who seems to be saying that sympathy is merely disguised self-love).

So, in assessing personal development as a feature of morality we need to reflect on three possibilities:

1 That people are basically selfish, and if they are honest they will admit it.
2 That people think they are unselfish and considerate to others but, in fact, they are really just satisfying their own deeper needs.
3 That people can genuinely feel and respond to the situations of others, and can show honest altruism.

There is one other important feature of Hume's idea of 'sympathy' to keep in mind. When we looked at Aristotle in Chapter 03, we saw that he attempted to get some objective criterion for moral statements. His idea of what was right stemmed from reason, and an intellectual conception about the purpose of human existence. Hume, by contrast, has no such rational basis for his morality. It is not based on intellectual argument, but on experience. In this respect, it is parallel to Kant's categorical imperative, which is understood only in the moment of being aware of a moral demand.

If a person is to develop, that development takes place within a social context. In other words, personal development implies personal worth in terms of relationships. It would be difficult to develop personally in total isolation from others, and if a person could achieve a high degree of personal growth in isolation (for example, through some form of religious asceticism), it would still depend upon the religious and social ideas that set up the conditions for that growth in the first place. This social context was emphasized by F. H. Bradley in an essay called 'My station and its duties' (in *Ethical Studies*, 1876). Bradley argued that self-realization was the basis of ethics, and he followed the philosopher Hegel in pointing out that people need both self-expression and recognition if they are to enjoy the good life. That recognition can come through family relationships, through local society or through the state, because (according to Hegel) these are the basic spheres of influence.

Central to Bradley (and Hegel) is the idea that self-realization (achieving one's full potential as a unique human being) takes place in society, not in isolation. If freedom is needed to allow for the personal development and autonomy of an individual, we need to remember that it comes with a price, and that one person's freedom may well curtail that of another.

Nietzsche

The thinker who most radically challenged traditional moral thinking and placed human development at the centre of a value creating system of thought was Friedrich Nietzsche.

It is often valuable to consider a thinker's work against the background of his or her personal circumstances – although with many philosophers this is discouraged by the way that they present ideas in a cogent fashion, inviting logical comment only. Nietzsche is different. His writing is vivid, and his ideas are sometimes presented as images. It may be worth reflecting therefore that he was born in 1844, the son of a Lutheran pastor and of the daughter of a country vicar, and that as a young man he was a lover of solitude, enthusiastically religious, and also highly talented. (He composed a motet at the age of 10, and by 14 had written some 50 poems and had decided that he wanted to be a writer.)

We shall approach Nietzsche's work through four key features.

'God is dead'

The first of these is the idea that God is dead. This is not a casual comment from one who has not taken religious seriously; it is a conclusion about the state of things as Nietzsche saw them in the 1880s. In *The Joyous Science* he has the image of a madman who comes into the town with the message that 'God is dead': not that God had never existed, but that people had killed him. The character asks if his hearers do not sense that it is growing darker, that they need lamps, even at noon. He tries to explain that people have cut the world loose, and that (without God) it is wandering without fixed values and without direction.

This is perhaps the starkest recognition of what had taken place, almost since the Reformation – the replacement of an authoritarian and metaphysical structure of thought, believed to have been given by God, by human reason. His point was that, whatever they may claim to believe, people in fact create values based on themselves, not on God. They are the centre and measure of life.

It is presented, not as something good or bad, but as an observation – something that he is amazed others have not realized.

Superman

The next feature is the **superman** (a rather poor translation of *Übermensch*, which means something that goes over or beyond man). In *Thus Spoke Zarathustra*, the sage Zarathustra comes down his mountain. He opens his teaching by saying:

> I teach you the Superman. Man is something that should be overcome. What have you done to overcome him?

> All creatures hitherto have created something beyond themselves: and do you want to be the ebb of this great tide, and return to the animals rather than overcoming man?

> (translated by Hollingdale, Penguin, p. 41)

Here the context is evolution. As the ape is to humans, so humans will be to the superman. He then takes an important step: 'The Superman is the meaning of the earth. Let your will say: The Superman *shall be* the meaning of the earth!' In other words, from this moment on humanity is to choose its values and its direction by an act of will. We humans are to be the creators of value. Nietzsche is critical of those who sought some heavenly goal, accusing them of being poisoners, weakening humankind. Instead, the true goal is to be found in the future – the *Übermensch*. It is an affirmation of life, and of the human will that shapes and determines that life. In other words, you are free to define your world!

'The will to power'

The third feature is the **will to power** – which is the force behind Nietzsche's moral thinking. It does not mean a crude attempt to get power, but the affirmation of life, and the will to develop and move forward. It is the will to power that, for Nietzsche, is the source of all values and therefore the source of morality.

Nietzsche's thought is highly individualistic. Wanting to be equal with others and showing humility – key features of democracy and Christianity, as he sees them – are signs of decadence and weakness. They sap the will to power and desire for personal development. For this reason, Nietzsche opposed both democracy and Christianity. According to Nietzsche, exploitation is one of the basic features of life, and self-development is fundamental. Therefore we should be free to adopt whatever means we need in order to secure that power. In *Beyond Good and Evil*, he sees the world as divided into masters and slaves, and he holds that the morality that suits the one will not suit the other. Masters are free to do what their own creative development requires. Nietzsche rejects both democracy and Christianity because they are associated with slave values, not with master values. Both democracy and Christianity cause the decay of the state because they are based on the false assumption that all are equal. He attacks Christianity because it allows people to deny themselves on Earth for the sake of God and a heavenly reward.

This is perhaps where it is important to recognize Nietzsche's background in nineteenth-century Protestantism: not everyone taking a religious position today would view Christian values in quite the way he did. Nevertheless it is true that some moral principles emphasize humility and co-operation while others stress personal development and the competitive spirit. Nietzsche's is one of the latter.

'The eternal recurrence'

Finally, there is **the eternal recurrence**. This is a difficult and complex idea. Perhaps it may be approached by contrasting it with the ideas of Aristotle or traditional Christian views. To Aristotle, everything has an end or a purpose. It achieves its goal once it fulfils that end. The world looks to something outside itself to justify its existence. In the traditional Christian scheme, this is God. But for Nietzsche, God is dead. There is no way that this present life can be simply tolerated because it leads to or points to something beyond itself. One should therefore be prepared to accept life as it is; to affirm it and work with it.

His graphic way of presenting this is to pose the challenge of accepting that everything that happens will be repeated over and over again. Can you look at such an endlessly repeating life and still affirm it? Can you enjoy it just as it is, without asking for some external compensation or explanation? Nietzsche presents a challenge – a necessary challenge in any world that has consciously or unconsciously discarded religious belief and the old metaphysics that went with it. **The challenge of 'the eternal recurrence' is to accept life as it is.**

Nietzsche's writings *are* a challenge, and these notes hardly touch the surface of what he has to say on the topic of morality. They are included here because Nietzsche looks at morality in a way that is very different from the older 'natural law' and 'utilitarian' arguments – in place of a fixed purpose or happiness, the key to Nietzsche's morality is the development of humankind.

A point for reflection

Through the 'will to power', one should 'give style' to one's character and the greatest enjoyment is 'to live dangerously!' In *Beyond Good and Evil*, Nietzsche said of morality: 'Every morality is a rationalization of fear, a set of safety instructions on how to live at peace with the most dangerous aspects of one's self.'

- What might a modern psychologist make of this?
- How is it possible to be afraid of aspects of oneself, or to regard oneself as dangerous?
- What might be the ethical implication of admitting that, consciously or unconsciously, we have a 'will to power' and that it is the source of our values?

Virtue ethics

Rather than starting with questions about whether a particular action is right or wrong, it is equally possible to approach ethics by asking what it means to be a 'good' person. In other words, we ask what virtues or qualities a person should possess if they are to live the good life.

This 'virtue ethics' approach goes back to Aristotle, who was concerned to understand what constituted the good life. Virtues are those qualities that can enable someone to live well and fulfil themselves as a human being. There are various lists of virtues, but the 'cardinal virtues' listed by the Ancient Greeks were temperance, justice, courage and prudence.

If these qualities enable a person to express and live out his or her true – or essential – nature, then there will be parallels between virtue ethics and the 'natural law' approach that we examined in Chapter 03. Natural law understood morality in terms of conforming to one's essential nature; the virtues summarize the personal qualities that enable that to happen.

With the rise of utilitarianism and Kantian ethics, alongside the older Natural Law approach, the virtues had not featured much in ethical debates until the 1950s, when virtue ethics was examined again, particularly associated with the work of Phillipa Foot and Elizabeth Anscombe. Although the basic argument – seeing virtues as dispositions to act in a particular way, and as a means of self-fulfilment – was not new, what *was* new was that it shifted moral debate away from general rules and principles of behaviour and towards more general questions about value and meaning in life, and the qualities that were worth developing and encouraging.

In particular this appealed to feminist thinkers, who had seen the rationalism of other ethical theories as being influenced by particularly male ways of approaching life, based on rights and duties, whereas they sought a more 'feminine' approach that included a recognition of the value of relationships and intimacy.

It also had the advantage of being a **naturalistic** ethic, in that it moved away from the idea of simply obeying rules, to an appreciation of how one might express one's fundamental nature and thus fulfil one's potential as a human being. That had a great appeal to those who were critical of the narrowness of ethical debate, and who wanted to explore human potential in a much broader context.

There are important questions raised by virtue ethics:

- Do we have a fixed **essence**? Are there, for example, particular feminine qualities that all women should seek to express, and which constitute feminine virtues? Or is our nature dependent upon our surroundings and upbringing?
- If our actions express our essential nature, and if our nature has been shaped by factors over which we have no control (e.g. the culture into which we have been born; traumatic experiences in childhood) are we **responsible** for our actions?
- How do we relate the expression of an individual's virtues to the needs of society?
- If there are different ways of expressing the same virtue (e.g. out of love, one person might seek euthanasia, another seek to prolong life), how should you choose between them? At that point, is is necessary to fall back on one of the other ethical theories?

> **Example**
>
> Consider the difference between murder, committed in the course of a robbery, and killing a loved one who is seriously ill, in order to prevent further suffering. The latter – euthanasia – is treated differently, because the intention of the person doing the killing is quite different. In the first example the vice displayed is greed, in the second, the virtue displayed is compassion, and that makes a fundamental difference to the moral significance of the act itself.

Notice here that moral praise of blame focuses on the virtues or vices of the people concerned, not on the absolute legality or results of their actions.

Existentialism

Existentialism is the term used for a school of philosophy, developed during the nineteenth and twentieth centuries, concerning human existence and its meaning. The basic idea of existentialism is that our life is shaped by the choices that we make. We are all in a process of becoming, of changing and developing as we respond to our circumstances. We are free to choose what we shall become, but that freedom can be seen as terrifying in its implications.

Although existential questions had been raised earlier, Søren Kierkegaard (1813–55) is regarded as the originator of existentialism. He emphasized the inwardness, the subjective importance of choice. It was less a matter of *what* one chose to do, as of *how* one chose it – not in a superficial way, but with earnest integrity.

There are two other major contributors to this tradition. The first of these is Martin Heidegger (1889–1976). He pointed out that we are 'thrown' into the particular circumstances of our life, and we respond to them. While it is relatively easy to wear particular masks to fit the roles that we perform (as a son or daughter, a student, a worker, and so on), to hide behind a mask is to opt out of our real task, which is to live in an authentic way – being ourselves, in all our uniqueness, not what others expect of us because of our social or family role. Thrown into life, Heidegger considered that we are also all too aware of death. We are finite, and it is therefore a challenge to find meaning in our lives – meaning that is not negated by death.

Clearly, there is much in Heidegger's thinking that relates to ethics – quite apart from his controversial support for the Nazi movement, and his later examination of issues concerning mechanization and the environment. Notice the key feature here is *authenticity*. Heidegger does not tell you what you should choose to do – but he does argue that, whatever you choose, you should do it with integrity, as an expression of your authentic self, not simply to conform to the expectations that society might impose upon you.

A similar emphasis is found with the other major contributor here, Jean-Paul Sartre (1905–80). The key phrase that encapsulates his existentialism is 'Existence precedes essence.' In other words, I do not have an essential nature which is then expressed through what I do. Rather, my life and its choices shape who I am; I am the creation of my life, the result of the choices I make. Life is fundamentally absurd, in that there is no basic rational justification for what motivates us – there is no God to guarantee and explain what life is about. There is no meaning to be found in it, other than the meaning that we choose to give it.

As with Heidegger's masks, Sartre emphasizes the difference between authentic and inauthentic human existence. Human consciousness is a matter of *être-pour-soi*, being for itself, as opposed to the world of objects *être-en-soi*. The danger for human authenticity is the temptation to opt out of the responsibility of human development – to see oneself and others as objects, rather than as individuals able to take and shape their world.

Existentialism is a huge and fascinating area of study, and there is no opportunity to examine it in any depth here. However, we should be aware that the significance for ethics is that it makes personal development – learning what it means to live an authentic existence – the fundamental value. There is one huge problem with this, of course. If there is no fundamental rationality – if there is no fixed essence that natural law or virtue ethics can take as an objective starting point – then how do you decide whether the self that you choose to shape is good or bad? Integrity and authenticity may be fine, but if that authentic self is one that exploits others without hesitation and without shame, one might claim that, integrated or not, there is something fundamentally wrong. If there is no rational basis or essence for human existence, then we are free to make whatever we like of ourselves – and doing that authentically seems to be the only guideline that existentialism is able to offer.

In Chapter 07 we shall be looking at the social and political aspect of ethics. We should note here that existentialism really contributes nothing to that but is focused on the individual, in a way that the more politically minded ethical thinkers are unlikely to accept.

For reflection

In response to the sense of gloom in Germany that followed the defeat in the First World War, Heidegger looked for some figure that could give people self-respect, direction and hope for the future. He saw just such a figure in Hitler. Like Nietzsche, who saw the *Übermensch* as the direction of the future, in the absence of God-given value and direction, so Heidegger saw self-respect in following a leader who could promise a positive and self-affirming future.

- Are there any existential grounds for condemning Hitler?
- Is the promise of personal success its own justification?

Humankind, Marx and Freud

If we are to use the personal development of individuals as a criterion for morality – in the sense that what is 'right' is what enables individuals to develop to their full potential – then we need to look at the broader context of human life and motivation. What are the circumstances that influence moral choice? What motivates such choice?

Clearly, if you accept that humankind has a fixed and knowable 'essence' then, following the 'natural law' approach, it is relatively easy to set about evaluating what human development means – it is whatever enables people to express their true essence or nature. However, if you accept that human nature is something to be developed, rather than something given, then there will be other factors to consider. One of these – but quite beyond the scope of the present book – is to look at the biological and evolutionary aspects of humankind. It could be argued, for example, that certain traits in behaviour give the species a biological advantage, and will therefore be promoted by the process of natural selection. Hence you could argue that there is a biological basis for ethics – in effect, that the 'good' is what enables your species to develop.

However, that raises another problem. On what basis can we argue that the 'good' is what benefits the human species rather than any other? Is there a criterion that stands over and above the competing claims of different species in this world of competition for limited food and space? If not, then, if we opt for saying that human development is what counts, we need to recognize that our ethical system is based on a preference rather than a logically defensible argument. After all, the world was developing for millennia before the appearance of humankind; why should we assume that, having arrived, humankind will be a permanent feature of global evolution? Nietzsche spoke of creating a higher form of man. Why not accept that there may be other species now in existence that will one day take over the dominant position held now by humankind?

But quite apart from such global, environmental and biological issues, there are two other factors to be taken into account when we consider the personal development of individuals as a moral criterion: the Marxist and Freudian perceptions of humankind. Both Marx and Freud (along with those who followed and developed their work) have had an enormous influence on modern ethics, and both of them look to self-realization of the individual as a criterion in evaluating their theories.

Marx

Marx saw the proletariat suffering from the way in which the wage labourer was separated off from the product of his labours. In factory conditions, the worker could no longer get pride or personal satisfaction from his or her work, but was simply a function in a process from which someone else made a profit. This Marx called 'alienation'.

Whatever the practical consequences of Marx's thought – and, indeed, the huge moral issues that arise when we contemplate the application of this thought in the twentieth century – we can at least acknowledge this fundamental problem of alienation. Being recognized and valued for what one creates is an important element in maintaining self-worth. To be alienated in the workplace is to be cut off from an important feature of life, namely the acknowledgement of one's role in creating goods and services, in other words, of participating creatively in the social sphere.

When it comes to applied ethics, the area that might be influenced by this is business and work ethics. How should employees be treated? What is the status of wage labour? We saw that the second form of Kant's categorical imperative was the fundamental statement that everyone should be treated as an 'end', never only as a 'means'. Clearly, a fundamental problem with all forms of work that alienate the worker is that the worker becomes de-humanized (theoretically replaceable by a machine), a mere mechanical function. Workers, following Kant, should be regarded as autonomous human beings and therefore ends in themselves, not simply means to a corporate productive end.

Freud

In his analysis of the self, Freud introduced a threefold division – the id, the ego and the super-ego. Of these, the super-ego was the 'conscience', the source of moral commands, taken in as rules during childhood and now (for those who are psychologically unhealthy) unconsciously inhibiting the free expression of the rational self, the ego. For health, according to most psychological theories, the ego needs to be in control. Health is the freedom to understand one's needs and wants, to see how one might develop to achieve them, and then to take steps in that direction, free from neurotic guilt.

That approach – and it is, of course, not limited to Freud – takes the personal development and fulfilment of individuals as its fundamental aim. Whatever inhibits that development is 'bad', whatever enables it is 'good'. Might it be good or morally right to be inhibited, or to bring up children in a way that makes it more likely that they will grow up inhibited? Clearly not. Conscience, the super-ego, and all the structure of moral claims and principles that the super-ego looks to for support, are therefore subject to self-development as their criterion.

There is far more that both Marx and Freud could contribute to our study of ethics, but for now it is important only to recognize that they both emphasize this central feature of personal development. They also follow Nietzsche in seeing the moral self as creating something positive, and not just responding to circumstances. Marx sought to change the world rather than simply to understand it, and psychotherapy of all sorts seeks to set clients free from all that inhibits the natural flowering of their personality.

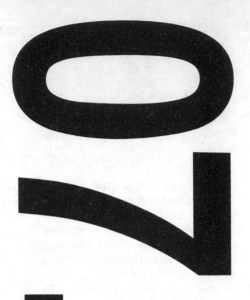

07

law and order

In this chapter you will learn:
- to explore the political and social aspects of morality
- about some key thinkers on the topic of law and order
- to examine the issues of punishment, self-defence and civil disobedience.

Society and moral choice

Some people might want to argue that there is no such thing as 'society': there are just collections of individuals. You cannot ask 'society' what it thinks; you can only ask particular people. Yet people who live together tend to develop sets of principles, expressed sometimes through laws, to make their common life easier. This means that an individual can take these agreed principles or laws into account when faced with a moral dilemma. These can be thought of as conventional morality, expressing the views of society as a whole, and it will vary from one society to another.

In the fifth century BCE, the Greek Sophist Protagoras argued that moral rules were conventions created by society, rather than absolute truths. He believed that they were necessary in order for society to function, but that they could be challenged and changed. However, both Plato and Aristotle wanted to go beyond this idea of conventional morality, to show a link between virtue and happiness in order to find a more objective basis for moral rules – showing them to be in accord with nature. We have already seen the way in which Aristotle's views on this formed the basis of the 'natural law' argument.

In Plato's *Republic* there is a debate about the function of rules within society. As we saw in Chapter 01 (when considering freedom), Thrasymachus argues that conventional justice promotes the interests of the rulers (Marx was not the first to examine society in terms of the struggle between rulers and ruled!), and that the only reasonable basis for ethics is self-interest. Glaucon, in reply, points out that, if everyone acts from selfish motives, then all will end up suffering in some way, exploited by others. The conventional rules, imposed by society, are therefore a way of protecting everyone from the basic selfish desires of everyone else.

Phone tap evidence?

At the time of writing, evidence gained by the police or intelligence agencies in Britain through phone interceptions is not allowed to be presented in court. In March 2006, however, the Home Secretary was said to be considering allowing it, particularly for terrorism and serious, organized crime.

Here there needs to be a balance between the rights of the individual to be free from intrusive investigation, and the need to

> secure convictions. Since the latter is intended to make society safer, the individual might benefit either way. Most social legislation requires a balance of benefit and harm. A moral case can be made for either side of the argument.

Plato wants to take the debate further, and presents the idea that all elements in society (like parts of a human body) need to work together for the general health of the whole. He takes the view that justice offers the happiest life, because it is the expression of health. Injustice is a sickness that is liable to cause suffering in all parts of society. Controlled by reason, Plato considered that happiness lay in achieving a harmony within one's life, and thus also within society.

Of course, not everyone is willing or able to think rationally about the moral and social implications of every action. Plato considered – in *Republic*, Book 11 – that society should therefore be ruled by philosophers (because they are able to look at the needs of society as a whole in an unbiased way), and that ordinary people should be required to obey the laws that they devise. But are philosophers really as objective and rational as that? Do they not have presuppositions and values of their own to impose?

Both Plato and Aristotle could be said to base their ethics upon reason, but one should beware of assuming that they were therefore free from the prejudices of their day. For example, Aristotle (in *Politics*, Book 1, Chapter 5) is quite prepared to say that the proper function of slaves is to obey their masters, and that women should naturally obey men. These are huge social presuppositions that slip into the rational argument, illustrating the way all philosophy (and therefore all ethics) takes place within a particular society and reflects its values.

We cannot have value-free ethics, for in a value-free situation most ethical debate would be meaningless. It could be argued that ethics is based on experience and reason, but these alone do not provide the stimulus for the questioning of morality. Computers can handle experience quite effectively, and are also efficient at the application of logic. A computer cannot be moral or immoral, however, because it lacks an inherent set of values with which to assess its choices.

This brief look at early debates on social ethics illustrates three points:

1 Society imposes laws, and encourages moral principles, in order to maintain social cohesion and minimize the damage that would be done by the exercise of unbridled individual desires.
2 Any moral or legal system will therefore be the result of a negotiation between the needs of society as a whole and the freedom of the individual.
3 Rational arguments about the needs of individuals or of society spring from (but may well hide) value judgements and presuppositions.

When we look at moral issues concerned with law and order, and the punishments that society imposes on those who break laws, we need to keep in mind three questions:

1 Does society need this particular law for its own well-being?
2 Has this law achieved a suitable balance between any conflicting needs of the individual and society?
3 Upon what values is it based, and are these values widely accepted within society?

In whose interest?

In Plato's *Republic*, Thrasymachus argues that justice is the interest of the stronger. A ruler controls his or her subjects simply because he or she has the authority, backed up by power, to impose chosen laws. Justice therefore depends on the form of government; an absolute monarchy will be different from a democracy in the way that its laws are framed and applied.

In modern times, Thrasymachus' views have been reinforced by the Marxist critique of society, in which society progresses by way of conflict between classes. For Marx, the ideal is a classless society in which such struggles are overcome, and in which no one group is able to impose its will on others. His assumption is that, in such a society, the free development of each individual depends upon, and enhances, the development of all.

But how, in a society of many different people and interests, are you to find a common basis for social ethics? Each person and each group will have particular goals and aspirations. Plato, in *Theaetetus*, ascribed to the Sophist Protagoras the idea that the wind feels cool to one person but warm to another – and in the same way values depend upon the society within which they are encountered. If there is no general set of values, independent of the form of society in which they are found, how do we assess or criticize any existing legal or social situation?

We therefore need to ask two basic questions:

1 Does this imply that there can be no objective standards in law and social morals?
2 Is any political system as 'good' as any other? If not, by what criterion can you decide which is better?

Beneath these there lurks another, more general problem. If all social controls are evaluated in terms of their impact on individuals and what they enable to happen within society as a whole, then we need to ask how the balance between the individual and society is to be achieved.

Example
Clearly, terrorism is a threat to individuals who may become caught up in an act of violence, as well as to society as a whole. The protection of society therefore requires some loss of individual liberty, in order that the threat of terrorism may be contained. Hence the balance between freedom of the individual, freedom of information, and the imposition of laws to enable measures to be taken against terrorists. Like Protagoras, however, what feels like a major infringement of civil liberties to one person may be of almost no concern to another.

Is equality possible?

David Hume argued that it was impossible to achieve a justice based on what people deserve, simply because people never agree about what each deserves. But he also felt that it was not practically possible to seek a justice of equality. He sought to protect the property of each person, even though people were unequal in what they owned. He does not say that it would be *wrong* for people to have equal shares, but that it is impractical to expect that such equality could be enforced. The reason he gives is that people are by nature unequal in their abilities, and some will prosper more than others. Whereas an individual act of redistribution might be beneficial (e.g. stealing something that a rich person will not miss to benefit someone who is poor), the application of that principle to the whole of society would not be practicable, and would have harmful consequences.

In this, Hume uses a 'rule utilitarian' argument (see Chapter 4). In the example given above, the point to consider is not 'Will I actually benefit someone by breaking the law of theft in this particular case?' but 'What will be the result of everyone breaking the law of theft in this way?'

Social rules

Laws are created artificially. They are devised by legislators (with or without the consent of the people) and imposed on society. The way in which laws are applied, and the punishments that are deemed to be appropriate for those who break them, may be established and refined, as particular cases are brought to court.

Some social rules do not have the force of law, but may become established over a period of time by custom. But these too are artificial, and may vary from one society to another.

Some philosophers have put forward ethical theories based on a social contract, an agreement made between people to abide by certain rules, which limit what they are able to do, in order to benefit society as a whole and to allow everyone a measure of freedom and security.

Hobbes (1588–1679)

Thomas Hobbes argued for a contract to be made between people and their ruler. In such a contract, the ruler should agree to protect the natural rights of the people, to act as an arbiter in disputes, and to establish just laws. In return, all who live in the area of the ruler's jurisdiction agree to accept the authority of that ruler and of such governments and laws as are established. Hobbes thought that, if the ruler did not have absolute power, there was a danger of social disintegration – something all too obvious in seventeenth-century England. He therefore placed the ruler above the law.

For Hobbes, someone taking a minority view, or refusing to agree to any social contract, could not 'opt out' of this arrangement. Simply by living in the geographical area covered by that political regime, a person became bound to accept the contract.

Locke (1632–1704)

Locke took a different view. In *The Second Treatise on Civil Government* he argued that people are required to surrender some of their individual rights to the community, but that nobody (not even the ruler) should be above the law. Authority should reside in the institutions of state, as chosen by the majority of the people. Individuals are given rights – free speech, freedom to worship, freedom to hold property – and it is the duty of government to uphold these rights.

The general principles of individual rights, coupled with democratically supported responsible government, set out by Locke, are basic to modern democratic systems. Locke was anti-monarchist and against any one person having absolute power.

Rousseau (1712–78)

Ideas put forward by Locke are found also in the works of Rousseau. Social contract forms the basis of individual liberty, and in a democracy people and rulers have the same interests – they work together for mutual benefit. Rousseau was therefore against the divine right of kings, and his ideas influenced the French Revolution, although he did not live to see it.

He argued that primitive people have two basic emotions: self-preservation and repugnance at the sufferings of others (sympathy). These appear to form quite a reasonable basis for co-operative living. He felt that civilization, and the rules that go with it, tend to corrupt people (e.g. by imposing ideas of private property, thereby creating inequality and consequent resentment), which destroys the simplicity and co-operative possibilities of the primitive state. He argued that, under a social contract imposed by 'the general will', people would agree to give up some of their natural liberty in order to establish 'civil liberty'. In this way, an individual subsumes his or her will to that of the community as a whole.

Mugging for iPods

Crime figures in Britain for the third quarter of 2005 showed an 11 per cent increase in muggings over the previous year; a total of 23,500 street robberies. This increase has been blamed on the targeting of young people carrying mobile phones and iPods.

Latest phones and iPods are there to be seen – and their ownership conveys status. But this increases the desire for them, and hence the incidence of robbery.

Rousseau would, no doubt, claim this as endorsing his view that the proximity of desirable goods only encourages resentment, which leads to temptation and theft.

Thomas Paine (1737–1809)

Paine developed a similar view of the social contract. He argued that an individual should be given liberty, and allowed to do anything (including the right to pursue his or her own happiness) as long as no harm is done to others in the process.

Paine's views lie behind the American Declaration of Independence, which allows to each person life, liberty and the pursuit of happiness as a fundamental right.

J. S. Mill (1806–73)

Mill highlights another feature of the social contract. In *On Liberty*, he is concerned that, under a social contract, individuals and minority groups might suffer by being made to conform to the wishes of the majority. His answer to this is that a majority should interfere with a minority only if that minority is doing something that is directly harmful to the interests of the majority.

Therefore, free speech should be allowed, even if the person speaking is thought to be clearly wrong or misguided. He considered that this was less dangerous than allowing an authority to decide what could or could not be said, which would result in loss of liberty for all.

Jailed for Holocaust denial
Denying that the Holocaust took place is illegal in some countries. In February 2006, the historian David Irving was sentenced to three years in jail for having denied, in speeches he make 16 years earlier, the murder of six million Jews and the existence of the gas chambers. This was in spite of the fact that he expressed regret for some of the statements that he had made earlier, and accepted that there had been gas chambers in Auschwitz. The state prosecutor called Irving a 'dangerous falsifier of history'.

There is a mixture of ethical issues here. One is the responsibility of a historian (or any non-fiction writer) to give the best available interpretation of the facts. Another is the utilitarian assessment of the damage caused if deliberately false information, or unsound interpretation, is given credibility by being published. (In this case, there was the danger of neo-Nazis using such ideas to justify their political views.)

But, at the same time, there is the issue of free speech. In democratic countries it is generally considered better to allow free speech than to forbid it. There are exceptions, however. Any speech that is likely to incite racial hatred or soliciting to murder is illegal (as was made clear in the case against the radical Muslim cleric Abu Hamza in Britain in January 2006). Here a utilitarian assessment is that the harm caused by such speech outweighs the right of an individual to express his or her views.

There is a further issue: Is it right that some things are protected in this way, but not others? However horrific the historical events surrounding the holocaust, they – like all historical events – are subject to interpretation, and no subsequent account of an event is guaranteed to be 100 per cent accurate.

Under the heading *'What price free speech?'* a newspaper front page on Friday 3 February 2006 shows two photographs. On the left, masked gunmen point their weapons towards a 'European Commission' plaque on the wall of the EU compound in Gaza, as Muslim outrage over cartoons depicting the Prophet Muhammad. On the right, the British National Party leader, Nick Griffin, is cleared at Leeds Crown Court of race-hate charges. Both issues concern the rights of individuals to express themselves in a way that may give offence to others.

John Rawls (1921–2002)

A modern version of the social contract theory is found in the work of Rawls. In an article entitled 'Justice as Fairness' (1957) and in his major book *A Theory of Justice* (1972) Rawls introduced the idea of 'fairness' into social morality.

He imagines a situation in which a number of people gather to decide the rules under which they are to live. But (by some curious form of amnesia) they forget who they are. They do not know their age, their colour, their wealth, their social position. They decide what they want from society, therefore, without any reference to any special interest group that they might otherwise represent.

He presents two principles upon which justice, so framed, would be based:

1 Each person has an equal right to the maximum amount of liberty compatible with allowing liberty for all.
2 Inequalities are to be allowed only if there is reason to think that such inequalities will benefit the least well-off in society.

He introduced what he called 'the principle of priority', by which liberties come first and social equality second. You should not therefore surrender a liberty even if, by doing so, you could argue that the least well-off in society would benefit.

Rawls thought that people would choose to help the poorest in society because – not knowing whether they themselves were poor or rich when they met to decide their rules – they would play safe, in case they found that they were in that poorest category.

A situation

The public provision of health care would seem to be based on a social contract: people pay money in taxes with which the government provides a service. Since nobody knows the extent to which they might need medical help, it is perfectly reasonable that all contribute on the basis that it will be equally available for all who need it.

But life is never that easy …

At the time of the first edition of this book, in the early 1990s, there was a debate about whether doctors should be allowed to refuse to operate on those who, by continuing to smoke, were making the outcome and recovery from an operation more problematic. The argument in favour of offering smokers surgery on the same basis as for non-smokers is that it is wrong to deny treatment to any group of people, even if they have an added (and voluntary) risk factor. Other people are treated for self-inflicted injuries – hospitals do not require that sportsmen give up their sport before they treat their injuries. Why should smokers be refused treatment on that basis?

In January 2006, the same argument could be made in terms of the increase of instances of cirrhosis of the liver as a result of binge drinking. The same could apply to those who, by their diet and lifestyle, contribute to problems of obesity and diabetes. Should only the healthy be entitled to full treatment? Should treatment be conditional upon lifestyle changes?

- Do you start with the rights of the individual to equality of treatment, irrespective of his or her lifestyle?
- Or do you take a utilitarian approach, looking at how the limited resources of the health service can be used most effectively to bring benefit to the greatest number?
- Over eating, over drinking and smoking are not illegal. Would it be different if they were? What responsibility does society have towards those who have a lifestyle that takes them outside the law, e.g. by drug taking?
- Do those who go against advice, or act unlawfully, effectively opt out of the social contract? If so, can they make demands upon resources provided for society as a whole?
- Is there a basic responsibility to provide care for human individuals, no matter who they are and what they may have done? If so, how is that responsibility defined? Does it have limits?

In these social contract arguments there is a balance between the rights of an individual and the needs of society – and for the democratic and liberal approaches to social morality it is the individual who takes priority, by being given rights and by being allowed a say in the process of government. Any utilitarian assessment of a situation (e.g. about the allocation of health service resources) is therefore tempered by the sense that there are rights to which every individual has a just claim.

Crime and punishment

There are, in general, five reasons why society may impose a punishment on those who break the law.

1 To protect society from those who have committed crimes, in order to stop them repeating their offences.
2 To deter others from breaking the law.
3 To reform the criminal.
4 As retribution for the wrong that has been done (i.e. it is felt that the person deserves punishment for what he or she has done).

5 To vindicate the law (i.e. unless punishments can be imposed, people will stop having respect for the law, and the result will be anarchy).

Of these, 1, 2, 3 and 5 can be justified on utilitarian grounds. They see punishment as a means of minimizing suffering and protecting society. The punishment imposed on one person allows many others to live unmolested.

Reason 4 tends to be defended on the basis of what might be called 'natural justice'. In a natural state, people might be expected to take revenge if they are wronged. Unlimited revenge leads to anarchy. Therefore society limits what is appropriate by way of punishment.

Just as Kant pointed to a sense of 'ought' that does not depend upon results, so there is a sense that justice requires punishment, irrespective of whether or not anything positive by way of reform or restitution can be achieved by it.

Example

In August 1993, following the leak of a memorandum about standards of comfort in prisons, there was considerable debate about how prisoners should be treated and how effective different prison regimes were in preventing prisoners from re-offending. Here is a selection of comments:

What the public expects from the prison system is that it will be frightening enough for potential offenders to deter them from crime.

(Chairman: Commons Home Affairs Select Committee)

So much for deterrence, but do severe prison regimes actually reform prisoners? This comment is from the director of the Prison Reform Trust:

Candidly, there isn't hard and fast proof one way or the other, but we do know there is a strong relationship between the kind of employment and housing ex-prisoners obtain and whether people re-offend. Common sense tells you that if people feel they are being given opportunities to prepare for that, then that will produce a better result than if they are treated harshly and simply emerge full of resentment and anger.

And a prison governor commented:

We have to ask: will treating them in a beastly way make them better citizens when they return to ordinary life? I don't think that there is any evidence that if you treat people in a capricious, punitive and uncaring manner they turn out any better than if you treat them with care, consideration and support. It seems clear that the way people are treated affects the way they behave.

Adding that loss of liberty was punishment in itself:

Going to see your kids on sports day, going out for a meal or down the pub, seeing a football match, having a sex life, going on holiday – they have been deprived of all that already. It's a pretty sterile life they lead.

With these comments the need to reform must be balanced with the natural sense that punishment should be unpleasant if it is to deter. Is it possible to run a prison service in which these two goals of punishment are equally balanced? Is it not inevitable that one will always take priority over the other in any one institution?

A suggestion – 'Prisoners must earn wages and pay rent.'

In November 1999, the Conservative party policy 'Common Sense on Crime' proposed that prisoners should work for realistic wages in prison workshops, which would be placed on a self-financing basis. Prisoners would have money deducted to help pay for the cost of their upkeep, and build up savings for their eventual release, and to help both their families and their victims. This, it was argued, would help with their rehabilitation.

Various crimes require various forms of punishment – depending on their severity, on the danger posed to society by the person committing the crime, and on the practical implication of the punishment – in terms of whether or not it can reform the criminal, and whether it is necessary to deter others, or to vindicate the law. In terms of the moral issues involved, one form of punishment deserves some special attention: capital punishment.

Capital punishment

As with other life and death issues, there are three main lines of approach.

1   One is to affirm that there is an absolute right to life, and that nothing can justify taking the life of another human being (this also underlies opposition to abortion and euthanasia).

2 Another is to take a utilitarian approach – balancing the loss of life against the cost to society of keeping a person in prison for life, or the potential suffering that could result if that person is released from prison and offends again.

3 There is also the need to deter others from committing murder or other serious crimes.

The first of these is based on an absolute moral conviction – either of the 'natural law' or the 'categorical imperative' variety – and is thus not swayed by the nature of the crime or the needs of society. If human life is paramount, then other forms of punishment and protection of society are necessary.

The second and third points are made more difficult by the great variety of serious crimes. Many murders are committed in the course of arguments between close relatives, others take place in the course of robbery or drug dealing, still others are politically motivated, as where a terrorist plants a bomb, or carries out a shooting. It is difficult to balance the effect of a custodial sentence or capital punishment on any of these – a political murderer may well be prepared to face capital punishment, thereby achieving martyrdom. On the other hand, a domestic murder may lead to profound remorse, and it is highly unlikely that the person involved would offend again.

Generally, where capital punishment is legal, there are a number of special conditions that apply. In Texas, for example, not every act of murder carries the death penalty. It applies to murder of a public safety officer or fire-fighter, murder while carrying out a serious crime, murder for financial gain, murder of a prison guard or during an escape, multiple murders and murder of anyone under six years of age.

In considering the utilitarian and deterrence arguments, two things need to be kept in mind. The first is that, from the operation of capital punishment in the USA, it may eventually cost up to six times as much to execute a prisoner as to keep him in prison for life. The reason for this is that execution takes place only after a lengthy series of appeals, which may last many years and are very expensive. For example, Excell White was executed in Texas on 30 March 1999 after spending 24 years on death row. The second point is that, although it is reasonable to assume that the existence of capital punishment should be a deterrent, there is no firm evidence that it actually works as such. Countries with capital punishment do not automatically enjoy a lower incidence of murder.

A further moral point for consideration is whether or not a prisoner should be allowed to choose to be executed, if it is genuinely his or her wish, rather than be kept alive in prison for life. In this case, the utilitarian or deterrence arguments are less relevant – the issue becomes that of the 'right to die', and therefore of the autonomy of the individual.

In self-defence?

The law does not consider whether something is morally right, but whether or not it is legal. Nevertheless, in looking at evidence in court, a judge and jury have to decide both what actually happened and whether the person accused intended to commit the crime for which he or she is accused. In this, the intention to do something illegal is crucial. This is particularly well illustrated in cases of murder. If the accused killed deliberately, then it is murder. If the killing was done while the person was deranged, or provoked to a point at which he or she lost control, then a charge of manslaughter is considered. If the killing is done in genuine self-defence, then the killing is not a crime. The courts must therefore ascertain a person's intention, as well as his or her actions.

A situation

In December 1997, a woman of 30 was given a life sentence for the murder of her apparently loving partner, having stabbed him in the course of an argument.

After serving a year of her sentence, and having also suffered from being separated from her 10-year-old son, she secretly admitted to the one person she felt she could trust, a psychiatric nurse, that she had suffered sexual, physical and mental abuse at the hands of her husband. She had felt too ashamed to reveal it at her trial but was eventually persuaded to reveal the details to her lawyers. As a result her murder conviction was quashed, and she pleaded guilty to manslaughter on grounds of diminished responsibility. Having already served a year in prison, she was sentenced to three years' probation.

This case raises an interesting issue: if she had killed her husband in self-defence while he was attacking her, it would not have been a crime. Her case was subsequently considered to be one of 'diminished responsibility' because she was aware of what she was doing, and not (apparently) in immediate danger, but had been provoked to such an extent that she was not wholly responsible for her action.

In this case, therefore, the husband takes partial responsibility for the situation that led to his being killed – in that he had provoked his wife to the point at which she stabbed him. But if that argument is extended to the situation before the stabbing, one might argue that the wife (morally, but not legally) should take some responsibility for allowing the situation to develop in which her husband became increasingly violent. Is allowing such a situation to continue the reason why she felt 'ashamed' and was unwilling to speak of it in court, even though her silence meant that she was found guilty of murder?

Legally, blame and punishment are related to an action, and this is generally also the case with ethics. But in the case of domestic or marital issues it may be unrealistic to single out actions rather than consider the dynamics of the underlying relationship. What you appear to have here is a person who feels shame and guilt about the state of a relationship, and for whom that takes priority over the issue of whether or not her action in stabbing her husband should be considered murder.

A further example

Two men from a Norfolk village (referred to in newspaper reports as 'village vigilantes') lay in wait for a local teenager, whom they suspected of stealing. They forced him into a van, tied his hands and threatened him with violence. They freed him, unharmed, 20 minutes later.

They were sentenced to five years in jail for kidnapping. On appeal, their sentences were cut to six months, much to the satisfaction of a large number of villagers, who had campaigned on their behalf.

The argument against the vigilantes was that you cannot uphold the law by breaking it – which they did by kidnapping the youth. That argument is independent of the issue of whether the youth was actually guilty of any offences.

Notice that with the earlier situation the intention was all important. To commit murder you have to intend to kill. Here, however, the intention is overruled by the action. It is not enough to say that the men 'intended' simply to warn the youth about what would happen if he stole things because they actually carried out (and pleaded guilty to) the crime of kidnapping.

This case raises an important issue of social morality. There are things that one person can do but another cannot. A surgeon can cut a person open with a knife; his or her social function makes that quite reasonable. However, if I were to walk into a hospital wearing a white coat and brandishing a scalpel, I would not be morally justified in going to work in the operating theatre!

On this basis, it is quite lawful for a policeman to arrest a suspect, to bind his hands in handcuffs, and to take him to a police station. There the suspect may be spoken to very sternly, threatened with legal action if he is apprehended committing a crime and then (following a formal caution, if he has been caught actually committing a minor offence) released.

Equal treatment on the street?

Police stopped and searched 35,776 people in Britain in 2005 under Section 44 of the Terrorism Act. Of these, only 455 were arrested. Under conventional law, police can only stop a person if they have suspicion that he or she may have committed a crime, whereas under the anti-terror legislation, no such suspicion is needed.

In assessing whether it is right for police to be able to stop and search without reasonable suspicion of a crime, one has to balance the loss of personal privacy against the perceived threat to society posed by terrorism – a utilitarian approach, weighing up the benefits to all concerned.

But even if a utilitarian argument comes down on the side of the legislation, there is a further question of whether it can be implemented fairly. Some might argue that it opens the way for superficial assumptions about people, based on age, sex and ethnic origin.

The problem with the vigilantes is that *they* were taking on a role for which society has agreed that only certain people are to perform. Of course, if the two vigilantes had caught the youth in the act of committing a crime and had forcibly taken him to a police station (provided that no unreasonable force was used), they would have been carrying out a citizen's arrest, which is legal.

Civil disobedience

Do you have an absolute duty to obey the law of the land? Are there occasions when it would be right to break the law?

You could argue, for example, that if a law goes against fundamental human rights the law is wrong and should be opposed. Remember that laws are artificial things, devised and imposed. Even though, according to the theory of social contract, they may have been established by the agreement of a majority of people, that does not mean that they are absolute – they are not created by logical necessity, and do not apply to all people at all times.

Those who contemplate civil disobedience might want to take the following into consideration:

- Is the law the product of a democratic process? If there are no democratic controls on the law then you could argue (on utilitarian grounds) that it is right to oppose the law for the benefit of the greater number of people. This would be the case if there was a law that was imposed on people, but benefited only the ruler or small elite rather than the people as a whole. On the other hand, if the law is established within a democracy you cannot argue that opposing it will be in the interests of a majority unless you can show that the majority were duped by the rulers or legislators. 'We didn't realize, when we elected this government, that this would be the result' would launch an argument of this sort.

- Is there any other way in which you can pursue the cause that you are supporting? For example, could the law be changed? If so, by whom? Can you influence those who could do so?

- Is there a categorical imperative – a sense of moral obligation that is absolute, and that opposes the law in question? In this case, you may feel justified in challenging or breaking the law. Although, of course, you will need to be prepared to take the consequences in terms of any punishments that society may impose on you.

A situation

It is illegal to trespass onto private farmland and to destroy crops. Yet in the late 1990s, faced with increasing field trials of genetically modified crops, protesters from a number of environmental groups broke the law in this way, gaining publicity for their argument that large-scale trials of such crops were a threat to the environment.

This publicity, and increasing recognition of the scale of GM ingredients in food, led to customer resistance. In April 1999 several major food manufacturing companies announced that they would be phasing out the use of GM products, and supermarkets followed, amid calls for clearer food labelling and customers seeking non-GM alternatives.

Quite apart from any technical questions about the safety of GM crops or issues of environmental ethics, it is clear that the act of breaking the law contributed significantly to the overall change in the perception of GM crops.

Ethically, several areas are touched on here. One is the conflict between one's duty to obey the laws of the country within which one lives, and one's duty towards the global community – concern about long-term adverse effects on the environment should take precedence over respect for the legal status of private property. Another is the justification of illegal acts performed in order to gain publicity for a cause. A third concerns business ethics. For example, the dialogue between a major producer of GM crops (Monsanto) and environmentalist groups was initiated by the company in response to falling sales and share prices by late 1999 caused by consumers refusing to buy GM products. The question here is the extent to which a company has a responsibility both to make profits for its stockholders and also towards the environment.

Revolutionary change

Although there *are* acts of civil disobedience from time to time, it is more usual for laws to change through the normal legislative procedures of the democratic process that framed them. Changes like this come because of practical or scientific advances (e.g. the time limit on termination of pregnancy was lowered in Britain in 1990 because scientific advances were allowing the survival of foetuses at an earlier stage), or because the attitudes of society change (e.g. the legalizing of homosexual acts in private between consenting adults).

• If laws can be changed peacefully then – on the basis of utilitarianism or social contract – it would be right to avoid any violence or revolution.

- If the law cannot be changed peacefully, then (on a utilitarian basis) an assessment should be made about whether the cost of that revolutionary change, in terms of suffering or loss of life, is worth the benefits to be gained by it.
- Violence could be justified on a utilitarian basis if it were to be shown that it is simply a defence against an already existing violence. For example, it might be argued that a repressive regime imposed such financial hardship on its people that it amounts to 'economic violence'. In this case, some might argue that it could legitimately be opposed using physical violence.

Assessing results

Changes in society come about for a variety of reasons; some political, some economic, some because of a gradual change in attitudes and values. It is sometimes difficult to assess exactly how much change has been brought about by exactly which political actions.

A violent demonstration against a law could take place at a time of growing sense of general dissatisfaction with it and recognition on the part of a democratic government that it will not be re-elected if it does not change the law. Are those who took part in the violent demonstration therefore entitled to claim that their violence was justified because their chosen end has actually come about? Might the change not have happened anyway?

Who takes responsibility?

When people are involved in civil disobedience or in the violent overthrow of a government, they tend to become bolder as they act together in a group. In the course of a demonstration, for example, there might be a great deal of damage done, looting of shops, etc. The general atmosphere of violence and change appears to sanction the sort of actions that individuals might not contemplate in more peaceful times.

Does this loss of social restraint justify individual acts of violence against people or property?

If Nietzsche were a civil servant ...

Civil servants generally operate along carefully controlled and monitored lines.

First of all they gather data. They produce reports, setting out statistical evidence. To do this they gather together advisers, experts in particular fields. They are required to be well informed. Based on that information, they set about implementing the will of their political masters. In doing this they are governed by two things – the laws of the land, and the goals that politicians have set. What they do may be monitored through the checking process within the civil service, and through select committees, which can require them to explain their actions.

A good civil servant is meant to have no political views. His or her task is simply to act on the guidelines given, within the constraints of budgets, national and international law. The criterion upon which a civil servant is often judged is not whether the decisions implemented were right or wrong – that is something for politicians to sort out – but whether he or she was effective in putting them into practice.

Civil servants, like chess players, work creatively within carefully controlled and defined structures. They are answerable only for decisions made within a very specific brief. Ultimately, they have no 'I' that operates in choosing what to do. They use personal judgement, of course (which is why they cannot be replaced by computers), but their judgements are based on values that are given to them, not generated by them. That does not mean that civil servants are without power, but their power lies in their ability to manipulate rules and values to achieve their chosen result.

Contrast the civil servant with the campaigner. He or she is someone who takes up an issue, decides on a particular point of view, and argues it with moral conviction. Campaigners lobby politicians. They present one side of an argument, the side about which they feel strongly. They tend to be visionary, to think long-term, to be idealist in their aspirations. They are frustrated by bureaucracy and restrictive legislation. They wish to change laws by changing the values and priorities upon which those laws are based.

Between the civil servant and the campaigner lies the politician. Some might be presented as genuine transmitters of the values and aspirations of those they represent, seeking to frame laws that will benefit their constituents. Others seem to be followers of Machiavelli, seeking their own power, and ruthless in maintaining their establishment. In either case, in order to survive, a politician has to take a line that is half-way between the campaigner and the civil servant. He or she has to explore situations and values, and use them as the basis of legislation.

One could imagine a television sitcom involving a civil servant and politician and a campaigner – in a caricature, their styles of speech, dress and lifestyle would be quite different from one another.

Alongside the political and civil establishment is the judiciary. Judges, magistrates and lawyers seek to implement law, but they do so with a degree of flexibility that allows the particular situation to influence the application of the general rule. Moral questions are sometimes raised when it is considered that a particular legal decision strays too far from the general rule (e.g. when a man found guilty of rape is given a very light sentence, or someone is fined heavily for dropping litter). The judge is required to be an expert in law, a balanced assessor of what is appropriate in terms of punishment, and also a subtle inquisitor of human nature and of the way in which values and laws impinge on each individual.

These characters are introduced here (albeit in the form of caricature) to illustrate different positions that may be taken in terms of the ethics of law and society. All are needed in society. Without the campaigner, there is no direct application of values to practical issues. Without the politician there is no way of formulating laws for the common good based on those values. Without the civil servant, there is no application of laws to specific situations. Without the judge there is no application of law to individual situations in a way that allows justice to operate on an individual level.

Some thinkers might easily be typecast as one or other of these characters. Machiavelli, for example, would clearly do better as a politician than as a judge or campaigner! He might also do well as a civil servant – but he would have to be very skilled in achieving his goals without appearing to break too many of the rules under which he would be required to operate.

But what about Nietzsche? Is it possible to act as a civil servant if one's ultimate criterion of right and wrong is defined in terms of the ability of individuals to overcome themselves and develop something higher? Is it possible to promote personal evolution at the same time as maintaining social cohesion?

Nietzsche was a shrewd observer of the loss of faith in the nineteenth century, and he was not afraid to explore the consequences that this might have for morality and for human values in general. His 'will to power', like Hobbes' or Bentham's view that everyone seeks his or her own good, is an observation of what actually appears to take place as people make choices.

It is grossly unfair to see Nietzsche only from the perspective of those who later took some of his ideas (particularly that of the *Übermensch* or 'Superman') as the basis for racist elitism. The Nazi party in Germany, seeking to promote the idea of a superior Aryan race, exhibited a ruthless disregard of human life in the extermination of Jews, of gypsies, of the mentally ill. Nietzsche, by contrast, was against any form of racial or sectarian elitism. Yet the central challenge of Nietzsche remains: in the absence of God (who might have guaranteed and fixed a set of values), by what criterion – other than the development of that which is 'beyond' each individual in terms of personal development – can one judge what is right? Is society there fundamentally as the environment in which each individual can grow to his or her full potential? Or is the individual simply one part of a social pattern, defined and valued within it?

Both perspectives – the personal and the social – are needed. Neither makes sense without the other. But in moral debate there is a constant process of balancing the two: too far one way and the result is anarchy and chaos; too far the other and there is authoritarian rule and loss of personal freedom.

In an ideal ethical system (and an ideal world within which to operate it) every social contract would allow the personal development of each individual. Equally, personal development would enhance the relationships of which society is made up. If (like Rawls) we could see the world from a completely selfless point of view, then the ideal system might be devised. Unfortunately, no such global amnesia exists, and self-interest remains a powerful feature in human choice.

08

religion and moral values

In this chapter you will learn:
- how religion is related to ethics
- about the ethical norms of the major world religions
- to explore the issue of religious freedom.

The moral choices people make, and the values they express through them, depend (consciously or unconsciously) on their understanding of the nature of the world and the place of humanity within it. But these are also things with which religions are concerned. Each religion:

- presents a particular view of the world
- promotes a set of values by which its followers should live
- gives specific advice on how to live – in terms of either rules to be followed or attitudes to be taken.

Religious rules or values may be based on:

- the authority of a religious leader or holy book
- the cumulative experience of that religious community
- rational thought, or an understanding of what is 'natural'.

Religious values may influence society in general, not just practising members of that religion. For example, many of the ethical arguments that we have examined so far are based on ideas and values that have been promoted by the Christian religion. This does not mean that every ethical thinker is Christian, but that everyone who lives within Western culture is liable to be influenced by Christian ideas, simply because they have come to pervade so much habitual thinking. The same would be true for someone living in a predominantly Jewish, Muslim, Hindu, Sikh or Buddhist society. The assumptions people make about the nature and value of life often reflect their religious background, or a deliberate reaction against it.

How are religion and morality related?

There are three possibilities:

1 **Autonomy** – morality may be autonomous if it is based on reason alone, without any reference to religious ideas. If its values are the same as a particular religion, that is seen as purely coincidental.
2 **Heteronomy** – morality may be said to be heteronomous (i.e. rules coming from outside itself) if it depends directly upon religious belief or on a set of values given by religion.
3 **Theonomy** – morality is theonomous (i.e. comes from God) if both it and religion are thought to come from a common source of inspiration and knowledge, a source that religion refers to as 'God'.

Some arguments in favour of autonomy

- Responsible moral choice depends on freedom and the ability to choose rationally. But some religions have inculcated rules that may be obeyed out of fear of punishment. Rewards and punishments may be offered after this life – in terms of heaven or hell, or in terms of rebirth into higher or lower forms of life. With such religious pressure, can a person be truly free or moral?

- Different religions (or even different sects within a single religion) may take different approaches to moral issues. In order to choose between conflicting religious views, a person has to use his or her reason as the ultimate deciding factor – which is autonomy!

- If I subscribe to one of the theistic religions (i.e. I believe in God), then I will believe that God already knows what I will choose to do before I do it. If he is all-powerful, he should be able to prevent me from doing what is wrong. If he does not do so, he is responsible for the consequences of my action, aiding and abetting me through divine negligence! In which case, I lose my moral responsibility.

Some arguments in favour of heteronomy

- People cannot escape from the influence of religious values and attitudes. They have an unconscious effect, even for those who reject religion. Better, then, to acknowledge that influence than try to deny it.

- As soon as you try to define moral terms (such as 'goodness' or 'justice') you are using language that has been shaped by the prevailing religions. Natural law, for example, may have come originally from Aristotle, but today it is understood largely through the use made of it by Aquinas and the Catholic Church. Religion has largely supplied the language of ethical debate.

- It is one thing to understand what is right, quite another to have the courage or conviction to put it into effect. It can be argued that religion is the source of such courage and conviction, and that it provides a community within which values and moral attitudes can be shared and reinforced.

- Philosophers often assume that everyone is reasonable. Religions, by contrast, are well aware of human selfishness and unreasonableness. Religion is likely to offer a more realistic view of human nature than philosophy, and therefore be better able to guide moral choice.

Religion or politics?

Sometimes headlines can suggest that an issue is religious when it might equally be regarded as political. Take this one, from *The Independent*, 24 February 2006:

> *Five days of violence by Nigerian Christians and Muslims kill 150*

On the face of it, this is a clash between religious groups, sparked by Muslim protests against the publication of cartoons of the Prophet Muhammad. Mosques and churches were burned; dead bodies were left in the streets. But beneath this is the fact that the Muslims are mostly from the Hausa, and the Christians from the Yoruba and Ibgo ethnic groups. Hence the clash is as much ethnic as religious. Neither Christianity nor Islam, considered as religions, would condone such violence, but that does not prevent the religious differences becoming an opportunity for other resentments to be sparked into life.

Some arguments in favour of theonomy

- Intuitionism was right in saying that there are certain things that are known, but cannot be described. We have an intuitive sense of the meaning of the word 'good'. This intuition lies behind the ideas and practice of religion and the impulse to understand ethics.
- It can be argued that religion and morality have a common source in 'mystical' experience – moments of intuitive awareness of a sense of meaning, purpose or wholeness in life, of well-being and acceptance. This is a basic feature of religious experience, and gives the impetus to act in a purposeful and moral way.
- Metaphysics (the rational exploration of meaning and purpose in the world) can be seen as a basis for morality (as in Greek thought, in the 'natural law' tradition, and as explored today by, for example, Iris Murdoch in *Metaphysics as a Guide to Morals*) and as fundamental to religion.
- Ideas like 'categorical imperative' and 'conscience' imply the personal awareness of obligation and meaning that are also fundamental to religion.

The essential difference between secular and religious ethics is that secular ethics justifies moral choice through rational argument, whereas religion regards moral choices as an expression of the fundamental beliefs and values that its followers hold. Each of the world religions has a distinctive way of presenting the values by which its followers seek to live, so it is important to explore the religions individually.

Religion and society

Before looking at the principles that lie behind the moral decision-making process for members of each of the major world religions, we should step back for a moment and recognize the danger of over-simplifying the situation.

The moral choices that a person makes, and the attitude of a society as a whole to accepted moral norms, will depend to some extent on the vitality of the ethical life of that society. Some societies are clearly defined by a single religious and cultural matrix, but in today's world they are becoming the exception rather than the rule. It is more normal these days to encounter societies in which there is a mixture of religious and ethnic groups. What is more, it might have been assumed at one time that the ethical views of a particular religion would be the same wherever it was practised. This again is now in question. Members of a single religion, bound together by a shared religious tradition, are nevertheless divided by the lifestyle and expectations of the societies within which they live.

Hence there is real scope for problems of commitment and the acknowledgement of ethical norms. Someone who belongs to a religion, but lives in a largely secular society, is likely to respond to that situation in one of two ways:

1 By making a clear distinction between the lifestyle and ethics of his or her religious community and that of the rest of society. The temptation then is to define by difference, and to emphasize those things in which the religion differs from the accepted secular norm.
2 By compromising on, or re-interpreting religious rules in a way that brings them into line with the prevailing lifestyle. Once that happens, members of the same religion, living in different societies, start to disagree about their religious ethics.

In a sense, one's ethical vitality – one's sense of the importance of making responsible moral choices, and living by them – depends on weighing up all the factors that influence self-understanding. Are you basically a member of a religion, who just happens to be living in this secular society? Or a secular person and an atheist, who happens to live in a society dominated by religion? Or are you a member of this society, who happens to find the teachings of a particular religion helpful? How you weigh up such conflicts (or potential conflicts) in interest and commitment, will determine the way in which you balance secular and religious moral arguments.

Note

There is no scope within this book to look in any systematic way at the actual lifestyle, attitudes or values of each religion; these can be found set out in books on the individual religions (e.g. the *Teach Yourself World Faiths* series). Our task here is to examine not so much what they hold to be of moral value, as why they value it, and how they therefore justify their moral principles.

Judaism

Jewish morality is based on the Torah, which means 'teaching' or 'law'. It is found in the first five books of the Hebrew Bible, and includes many rules for ethical and social matters. The most famous of these rules are the Ten Commandments (Exodus 20:1–17), and the Torah was famously summed up by Rabbi Hillel in the first century BCE in one of the various forms of the 'golden rule': 'What is hateful to you do not do to another.'

The body of the Torah developed over the centuries, as each law was applied to new situations. Eventually (by about 600 CE) a complex encyclopaedia of rules and traditions, the *Talmud* was completed. It contains the *Mishna*, a collection of oral traditions believed to have been originally given to Moses by God, along with the written Torah, and further commentaries on the *Mishna*, called the *Gemara*.

Jews are required to follow these in the correct way; this is called the *halakah*, or 'path'. Different groups within Judaism vary in the strictness with which they put these rules into effect. Some take them literally in every detail, others follow rather more general principles, adapting where necessary to some perceived requirements of modern life.

In terms of morality, the Jewish approach is one of rules. Reason and conscience have their part to play, but mainly in terms of interpretation and application. It is important to emphasize, however, that the rules are not regarded as arbitrary. They are seen as having the authority of God, given to humankind for its benefit. The many layers of tradition that surround the original

Torah represent the cumulative experience of generations. There is a real sense that, in keeping the rules of his or her religion, a follower of the Jewish faith is not simply adopting a particular style of life, but entering into a community and a tradition.

With any monotheistic religion, the issue of free-will is relevant, because if an omnipotent God can overrule human decisions, moral responsibility is taken away. It is clear that, for Judaism, this is not the case. Here is Moses Maimonides (1135–1204) on free will:

> Free will is granted to every human being. Should he so wish, he has the power to incline himself to the good way and to be just; should he so wish, he has the power to incline himself to the evil way and to be wicked ...

(as quoted in *Making Moral Decisions*, ed. Jean Holm with John Bowker, Pinter, 1994, p. 133)

Christianity

Because it developed out of Judaism (Jesus was a Jew, and his first followers formed a sect within Judaism rather than a separate religion), Christianity accepts the moral basis of the Ten Commandments and the Jewish Torah as part of its own scriptures.

Christianity interprets the rules of the Torah in the light of the life and teaching of Jesus Christ. In the New Testament, a significant feature of this is that Jesus was prepared to set aside the detailed requirements of the Law, but insisted that in doing so he was not setting the Law aside, but rather fulfilling and completing it. This has allowed Christian morality a measure of interpretative flexibility.

Early in the history of the Christian Church it was agreed that its members should not be required to keep all the rules of the Torah (the crucial issue being the distinctively Jewish practice of circumcision), thus allowing Gentiles to accept an equal place with Jews in the new religion. Nevertheless, Christians and Jews hold a common core of moral tradition.

Christianity emphasizes faith in God and in Jesus Christ, rather than obedience to religious rules as the basis of its way of life. It is therefore less rule-based than Judaism, even where it shares the same values.

Forgiveness

A key feature of Christian spirituality is the ability to forgive those who wrong you. When Anthony Walker was murdered in July 2005, his mother said of those convicted of the racist killing 'At the point of death, Jesus said: "I forgive them for they know not what they do." I have got to forgive them.' The following March, the Revd Julia Nicholson resigned from her post as vicar of a parish, because she could not bring herself to forgive the person who killed her daughter Jenny in the London bombings of July 2005. Her bishop appeared on television and praised her integrity and courage in making that decision.

It is argued that the courage to forgive sets the action – however terrible – in the broader context of recognition of what Christians describe as the universal human phenomenon of 'sin' – a falling short of what humans are designed to be.

Sources of authority for Christian morality vary from one Christian denomination to another. But they include:

- the authority of the Church (believed to be inspired by the Holy Spirit), including the Pope, the Bishop of Rome
- the authority of the Scriptures
- human reason (used in applying a 'natural law' basis for morality)
- conscience
- the direct inspiration of the Holy Spirit.

The fact that there are a number of different sources of authority is significant. Thus, at the time of the Reformation, the authority of the Church was challenged on the basis of the authority of the Scriptures. Reason and conscience are significant in re-examining the relevance of particular teachings to changing cultural and social circumstances.

Islam

The word 'Islam' means 'submission'. Muslims believe that most things in the world submit naturally to God, the source of life. Humans are the exception, for people can either choose to submit to God, living in a natural way, or refuse to do so. Fundamental to Muslim ethics is the idea that everything should submit in a natural way to the life of the universe. Indeed, Muslims believe that every child is born a Muslim, and only later may adopt another religion or decide to have no religion at all.

Muslims believe that Allah (the Arabic term for God, the source of life) revealed his will for humankind through various prophets (including Jesus, and figures from the Jewish scriptures), but that his final revelation was given through the prophet Muhammad.

Muslims have two written sources of authority:

1 The **Qur'an** – this is believed by Muslims to be the revelation of the will of God, given to Muhammad in a series of visionary experiences. It is traditionally thought that Muhammad was illiterate, but that he was told to recite what he heard. The Qur'an is the written record of that recitation.

2 The **Hadith** – this is a collection of the sayings and deeds of the Prophet Muhammad.

These form the basis of *Shariah*. This term, which means 'path', describes a natural law, created by God, which determines everything in the universe, from the movement of planets to the details of how people should act. It seeks to give expression to the fundamental Muslim belief in the unity of God (Allah), and forms not only an ethical system and legal framework, but effectively a whole way of life.

As they apply the Shariah to present-day situations, Muslims use the principle of analogy – linking a present issue to a decision found in the Hadith or Qur'an. Where there is doubt about what is right, a gathering of Muslim scholars (called the *ulama*) is called together to reach a decision on a point of law. Muslims believe that their community can never agree together upon something that is wrong and therefore decisions by the *ulama* are authoritative.

One particular feature of Muslim moral thinking is the requirement that Muslims should defend of the faith of Islam and of the community of Muslims. The term used for this is *jihad*, and it takes two forms. The greater *jihad* is the internal struggle that every Muslim is required to undertake to overcome his or her personal faults. The lesser *jihad*, however, is the requirement to defend the both the faith and the worldwide community of Muslims against external threats.

Examples

The term *jihad* has become known in recent years through its use by those Muslim groups who claim that Islam is under attack from secular (particularly Western) forces, whether that threat is seen in military, political, economic or social terms.

This is seen in the military situation in countries such as Afghanistan and Iraq. It is used by al-Qa'ida to justify its terrorist campaign – seeing Western society and its economic and military might as a threat to Islam that requires to be countered. It is found in terms of confrontation between radical Islamic groups and what they perceive as symbols of western culture and economics – as, for example, in the targeting of young western tourists in the Bali bombings in 2004.

It is also found in the clash between secular freedom of expression and any perceived insult to the Prophet Muhammad. This was the case when Salman Rushdie published *The Satanic Verses* in 1989, and most recently in the worldwide protests by Muslims against the publication of cartoons of the Prophet in a Danish newspaper, and their subsequent reproduction elsewhere.

For Islam, submission to Allah and the defence of Islam and the Prophet are paramount. In secular society, emphasis is placed on the rights of the individual and freedom of expression. This clash of values is fundamental, and it is difficult to see how a compromise can be achieved.

Notice how this view contrasts with the libertarian approach of J. S. Mill. For Mill, everyone should be free to express his or her own opinions, even if they are obviously misguided. For him, freedom of the individual takes precedence over the dissemination of right views. For a Muslim this can never be the case – defending the truth of Islam takes absolute priority. The autonomy of the individual within a democratic society is the basis of utilitarianism, and is the unquestioned assumption behind much discussion of right and wrong in a secular, western context. Notice that a Muslim, regarding submission to God as primary, cannot accept such a utilitarian perspective.

Hinduism

Hinduism is the name used for a variety of religious traditions that originated in the Indian sub-continent. People do not generally call themselves 'Hindu', but say that they are devotees of Krishna, Shiva or one of the other gods.

Because of this, it is difficult to set out ethical guidelines that will apply in detail to all who might be called Hindu. There are scriptures that are used by a large number of them – the *Ramayana* or the *Bhagavad Gita*, for example – but there is no set way of interpreting them, and some Hindus do not read scriptures, but depend on oral traditions for understanding their religion.

Nevertheless, there are certain features that apply widely, and concepts that may be used in understanding the personal and social values of Hindu society.

Dharma

This is the term used for 'right conduct' or 'duty', and it is this that determines what is morally right. Your particular Dharma depends on who you are, and what stage of life you have reached.

Caste

Hindu society is divided up into caste groups, within each of which there are various sub-groups. The main groups are:

- **Brahmin** – the priestly caste, generally the most highly educated, and traditionally much involved with education and religion.
- **Kshatriya** – traditionally the warrior caste, these tend to be involved in military and administrative posts and in the law.
- **Vaishya** – the 'merchant' caste, often involved with business and agriculture.
- **Shudra** – this is the caste for manual workers.

Today there is flexibility between the castes: some Kshatriyas, for example, hold university teaching posts. What is important to recognize is that those who are born into one of the three upper castes may be expected to have a sense of their duty and social position.

Below the four castes come those who are outside the caste system, who tend to take the most menial of work.

The Ashramas

The Ashramas are the four stages in life. Each of them has certain duties, and each implies certain moral choices:

1 **Student** – at this stage a person is expected to work hard, to show respect to parents and teachers and to develop self-discipline. Students are expected to abstain from sex, alcohol, tobacco and drugs.

2 **Householder** – during the middle years of life a person is expected to be involved with marriage, family and career. The social rules for this stage are the most lenient.

3 **Retired** – traditionally, from the time of the arrival of a grandchild, it is expected that both husband and wife may start to stand back from family and business concerns. At this point they can choose to hand over control of a family business, for example, to the next generation.

4 **Ascetic** – a few Hindus, in the last years of their life, choose to divest themselves of all possessions and devote themselves to the practice of their religion. Most remain in the retired stage, however, and continue to live with their families.

Hinduism recognizes that different people have different abilities and are able to take on different responsibilities. It does not pretend that society is uniform, or that an equal distribution of goods, or equal rights, will in itself produce happiness or justice.

There are situations in which the caste system allows people to remain in poverty, or favours those of higher birth even if they do not necessarily have the ability to match. However, the caste system is not meant to promote inequality, but difference. People are to be given respect, whatever their place in society. Nevertheless, although Hindus may be hard working and ambitious, their aspirations may well be determined as much by birth as by the opportunities afforded by society.

Buddhism

Unlike most other religious traditions, Buddhism is not based on a belief in God but offers a practical set of guidelines for spiritual development.

A Buddhist may say that his or her aim in life is to overcome the suffering caused by greed, hatred and illusion whilst developing in a way that leads to peace, joy and insight. Buddhists believe that all ethically significant actions (*karma*) have their consequences. What you do today will affect the sort of person you become tomorrow – not in the sense that there is any externally imposed law to that effect, but just because actions have their natural consequences. Those who are foolish remained trapped in a cycle of craving and unsatisfactoriness.

Buddhists are encouraged to cultivate qualities of compassion, gentleness and serenity, and to overcome the 'poisons' of hatred, greed and ignorance.

Buddhist moral guidelines are summed up in the five basic precepts, undertaken by all committed Buddhists.

1 **Not to destroy life.** This means avoiding killing other humans, and also (for many Buddhists) keeping to a vegetarian diet, so as to minimize the suffering of other species. It also implies that Buddhists should avoid a negative attitude towards life – denigrating people or situations – but should cultivate an attitude of *metta* (loving kindness).

2 **Not to take what is not given.** This requires avoidance of dishonesty and grasping for material goods in a way that may be honest, but implies craving. Buddhists should cultivate an attitude of generosity.

3 **Not to indulge in harmful sexual activity.** There is the general principle that sexuality should not be used in such a way as to harm people. Although many Buddhist attitudes are shaped by the cultures within which it has developed, in general, Buddhism takes a liberal and positive attitude to sex – although those who aspire to follow the spiritual path seriously may find that they are able to find personal fulfilment without sexual activity. This precept is sometimes taken in a broader sense of not harmfully over-indulging any of the senses.

4 **Not to speak falsely.** This is a general rule against lying, but also against anything that deliberately gives a false impression.

5 **Not to take those things that cloud the mind.** In order to increase their awareness, it is important that Buddhists should stay alert and be sensitive to their own and other people's feelings and responses. This cannot happen if the mind is dulled by alcohol or drugs, and so it is recommended to avoid them. Unlike in Islam, however, there is no absolute prohibition.

As well as these principles, Buddhists are required to cultivate four mental states, known as the *Brahma Viharas*, which may be translated as 'the resting places of the divine spirit':

- **love** – towards all creatures, and including oneself
- **pity** – compassion for all who suffer
- **joy** – an unselfish sharing in the happiness of others
- **serenity** – freeing oneself from anxieties of success or failure, and being equal minded in dealing with other people.

Buddhists do not refer to actions as 'good' or 'bad', 'right' or 'wrong', but as 'skilful' or 'unskilful'. This implies that an action is assessed by the intention of the person who does it rather than by any external absolutes. As action is skilful if it is the result of insight and loving kindness, it is unskilful if it is the result of ignorance, greed or hatred. That unskilfulness is shown both in the action itself and in the results that come from it.

Like Christianity, Buddhism is a religion that has been very free to adapt itself as it has moved from one culture to another. The oldest forms of Buddhism, as found now in the Theravada traditions of Thailand and Sri Lanka, for example, are very different from those found in Tibet or Japan. The basic teachings of the Buddha are a common factor, but it is considered wise to use 'skilful means' to adapt and apply teachings to the particular society and situation in which people find themselves.

Where there can be no externally imposed law, originating in a God, there is bound to be a greater degree of flexibility. Buddhism, although it does have cultural traditions and many Buddhists place great importance of the lineage of their teachings – the list of teachers who have handed down traditions from one generation to the next – it is essentially a process of self-examination, within broadly defined parameters. Hence it produces general moral principles and virtues, but does not offer narrowly defined moral rules. The main exception to this is the voluntary acceptance of rules by individuals who want to enter a regime of spiritual training for a period, as when a person becomes a monk or a nun, even for a short time. In this case, rules become 'hypothetical imperatives' – if you want to meditate well, you should abstain from alcohol; if you wish to gain merit from a time of monastic discipline, you must obey the rules that apply to monks and nuns.

Sikhism

Sikhs believe that, without the inspiration that comes from devotion to God, people live in illusion, and are dominated by the five evil impulses: lust, anger, greed, attachment to worldly things and pride. Sikhs are therefore required to cultivate their opposites: self-control, forgiveness, contentment, love of God, humility.

In practical terms, the guidelines for the Sikh way of life are set out in a book called the *Rehat Maryada: A Guide to the Sikh Way of Life*, a translation of a Punjabi work of 1945, produced by a group of Sikh scholars and regarded as authoritative for giving a summary of the Sikh way of life and the teachings of the ten Gurus upon which the Sikh faith is based.

The Sikh community is concerned to emphasize equality. Every Gurdwara (a place of Sikh worship) has a kitchen and a place where worshippers can sit and eat together. This is a way of demonstrating the unity and equality of Sikhs.

Sikhs who belong to the Khalsa (those who have committed themselves in a ceremony to follow the Sikh way of life – the word itself means 'pure') are required to carry a sword (*kirpan*), to be used in self-defence. It should be used only when all peaceful means of resolving a dispute have failed, and only to re-establish justice where there has been a wrong (for example, to defend the Sikh community), or in a direct act of self-defence.

The Sikh religion came into existence against a background of opposition between Hindus and Muslims, and countered this by emphasizing the unity of all people before God. This not only colours Sikh worship, and the sharing of food at the Gurdwara, but is a key feature of Sikh attitudes towards moral issues – seeking a justice that goes beyond any religious or political divisions.

Religious values and society

In this chapter we have attempted to show no more than the briefest outline of the way in which those who belong to the various faiths establish the principles and values upon which their moral views depend.

Notice the variety of approaches, not so much in terms of moral rules but in the way in which they are established. Some are imposed by authoritative teachers, or through the interpretation of scriptures; others depend more on the traditions of their own communities. Some have many specific rules (notably Judaism and Islam); others (notably Buddhism) avoid the concept of rules altogether. Some offer rewards after death for obeying the rules and punishments for those who disobey; others see actions as bringing about their own consequences without external agency.

Such values and moral principles make most direct sense within the faith communities themselves. The shared values and moral rules give cohesion to the community. Where members of a faith community live within a secular society, the moral principles by which that society claims to live may well be similar to those of the faith community, but the actual force of authority and the way in which those rules are justified may be quite different.

Example
The deliberate killing of another human being is against the law in almost all societies, except in particular circumstances (e.g. when war is declared, or where a person is legally sentenced to death). A Buddhist living in that society would also wish to refrain from killing; not because of the secular law, but from a profound respect for all living things. The Buddhist may also go beyond the secular law, opposing those forms of killing which are permitted by society (e.g. the killing of animals for food). The secular and religious viewpoints may or may not coincide in practical terms, but what is essentially different is the justification given in each case. Social observation is therefore inadequate in assessing the strength of religious moral influence.

Sometimes moral dilemmas reflect differences of culture rather than religious belief as such. Traditionally, Asian families have maintained close control over their young people, especially girls. The dilemma is that young Asians in the West may wish to go along with the prevailing culture, to the distress of their families.

A situation
A 23-year-old Hindu girl is disowned by her family because she has been working as a model, appearing in soft porn magazines. Although she was originally shocked and felt very uncomfortable about appearing topless, she came to accept it and found that it

ceased to bother her. She claimed that it did not change her traditional, conservative attitude to sexual morality.

- Is it possible to live equally in two cultures if they hold conflicting values? Can one be a devout Hindu and yet accept the values of a largely secular Western society?
- Which should take precedence: the individual or the family and cultural group?

This illustrates the problems of ethics in a multi-cultural society; it is not simply a matter of understanding the religious and cultural norms of each group, but of sorting out to which group a person is giving his or her loyalty at any one time. Such diversity also affects religions that cross cultures.

In the case of Judaism, Islam, Sikhism and Hinduism, the religion tends to promote its own culture, and is little influenced by the secular or cultural contexts within which it finds itself. Traditions of prayer, or the observation of Ramadan in Islam, for example, will be the same wherever in the world Muslims find themselves.

Buddhists and Christians, however, have tended to adapt their presentation of their fundamental beliefs to take into account prevailing attitudes and philosophies of the societies within which they have found themselves. Consequently, there is great variety within these religions to moral issues. Where the religion is established as the historical norm within a culture (e.g. Christianity in Europe or the United States, Buddhism in Thailand) it is sometimes difficult to distinguish what is an expression of secular culture and what has religious roots. Minority religious groups tend to stand out against their cultural background, and their ethical position may be more sharply defined.

Example
At the Lambeth Conference in July 1998, bishops of the Anglican Church agreed to turn a blind eye to polygamy in areas where this was accepted by society. African bishops had argued that it was wrong to force Christian converts who had several wives to become monogamous as a condition of church membership. Although the Church did not endorse polygamy, it recognized it as something it had to live with, and agreed not to make pronouncements against it.

Equally, there was considerable opposition of African Christians to the ordination of homosexual priests and bishops within the Anglican Church, since within the African context the pressure to accept equality between those of different sexual orientation was less than within Europe and North America.

Should religious freedom be restricted?

There are situations where religious beliefs lead to actions that go against the prevailing norms of the society within which they operate.

Two examples

1 In Waco, Texas, in 1993, a branch of the Seventh-Day Adventist Church, led by David Koresh, was besieged in its headquarters by federal agents, following a shooting incident. The cult members were heavily armed, and there had been considerable exchange of fire in which four agents had been killed. At the end of the siege there was a fire in which Koresh and many of his followers died.

2 Some people refuse to accept medical attention on religious grounds. For example, Jehovah's Witnesses may refuse to accept blood transfusions. Sometimes Christian Science practitioners may also refuse conventional medical treatment for themselves or their children on religious grounds.

Should a religious cult be allowed to operate outside the laws of the society within which its members live? Does society as a whole have a right to legislate about religious beliefs?

Historically, those who have deviated from the norms of religious belief have often been persecuted and killed. In contrast, there is wide acceptance today of the idea that the free practice of one's religion is a basic human right. To what extent is there a moral obligation on society, or on individuals, to monitor or take action to prevent the spread of beliefs which (on the basis of the ethics of society as a whole) are harmful?

The dilemma here is whether it is right, in the name of one set of moral values, to deprive any individual or group of the freedom to live by a different set of moral values.

- Does the value of allowing individuals or groups freedom to act according to their own moral or religious views outweigh any potential harm (from society's point of view) that such freedom might entail?
- Which is better for society overall: freedom, with the risk of minorities doing things that the majority regard as wrong, or an enforced moral code?

Recent freedom ...

Although the freedom to practise any religion or none is generally accepted in modern secular societies, we need to remember that this is a fairly recent phenomenon. Until the middle of the nineteenth century, Christianity dominated the establishment in Britain, and many positions in society, or even access to education, were based on a religious requirement. During the wars of religion, people were tortured and killed for holding religious views other than those of the government of the day. Those accused of witchcraft could be burnt at the stake. As recently as 1842 George Holyoake, a campaigner for secular humanism, became the last person to be sent to prison for denying the existence of God!

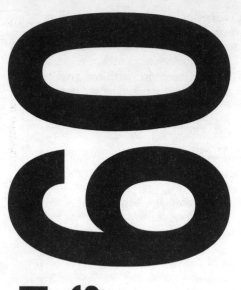

09

scepticism and relativism

In this chapter you will learn:

- to cast a sceptical eye over morality
- to examine the claim that morality is always culturally conditioned
- to explore whether moral absolutes are appropriate for a varied world.

In the context of ethics, **scepticism** is the view that there are no solid foundations for ethical theories or principles. It may take the form of a scientific argument for a determinist position – thereby suggesting that freedom of choice is an illusion, and therefore that moral responsibility meaningless. It may equally take the form of a logical argument that questions each assumption and attempts to show that there is no foundation for morality that cannot be challenged. Equally it may be expressed in the assumption that, whatever they may claim, people are motivated by their own self-interest.

There is, of course, a logical problem with being an absolute sceptic, namely that you can be sceptical about scepticism itself! Why should we not challenge the validity of challenging all moral norms?

Nevertheless, we shall look at one exponent of a political philosophy that comes as near as one might choose to scepticism, namely that of Machiavelli. Whether *The Prince* was taken to be serious advice for the aspiring ruler, or written with the wry smile of one who has long observed how people actually survive in the political jungle, need not greatly concern us. It does, however, offer a moral scepticism that verges on the cynical.

An equal threat to those who would espouse absolute moral principles is **relativism**. All ethical theories are relativist to some extent – in the sense that it is widely accepted that moral rules should be applied in a way that is sensitive to the particular situation and context. However, relativism can be pursued to the point of saying that all moral norms and principles originate within a social context. Hence they are not autonomous and cannot be applied universally. Society decides what is right or wrong, and may be free to change its mind.

Because relativism appears to be sensitive to the autonomy of the individual and the cultural context of human action, it tends to be more 'reasonable' and perhaps even more moral that scepticism. However, a thoroughgoing relativism makes moral debate very difficult, for debate depends on agreed principles and norms, and if these are culturally conditioned then they too can be challenged and dismissed.

Perhaps the question to ask in this chapter is whether the combined influence of scepticism and relativism invalidates the ethical arguments and theories that we have been considering so far, or whether they are simply a restraining influence on those who would define morality too narrowly.

Philosophers or politicians?

Kant was a professional philosopher, and by all accounts his life was regular and carefully ordered. There is an anecdote told of him that he took the same walk each day, and that his timing was so precise that housewives seeing him pass could set their watches by him! His thought is precise and logical, as we saw in the examination of his 'categorical imperative' (see Chapter 05).

- He looked at experience and realized that we play a large part in the ordering of what we see – we impose space, time and causality on the jumble of sense impressions that bombard us.
- He looked at the experience of behaving in a moral way, responding to a sense that there is something that one 'ought' to do, and analysed that too – in terms of both its implications and its presuppositions.
- He presents us with two simple rules – that we should be prepared to universalize the principles upon which we act, and that we should treat people as ends in themselves and not merely as means to our own ends, both eminently sensible criteria by which to assess our moral choices.
- He does not offer practical advice for specific situations, but the most general of guidelines.

Why then might one hesitate to accept Kant as the ultimate judge of acceptable action? Perhaps because in the actual world of crises and moral decisions, life is seldom as straightforward as it would seem from Kant's standpoint.

To get a realistic view of moral choices we need to balance what we feel 'ought' to happen by a study of what does actually happen. From Kant's perspective much of what happens – especially, perhaps, in the world of politics – might be regarded as immoral. But is that fair? Should we not look carefully at the actual choices that people make if they are to rule? Should we not balance the innocent simplicity of the categorical imperative against the experience of one who sees the consequence of always acting innocently?

For a very different perspective we shall therefore turn to a politician – a fifteenth-century Italian from Florence, a diplomat and shrewd (if cynical) observer of the realities of political life. His maxims are rather different from those of Kant, and he treats morality with a good degree of scepticism!

Machiavelli

Machiavelli was essentially a practical man. His book *The Prince* gives advice to one who would seek to rule a principality, and it is set against the political intrigues of fifteenth- and sixteenth-century Italy. It looks at the realities of political life, the need for stern action, the need to use power in a way that is effective, the need to act creatively and decisively, breaking all the conventional moral rules if necessary in order to deal in a pragmatic way with the demands of high office.

Machiavelli's views are suitable to balance against Kant's for three reasons:

1 Kant is concerned with the 'categorical imperative' – the 'ought' that does not depend upon conditions. Machiavelli is concerned almost all the time with 'hypothetical imperatives', such as what you need to do in order to retain power. The implication of this is that, in most practical situations, it is the hypothetical rather than the categorical that constitutes the normal sphere of 'moral' (to Machiavelli) operations.

2 Kant argues that you should always treat people as ends, not as means. Machiavelli recognizes that there are occasions when a ruler must act cruelly against one person or group of people in order to establish fear as a deterrent against lawlessness, for example. Treating people as ends in themselves, he might well argue, leads to anarchy and chaos.

3 Kant assumes that the right thing to do is judged by what I would wish other people to do. Machiavelli argues that the right thing to do is judged by what I know other people will try to do to me given half a chance.

Let us look at just a little of Machiavelli's advice. Here, for example, are his words to a ruler who has taken over a state, but it might equally apply to a Managing Director who has taken over an ailing company, or a politician inheriting a new ministry.

> So it should be noted that when he seizes a state the new ruler ought to determine all the injuries that he will need to inflict. He should inflict them once for all, and not have to renew them every day, and in that way he will be able to set men's minds at rest, and win them over to him when he confers benefits. Whoever acts otherwise, either through timidity or bad advice, is always forced to have the knife ready in his hand and he can never depend on his subjects because they, suffering fresh and continuous

violence, can never feel secure with regard to him. Violence should be inflicted once for all; people will then forget what it tastes like and so be less resentful. Benefits should be conferred gradually; and in that way they will taste better.

(The Prince, section VIII)

Like a surgeon, forced in some extreme circumstances to operate without anaesthetic, one is sometimes in a position where the inflicting of pain is inevitable and ultimately beneficial.

It might seem irrelevant to ask 'Am I prepared for everyone to operate without anaesthetics?' because clearly the actual decision is not based on a general theory but on the immediate and unique situation. The surgeon might say 'This is not how I would choose to act, but in the circumstances it is right for me to do so.' What Machiavelli is saying (and using a utilitarian argument to justify it) is that less harm will be done by decisive action than by a compassionate but indecisive muddle.

And here the advice to a ruler might be adapted for a new teacher, taking over an unruly class:

So a prince should not worry if he incurs reproach for his cruelty so long as he keeps his subjects united and loyal. By making an example or two he will prove more compassionate than those who, being too compassionate, allow disorders which lead to murder and rapine. These nearly always harm the whole community, whereas executions ordered by a prince only affect individuals.

(The Prince, section XVIII)

He acknowledges the traditional virtues, but comments:

… taking everything into account, he (the prince) will find that some of the things that appear to be virtues will, if he practises them, ruin him, and some of the things that appear to be wicked will bring him security and prosperity.

(The Prince, section XV)

Now this is not to dismiss entirely the idea that a ruler should do good, merely that a ruler should be flexible enough to recognize that it is not always prudent.

… he should have a flexible disposition, varying as fortune and circumstances dictate. As I said above, he should not deviate from what is good, if that is possible, but he should know how to do evil, if that is necessary.

(The Prince, section XVIII)

For our purposes, there are four features of Machiavelli's advice that we may need to take into account:

1 In many situations, traditional virtues may be set aside, and actions judged on a utilitarian basis. Keeping order and minimizing pain take precedence over traditional moral principles.

2 Actions depend upon the duties and responsibilities of the position you hold in society. A prince might be justified, therefore, in doing something that would not be acceptable in one of his subjects. Once you have accepted the position of ruler, you are obliged to seek the benefit and integrity of the state – your morality in other respects being subsumed beneath that overall obligation. Morality is therefore related to social position.

3 In practical terms, one needs to be flexible, adapting moral principles to suit particular situations.

4 What we do should depend on our awareness of the likely actions and attitudes of those around us. If everyone else were good, there would be no problem – but they are not, and so we remain naively innocent at our own peril.

Example

In December 1999, following long negotiations during which political parties in Northern Ireland, from both the Unionist and Republican sides, agreed and followed a step-by-step process, political power was devolved to the province after 25 years of direct rule from Westminster.

Hardliners on both sides of the political divide accused their leaders of compromise in agreeing to share power without first getting all their demands met.

Against this there was a general view that politics requires compromise, and that an absolutist view is a luxury enjoyed by those who do not expect to hold positions of power.

To what extent does this view of political reality negate the Kantian attempt to settle moral issues on the basis of pure practical reason?

There is, of course, an answer to Machiavelli, but it is not an easy one. One could say: 'I will do what I know to be right, no matter what the consequences, to myself, my family and friends, my country. I will not compromise my integrity, however much pain that might cause.' That is a valid moral position to take, for someone who holds his or her principles very dear. Martyrs take such a stand.

It is also possible to take this position for other reasons: out of fear of being in the wrong; out of pride or stubbornness; out of the conviction that future glory awaits those who stand by their principles (in heaven, in a new incarnation, or in the perspective of history). T. S. Eliot put onto the lips of the soon-to-be-martyred Thomas à Beckett in his play *Murder in the Cathedral*, when Thomas is tempted to accept martyrdom for the sake of future glory, that the foulest treason is to do the right thing for the wrong reason.

Let Machiavelli stand for those who are sceptical about the application of moral principles. This is not a total scepticism about moral values – which implies that there are no values other than those that individuals choose to impose on life – it is just scepticism about the application of general rules to individual situations.

In almost all moral systems there is scope for individual flexibility. In extreme circumstances you are morally justified in doing things that would be wrong in the general run of events. Machiavelli takes this seriously, but in political life almost all events are extreme and unique, all demand that normal rules be set aside. Just how flexible can people be before they are 'unprincipled'? Is Machiavelli really unprincipled, or just a realist, applying moral guidelines as best he can in the world of political survival?

Situation ethics

The natural law approach to ethics formulates rules and then applies them to individual situations. But is it right to apply rules in this way? Is not every situation unique? Does the practical scepticism of Machiavelli not suggest that we need to be far more flexible in our approach?

In the 1960s, largely as a reaction against what he saw as a paternalistic and imposed morality of traditional Christianity, Joseph Fletcher developed **Situation Ethics**.

He argued against the deductive method of ethics (in which you start with a rule or principle, and then apply it to various particular cases), and suggested that the individual situation should be paramount. He believed that there should be a **single moral principle** – that you should do whatever is the most loving thing. Ethical rules were of secondary importance; they might guide a person, but should not dictate right and wrong.

The requirement to do the most loving thing is not a rule or law – it does not say *what* you should do in any particular situation – it merely gives a motive and attitude that can inform moral choice. Of course, a person may act foolishly out of love, with disastrous consequences, but nevertheless, from a strictly situationist ethical perspective, it is still morally right. Each situation is taken and judged by what love requires, and if that means breaking some conventional moral rule, it is right to do so.

Other writers from the same period took a position half way between this radical 'situationist' approach and the conventional application of rules. Paul Tillich (in *Morality and Beyond*, 1963), pointed out that, if there were no rules, then everyone would have to work out what he or she should do on every individual occasion. This, he argued, was too much to expect. There should be rules to help people decide what love might require of them in any given situation.

For reflection

The principle of love may be fine as an ideal, but will it work in the real world? What would be the result if some people accept it and others do not? Are those accepting it not going to be at a disadvantage? And if they are, might they accept that disadvantage as part of the price they pay for following the value they hold most dear? How might Machiavelli have responded to that principle?

Situation ethics, in putting individual circumstances before fixed moral rules, is a straightforward and rather mild version of the more general issue: relativism.

Relativism and moral absolutes

Any **absolutist** approach to ethics is going to argue that it is possible to find a basic feature of the world, or human nature, or biology, or pure reason upon which a system of ethics can be built. Once that foundation is established, moral principles and the right or wrong of particular actions can follow by logical deduction and practical application.

That is not to imply that absolutist ethics is inflexible; all moral systems need to take some account of particular circumstances, intentions and so on. However, every absolutist ethic is based on something other than itself, some reality or shared value, by which it is justified. Looking at the ethical theories we have considered so far:

- Natural Law ethics is based on a rational interpretation of purpose within a rationally comprehensible universe.
- Virtue ethics is based on an understanding of the essence of what it is to be a mature human being, and the virtues that spring from that.
- Utilitarianism is based on the assumption that a rational person (whether from altruism or enlightened self-interest) will want a democratic sharing out of benefits.
- Kant based his ethics on the pure practical reason and the logical application of his categorical imperative.
- Even where personal development, whether with a fixed idea of the self or an evolutionary one, is used as a basis for ethics, it is based on an ideal of what a person can become and understands morality in the light of that.

This does not imply that any of these are 'absolutist' in any narrow sense, but it does show that they all depend on some prior commitment or understanding, by which right and wrong can be judged.

Relativism also starts with a couple of basic assumptions, but they are very different from any of those listed above. **It assumes that the only absolute rule is that there are no absolute rules. It also assumes that nobody should impose his or her morality on anyone else.**

Early in this book (see page 33f) we made the distinction between descriptive and normative ethics. The former simply described what people do in particular situations, without attempting to label that behaviour either right or wrong. The latter – which then became the subject matter of all that followed, was concerned with defining and understanding moral norms. **Descriptive ethics is relativist.** In other words, if you say 'People in such and such a tribe practise cannibalism' you are not making a judgement about whether cannibalism is right or wrong, you are simply noting that it is socially acceptable in that tribe.

What a relativist approach to ethics is doing is extending descriptive ethics into the territory that was previously held by normative ethics. In other words, it argues that all issues of right and wrong should be seen as culturally, socially and temporally conditioned. We should not take moral norms or rules from one society and impose them on another; nor should we assume that the rules that applied in one era can be continued into another.

Note

In looking at moral language, we saw that emotivism (arguing that moral language is merely expressing one's approval or otherwise) and prescriptivism (recommending a course of action) were logical ways of understanding what ethics is about, once you accept the Logical Positivism argument that moral language cannot be justified with reference to facts (see page 38f).

Relativism follows exactly the same logic. Because there are no facts that can decide between competing sets of moral rules or values, no one set can be any better or worse than any other.

Those who argue for any of the traditional ethical systems tend to regard relativism as a dangerous medicine; taken in small quantities it is useful (in warning against too rigid an application of ethical maxims), but overdoses can be fatal – in the sense that they tend to preclude the rational discussion of genuine differences of opinion.

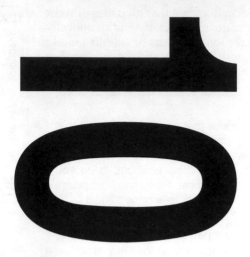

10

applied ethics

In this chapter you will learn:
- to apply ethical theories to a range of issues
- about the variety of moral issues today
- to understand how different arguments reflect different standpoints.

It may seem strange, at the end of a book that has already introduced examples of the way ethical thinking is applied to real-life situations, to have a separate chapter on 'applied ethics' – surely *all* ethics is 'applied'?

The reason for this is partly historical. Before the twentieth century, there is no doubt that ethical thinkers sought to apply their reasoning to practical situations. Bentham, for example, was concerned with prison reform and J. S. Mill campaigned for women to be given the vote. In the early twentieth century, however, in response to the 'logical positivist' claim that moral statements were 'meaningless' because they could not be verified empirically, it became increasingly common for ethics to be limited to the exploration of what moral statements might mean and how they might be justified – in other words, 'meta-ethics'. It did not presume to enter the real world and say what *should* happen. Philosophers were not expected to make pronouncements about what was right or wrong.

The last four decades of the twentieth century, however, saw a dramatic shift in emphasis, so that the range of ethical topics under consideration in the twenty-first century, both in an academic context and among the general public, is far greater than half a century earlier. The anti-war movements in the 1960s and 1970s, the coming of the contraceptive pill, the sexual revolution, feminism, and the environmental movements have all thrust ethics to the fore. In the professions (particularly medicine and nursing) there has been a range of very immediate ethical dilemmas, and pressure to define professional responsibilities in this area.

There has also been an increase in litigation. If people feel that they have been unfairly treated, they will sue; so companies and individual professionals have needed to define their responsibilities and be prepared to defend themselves when challenged. Equally, with the coming of the Internet and global television coverage of events, it has become far easier for people to review and compare the performance of the media. Censorship, political manipulation and the balance of news coverage all have ethical implications. There has also been an increase in interest in business ethics, again fuelled by the grievances felt when companies fail to deliver what they promise, or where corporate failure affects the lives of employees, who claim that they should have appropriate consideration.

In a world where newspaper coverage may be dominated by global warming and international terrorism, ethics is never far from the surface of public concern, as was illustrated in our 'One Day' section with which this book opened. All this has led to a resurgence of 'applied' ethics.

Clearly, applied ethics covers a vast range of subjects, and any one of these tends to spill over into others. Take issues about *race*. These may includes questions of legal and social equality, and the rights of ethnic minorities. Discussion of these can work both on the individual level, and also in terms of 'institutionalized racism' in organizations such as the police, as was revealed particularly by the enquiry into the murder of Stephen Lawrence in South London in 1993 and its subsequent investigation. Issues of race, like those of gender, tend to be rather different from other ethical issues, because they contribute an additional layer of complexity to an ethical analysis of a situation. For example, whether or not a police force investigates a crime adequately may be a matter of ethical debate (depending on the reasons for a failure of adequacy), but where it is suggested that there are racial or gender issues, these are superimposed over questions of existing rights and responsibilities. Ethical issues are seldom only about race or gender, they are about fundamental questions of human rights as well. Consequently, there is something slightly artificial about compartmentalizing moral issues – examine one and it has implications for many others.

However, this chapter will touch on some of the ethical issues in a range of key areas of human life, without attempting to give all the background details. Quite apart from the practical limitations of space, it is important to recognize that none of these issues is settled once and for all – some arguments may remain valid as circumstances change, others may become redundant and views may need to be revised. To keep pace with applied ethics, once you have a grasp of key arguments, it is necessary to scan the papers or Internet, for new examples are constantly being provided.

The natural environment

We have to recognize that the human species, both by its numbers and its technology, has a massive impact on the environment. Yet, in almost all moral thinking, the ultimate criterion has been human happiness; directly so in the case of utilitarianism, indirectly in the natural law arguments, intuitionism or the categorical imperative. We seek to benefit humans first of all, and then, by extension, may feel some responsibility towards other species or other elements in the natural environment.

A stone cannot feel pain, or express a preference; therefore, it has traditionally been ignored in moral debates. From a utilitarian point of view, care of the environment has therefore been seen as a moral issue first and foremost because destruction of the environment involved harm to humankind. The problem with a utilitarian assessment of our moral responsibilities to other species or to the environment as a whole is that the human happiness it seeks to safeguard may be of relatively short duration. We may not be able to assess the full impact of, for example, climate change on the human species, hence, as ever with a utilitarian argument, the results may be inconclusive.

Example

If rainforests are destroyed, we may be concerned because:

- global warming will affect us all
- many medicines are discovered through analysis of rare plant species, many of which are still to be found in the rainforests.

In both cases, this reflects a straightforward utilitarian argument. It does not imply any responsibility towards the rainforest in itself, nor to the other species who live in it.

A second approach is implied by what has already been said about the 'natural law' argument. Whether backed by religious convictions or not, there may be a sense that everything – humans, other species, the planet itself – has its place within an overall scheme of things, a 'final cause' that is its natural destiny. This approach is based on metaphysics, in that it goes beyond descriptions of the physical environment to consider issues of value, meaning and the fundamental structures of reality. It may conclude that the world and its many species should be valued, quite apart from any specific or demonstrable benefit to humankind.

For reflection

The human population is 6.5 billion, more than double what it was in 1960, and set to rise to more than 9 billion by 2050. It is increasing at the rate of 76 million per year. Whatever else is done in terms of environmental ethics, that fact stands ahead of all others. The planet cannot sustain such growth in one species. Whatever is done by way of ethically responsible lifestyle changes in order to reduce the 'human environmental footprint' – in other words, the impact of each person on the planet – it remains true that the only way to reduce that footprint to zero is for a person not to be born! Hence, although relatively little attention has been given to population reduction so far, it will have to be addressed soon enough.

Whether arguing from a utilitarian or natural law basis, it is clear that lifestyle options have a direct impact on the environment. Those concerned to preserve the ecosystems upon which life depends need to make a case for changes in our attitudes to those things that most people take for granted as part of an affluent lifestyle.

'All these flights abroad could end up costing us the earth'

The editorial in *The Independent*, 28 January 2006, highlights the fact that, in 2005, Britons took 65 million trips abroad, with huge ecological impact. Even those who are keen on the natural environment may be adding to its problems, for in 2005 there were 5 million eco-tourists worldwide, visiting exactly those places that need to be preserved!

Genetically modified foods

Although we shall look separately at the issue of human genetics, when it comes to GM foods the issues are closely linked to our views on the natural environment. We may argue that GM foods may carry long-term health risks of which we are not yet aware. Hence, on a utilitarian assessment, benefits (e.g. crops that resist certain diseases, or have better yields) are weighed against potential risks. But we then need to look at the wider issues:

- There is also the concern that GM crops may cross fertilize with other species in the environment, with unknowable effects on the natural environment. So, for example, those who farm organically near fields where trials of GM crops are taking place, may feel that the natural quality of their own produce is being threatened. Ethically, this approach may be justified on 'natural law' (showing respect for the environment) or utilitarian (we depend on a healthy environment) bases. But here the issue is still related to humankind.

- There may also be a deeply held view that the attempt to mix genes from widely different species is essentially unnatural, and (irrespective of its promised benefits) is therefore to be rejected. This may be justified on a 'natural law' basis, and it suggests that the natural order is of value in itself, and is not simply there for humankind to manipulate at will.

GM experimentation is sometimes justified on the grounds that selective breeding has long been a means employed to improve both crops and animal stock. This does not answer the anxiety of those who feel that it is 'unnatural', simply because breeding is carried out within the same or very closely related species. You can cross-pollinate two types of flower, or apple tree; you can interbreed similar kinds of dog. But you cannot cross a cabbage with a fish – they simply will not breed! On the other hand, you can introduce modified genetic material from a fish into plant DNA.

- It is precisely this 'unnatural' mixing of genetic material from very different species that is the main concern from the 'natural law' perspective. We are not simply speeding up a natural process, but doing something that is profoundly unnatural.
- The development of GM crops may also be challenged from a utilitarian perspective, if it is believed that there may be harmful effects of eating the resulting food. The problem here is that the potential benefits, in terms of the resistance of GM crops to disease, for example, are relatively easy to show. On the other hand, the potential dangers of eating GM products are as yet unknown. The balance is therefore not so much between known advantages and disadvantages of the product, but between positive claims for the new crops and unknown risks.

Interestingly, one of the key features here is economics. Since companies make money by selling what people want to buy, GM produce on the one hand and organic produce on the other may flourish or decline depending on market perception.

For reflection
- Is market economics a sufficient basis for deciding whether manipulating food is right or wrong? It is morally right to sell something simply because people are prepared to pay for it?
- Should government tax products that people want to buy in order to discourage them? (e.g. the levels of taxation of cigarettes)

Animal rights

So far, everything we have been considering has been concerned with the way in which human beings treat one another, but humankind is just one of many species on this planet, so we need to ask if the sort of moral considerations that have been applied to the treatment of other human beings should be extended to include other species.

This does not imply that animals should behave morally – without reason, morality makes no sense. A cat, offered the prospect of killing a mouse, acts instinctively, but (as we shall consider in a moment) humans can choose how they will behave towards other species.

But do we as a species have any moral obligations towards other species? Do animals have rights – and, if so, how are those rights assessed? Let us look at the way in which some ethical arguments might be applied to animals.

We may want to ask:
- Is it right to keep wild animals caged in zoos?
- Is the concept of making an animal into a 'pet' one that does violence to the animal's original nature?
- Should we breed favourite species on grounds of aesthetic appeal?

Fairness

Ethical theories that are based on the idea of a social contract drawn up between people are concerned with the fairness within a relationship. Each party accepts responsibilities and in return receives rights. Can this sort of theory be applied to other species?

A pet is accepted into a human social setting for the benefit of the humans. For example, looking after a pet hamster may be a way of encouraging children to take responsibility generally, as well as giving them pleasure. A dog or cat may be good company, especially for people living on their own. A family pet may be thought to offer something positive to the life and atmosphere of a family home. A relationship develops between the pet animal and the humans, through expressions of affection and shared enjoyments (like dog and owner taking walks together).

In what way does the animal benefit from this arrangement? By being given food and shelter, veterinary care and all else needed to enable it to live out its natural lifespan in a measure of comfort seldom offered in its natural habitat?

Where animals are treated cruelly, once accepted into the human environment, then it is clear that the humans have not acted fairly in terms of the implied contract between themselves and the animal. If you accept a pet, you have the responsibility to care for it in a way that is appropriate to its needs.

Natural law

It might be argued that humans have no right to be entering into such implied contracts with animals. The Islamic view of life, for example, is that animals should not be kept as pets or put into zoos. It regards this as basically unnatural, and therefore as violating the natural life and instincts of the animal. In this case, the argument being used is one of 'natural law'; that animals have their natural place within the scheme of things, and it is not to be treated as pets. Respect for the animal demands that it should be treated as an animal, not as a quasi-human, manicured, clipped and paraded!

On the other hand, animals in the wild feed on one another. Humans are omnivorous, and therefore have a choice – they can either eat animals or remain vegetarian. A natural law argument might well accept that there is a place for the eating of meat, and therefore also for the farming of animals. But if the eating of meat in order to sustain life is justified under natural law, what about the conditions in which the farming of animals takes place? Most species do not have any choice about their feeding habits; they simply catch what they can. The human species, on the other hand, controls the production of animals for food. Does such control imply moral responsibility?

Example

A cat will play with, kill and eat a mouse. The sight of this might be extremely distasteful, but it is a cat's nature to do so. However much the cat may have been domesticated, it is still a natural hunter with killer instincts. On the other hand, if I decide to take a pet mouse out of its cage, set it free in a room and then chase after it, biting it from time to time before killing and eating it, I would be considered to be acting in a way that is unnatural, and the morality of having such a supper would be questioned. My feeding habits might feature in a tabloid newspaper, and I might find myself under pressure to accept psychotherapy. I would certainly be banned from keeping pet mice.

- What distinguishes me from the cat in this respect?
- Does my rationality and ability to choose other sources of food mean that I have a moral responsibility towards the mouse?
- If I were starving, would I be morally justified in eating the mouse?

The treatment of animals is connected with questions about diet and standards of living. If fresh meat is enjoyed occasionally, and a roast chicken is regarded as a delicacy, it becomes more possible to breed chickens in humane circumstances – fewer are needed and people will pay more for what is considered a delicacy. On the other hand, if people expect to eat meat every day, and chicken is consumed on all occasions, then the demand for quantity of such meat goes up and artificial methods must be found to maximize the efficiency of meat production. A change in eating habits and expectations therefore implies a change in attitude to animals, even aside from the issue of vegetarianism.

How do you assess the fairness of an implied contract in which a member of one species is born, reared and fattened, and then killed to feed members of another species? All the gains would seem to be on one side. The animal used for food is not considered as an individual member of a species, but simply as a source of protein.

Experiments on animals

Animal rights activists target laboratories that conduct experiments on animals – and tend to do so irrespective of the purpose of the research being undertaken. In other words, they oppose the use of animals in this way, whether the aim is to find a cure for a serious human disease or whether it is to test cosmetics. In this, they are rejecting a utilitarian approach.

Using a utilitarian argument, the gains to be anticipated must outweigh the pain inflicted. Thus, if it is possible to use an animal in a test that might result in a cure for a serious disease, then many people would judge that a morally acceptable thing to do. Of course, it would need to be shown that as little suffering as possible was inflicted on the animals concerned. On the other hand, the testing of cosmetics on animals does not yield life-saving benefits. Cosmetics are not essential to life. The use of cosmetics that have been tested on animals is therefore optional, a matter of personal moral choice. One teenager, campaigning for the use of cruelty-free cosmetics, used the slogan 'Make up your mind before you make up your face' to highlight the nature of the choice involved.

Therefore, using a combination of a natural respect for the life of animals and a utilitarian approach to the expected gains from experimentation, the main moral questions about animal experimentation may be set out as:

- Is it necessary to use animals in these tests, or is there some other way to obtain the same information?
- Are the tests carried out in such a way as to minimize the pain caused?
- Are the anticipated results of the tests of sufficient importance to justify the suffering involved?

'Scientist backs animal testing for cosmetics'

A front page article in the *Guardian*, 4 March 2006, described a controversial statement, made in an interview with the newspaper, by Professor Aziz of Oxford, who had previously explained why he needed to use monkeys in his research into Parkinson's Disease. He suggested that it was not wrong to use animal testing in the production of cosmetics, if it could be shown to reduce suffering. Other scientists disagreed with this view, and made a clear distinction between animal testing for research into disease and testing for cosmetics.

The argument on both sides is broadly utilitarian. If the potential benefit to human health outweighs the consideration shown to the animals, then animal testing is acceptable. That might be the case for serious illnesses, but not for cosmetics.

However, there seems little prospect of Britain overturning its ban on animal testing for cosmetics, which came into force in 1998. Many cosmetic manufacturers, including the world's largest, L'Oreal, have developed other testing methods that do not involve animals.

An ethical approach to the treatment of animals has featured in the work of Peter Singer, and his book *A New Ethics for our Treatment of Animals*, published in 1975, became influential within the animal rights movement. His approach is utilitarian, in other words he wants to consider the happiness or benefit of all. Unlike earlier utilitarians, however, he sees no reason why the argument should be limited to humans. Just because animals cannot express their preferences, it does not follow that the benefit or harm caused to them should not be taken into account in a utilitarian assessment.

In general, the argument of the animal rights movement – and others, who want to consider the welfare of animals without considering themselves to be part of a campaign or movement – is that other species should be considered as worthy of consideration in themselves, and not used as the property of human beings. Hence, for example, some would argue that just as liberty and protection from the threat of cruel treatment is regarded as basic to the rights of a human being, so they should be extended to animals.

There is another school of thought, however, which points out that animals cannot act morally, cannot enter into contracts, and cannot therefore have moral duties, e.g. you cannot blame a hungry carnivore from committing murder! Hence we should not treat animals as though they were persons, but rather we should recognize that we have basic responsibilities to treat them fairly 'as animals'. Thus, for example, any gratuitous cruelty would be condemned, but in a utilitarian assessment of benefits, the welfare of the animal would probably not have equal consideration or weight to that of a human being.

Natural law sees everything – and therefore every species – as having a place within the overall scheme of things within the universe. Hence animals are regarded as having significance, but not the same significance as human beings, since they have a very different essence. Where a metaphysics is evolutionary, or emphasizes the interrelationship between all life forms – e.g. within Buddhism – the welfare of one species is bound up with the welfare of others, and the treatment of animals is therefore most definitely a moral concern.

Assessing rights

A key element in looking at the way in which humans treat one another is to consider which 'rights' a person should have – and such rights are based on their needs as a human being. When we consider rights for animals, we may need to consider what rights are appropriate for that particular species. Part of that may be a consideration of those things that animals seek in order to live and reproduce. An example (given by James Rachels in *Can Ethics Provide Answers?*) is that of a bird building a nest. Clearly, if we watch a bird build a nest and then take that nest away, or deliberately destroy it, we are depriving that bird of something that it needs, and it will have to start building all over again. Similarly, if another bird takes over a nest that is already built, we might tend to see that as unjust. Hence, by looking at the needs of a bird, we might conclude that the right to gain benefit from a nest that it has built would seem to be a fairly clear right. And that amounts to giving property rights to the bird, since the bird has invested effort in taking twigs (nominally the property of nobody and everybody) and investing energy and skill in constructing a property out of them.

This is further reflected in the fact that it is illegal to steal and sell rare birds eggs. A species of bird is deemed to have the right to reproduce itself, and that right is taken away if its eggs are stolen.

In this way, one can build up a case for some basic rights, appropriate to the essential needs of each species, the upholding of which will allow that species to survive and have the opportunity to flourish.

However, it is recognized that such giving of rights is a human phenomenon – in the natural order of things, species compete most ruthlessly, and no one animal species is likely to give much of a thought to ascribing rights to others! Where species co-operate, the basis is enlightened self-interest, based – as is everything – on natural selection.

And that view often predominates in arguments on animal rights. Kant is probably not alone in his view when he said:

> But so far as animals are concerned, we have no direct duties. Animals are not self-conscious, and they are merely as means to an end. That end is man.

> (from *Lectures on Ethics*, quoted by Rachels in *Can Ethics Provide Answers?*, p. 100)

International issues

The moral choices people make, and the laws by which they live, generally reflect the overall self-understanding and values of their society. Even when people use a widely accepted and logical argument to justify their ethics (e.g. natural law or utilitarianism) the application of that argument to their particular situation will still reflect on the underlying values they hold. You may seek the greatest happiness for the greatest number, but what counts as happiness of benefit in your eyes will reflect your own situation and society. The more closely defined your group, the clearer can be its moral rules, because people in the group are assumed to have a common outlook on life.

The problem with international ethics is that there is no single global ideology, religion or political system. An international ethic needs to be based, therefore, on those things that can be shown to be good and right for all people in all places and at all times – and that is difficult to establish.

Example

In medieval Christendom, it was considered right to torture heretics in the attempt to get them to turn from their 'erroneous' beliefs back to orthodox Christianity.

From a modern perspective, based on respect for the freedom and integrity of the individual, such torture seems barbaric and utterly wrong. But the torturer would have believed that the immortal soul of the heretic was at stake: if he or she died holding heretical beliefs, the result would be an eternity in hell-fire. A brief period of pain now, even if it led directly to death, would have been seen as a merciful alternative.

A medieval inquisitor, transported through time to a modern society where it is acceptable to hold any or no religious beliefs, would think such a society wilfully cruel, allowing so many to continue in their error and thus suffer eternal damnation.

You cannot separate ethical judgements from the prevailing beliefs and values of the society within which they are made.

Over recent decades there has been an explosion of information from all parts of the globe. If there is famine, war, or natural disaster, we see it live on our televisions, and have come to expect some international effort in response – 'something must be done'. The problem with such international efforts is the degree to which they are hampered by any prevailing political or social ideologies in the countries concerned. Thus, what may be seen as an international peacekeeping force from one perspective might be felt to be an unwelcome invasion of foreign troops from another.

Example

The justification for the presence of British and American forces in Iraq, three years after the invasion, is that they are there to assist in the rebuilding of the country, and the establishment of an Iraqi government and police force that so that the country can rule itself. In the eyes of the soldiers on the ground, they are there to help – and they point out the danger of allowing anarchy free reign with more bloodshed as Sunni, Shi'a and Kurdish sections of the population confront one another. However, their presence is seen by others as that of an invading force. Moderates might accept that their aim is to assist the rebuilding of the country, but still regret their presence, even suggesting that it exacerbates rather than helps the security situation by giving cause for resentment.

- Clearly, there are no easy answers. Simply abandoning a country to sort out its own problems is one option, but is that morally right?
- Equally, is it right to refuse to respond where there is political chaos or serious physical need, on the grounds that such help might be viewed ambiguously?
- How do you balance the value of international action against the claims of individual countries to autonomy?
- Is it right to invade a country in order to protect its citizens from its own government?

The international community

There are two ways of approaching the ethical guidelines for international relationships: one considers basic human rights, the other is utilitarian.

The first approach is to start with the basic human rights that should be allowed to every human being, irrespective of the sort of political, social or religious community in which he or she lives.

Examples of this are the United Nations Universal Declaration on Human Rights, and also the Geneva Convention, which deals with the conduct of war and the treatment of prisoners.

Such an approach also recognizes the integrity and national sovereignty of individual countries. For this reason, the United Nations will operate within a country only if it is invited to do so by those whom it recognizes as the legal government.

A major problem with this approach is that it is difficult to enforce. Without the equivalent of an international police force, capable of requiring individual nations to comply, all the international community can do is to try to exert political or economic pressure in the hope that an individual country may eventually come to the conclusion that it is in its own best interests to comply with the will of the majority. Where one nation invades another, the United Nations may be involved in an attempt at peacekeeping, but has no authority to threaten or carry out an invasion of the aggressor nation in its attempt to stop the conflict.

A utilitarian approach, however, seeks to take into account the preferences of the maximum number of people. But utilitarianism comes up against two major problems when applied to these global issues:

1 A person may have conflicting loyalties. I may think of myself as a citizen of a particular region, or of a wider grouping of nations, but I may first of all think of myself as coming from a particular county, or even village. In times of civil war, local loyalties conflict with national ones.

Examples

During the wars in Bosnia and Kosovo, people of different ethnic groups who had previously lived together peacefully as part of a village community were suddenly thrust apart, and regarded one another as enemies, each supporting a national rather than a local identity.

- Does being a Serb or Croat or Kosovar Albanian count for more than being a member of a particular village?
- Is it right to take action against former neighbours who are from a different ethnic, religious or national group, just because the majority of members of your own group demand that you do so?

Another dramatic example of this is Iraq, where the Sunni, Shi'a and Kurds see themselves as distinct, but yet also form a single nation. The fundamental question to ask of an individual looking at the political future is whether it is possible to think of oneself

first and foremost as Iraqi, or whether the first loyalty is to the
Shi'a community.

The same problem exists in Nigeria, where the north of the
country is mainly Muslim and the south Christian. During the
worldwide reaction among the Muslim community to cartoons of
the Prophet Muhammad in early 2006, there were clashes and
loss of life between Muslims and Christians in Nigeria – thus what
starts as one moral issue unlocks the deeper issues of a country
divided along religious lines.

Example

In July 1995, during the Bosnian war, certain places that had been
designated 'safe havens' for Bosnian Muslims and 'protected' by
UN troops, were overrun by Bosnian Serbs. In just a few days,
7,000 Muslims in Srebrenica were murdered, mostly shot in the
head and dumped into mass graves.

What became clear by October of that year, and was confirmed
by the publication of letters in November 1999, was that the UN
had effectively given up on the attempt to protect the Muslim
minority in the 'safe areas'. Britain was said to have played a key

role in blocking military action that might have stopped the Serbs, and the UN later admitted that the insufficient military response resulted from 'an inability to recognize the scope of the evil that confronted us'. It was feared at the time that the use of military force would have put humanitarian aid programmes at risk.

In a report on the Bosnian conflict, submitted to the Security Council in November 1999, the Secretary General of the UN, Kofi Annan, comments: 'The cardinal lesson of Srebrenica is that a deliberate and systematic attempt to terrorize, expel or murder an entire people must be met decisively with all necessary means, and with the political will to carry the policy through to its logical conclusion.'

The whole dilemma of the ethics of international relations is that there are few means of enforcing the decisions taken. There is a gap between what may be perceived as right, and what is possible. Whether it is in the field of national sovereignty or of destruction of the environment, argument, economic and political pressure, and exclusion from international bodies, are the only available means of persuasion – and some nations consider that their own internal perceptions and aspirations take priority over those of the international community.

International pressure is brought to bear, however, by the threat to withhold the normal process of international trade in the form of sanctions, or the cutting of international political or financial ties. The problem is that such pressure works long-term, whereas the issue it is meant to address is immediate.

For reflection

Machiavelli recommended that, if a ruler had to administer punishment, he should do it quickly and efficiently. This would produce least resentment. But sanctions – as a means of enforcing international agreements – produce their results only slowly, and maximize resentment. They affect all those who live in a country, not just its rulers, and may produce a sense of national solidarity. On the other hand, sanctions do not generally involve loss of life.

There seems to be no way in which an international moral code could be translated into enforceable laws without loss of the principle of national sovereignty. The nearest that the United

Nations would appear to come to such a situation is, for example, in the terms imposed on Iraq after the First Gulf War. These include 'no fly' zones over areas of the north and south of the country, seeking to give some protection for the Kurds and the Marsh Arabs respectively. But even so, without military on the ground, it is impossible to prevent persecution of minority groups within a state.

But here there is another dilemma. If you maintain national sovereignty, how do you deal fairly with those groups of people who do not form a nation? An example of this is the Kurds, who are found in Iraq, Iran and Turkey.

For reflection

- Is it better for a nation to keep its borders open to receive those who are fleeing persecution in other parts of the world, or to close them in order to preserve the standard of living of its own citizens?

- In a democracy, should people be balloted on whether or not to allow citizens from other countries entry permits?

- If its own citizens enjoy a far higher standard of living than that of the refugees, are they morally required to take a small cut in their own standards in order that their government can offer a considerably improved standard of living to the refugees?

Poverty and international aid

In his book *Practical Ethics*, Peter Singer argued that if deliberately allowing people to die is no different (in moral terms) from actually killing them, then we are all guilty of murder, because we allow a situation to continue in which millions of people starve to death. On the other hand, he recognized that cutting one's standard of living to the bare minimum in order to do all that might be possible to help others to life would require 'moral heroism' far greater than simply refraining from killing.

A point for reflection

Imagine a situation where people from various developed and developing countries are sitting in a single room, each in the exact situation that would apply in his or her home territory. In one corner people would be naked and starving, in another they would be well clothed and fed.

> In such a situation, it would not be too difficult to imagine sharing both food and clothes. Indeed, it would be very difficult not to do so because the emotional impact of the proximity of poverty and starvation would be intense.

But the single room situation is an unrealistic abstraction. In practice, it is easy to refrain from sharing necessities because:

- No one individual is to blame.
- Social pressures and expectations are connected with a particular standard of living: to give all that up and accept shared poverty would require great determination. It could also affect others, who might not share your personal commitment to such poverty.
- Although they can be seen on television, for much of the time the starving are out of sight. Although there is intellectual awareness of their plight, there is no immediate emotional pressure to respond to, in the way that there might be if they were visible and present.
- When confronted with a particular emotional challenge a person can take practical steps. For example, many people respond emotionally to appeals on the television: some make a practical response by donating money; a few take on a longer-term commitment, as when Bob Geldof was moved by reports of the starving in Ethiopia in 1984 to found Band Aid, and the Live Aid concerts, in order to raise money and awareness to benefit those who were starving.
- It is possible to justify inaction by arguing that much poverty is not caused by simple lack of food, but by the political situation. Most areas of starvation are also those hit by military conflict. In the absence of such conflict it is easier for people to move and get food, or for external agencies to give aid effectively. It is also possible to plan long-term agricultural development if there is peace.

Aid is therefore a complex issue: it cannot be reduced to the single room situation. Some major ethical issues connected with it are:

- How, on a utilitarian basis, do you determine what is an appropriate level of wealth or poverty? (One person aspires to a level of material support that another might fear, thinking it the most abject poverty.)
- How do you give aid, whilst maintaining the personal integrity and independence of the people who receive that aid?

(This is based on the moral principle that sees human autonomy and independence as of primary importance.)

- Can any one individual be held morally responsible for a global situation? If not, is there corporate guilt, shared by all people of a particular nation, class, or economic level? (This is a real issue, for there have been riots connected with economic and social groups, e.g. migrant workers.)
- Does the presence of a factor over which I can have no control (e.g. a civil war in a developing country) be justification for taking no action to alleviate a condition which, in theory, I can control (e.g. by giving a donation to an aid agency to help famine relief, even though that agency realizes that the underlying cause of the famine requires a political solution)?

It depends on what you produce!

The poppy fields of Afghanistan produce a large percentage of the world's opium, and it is the main source of heroin in both Europe and America. Drugs do harm and the money made from drugs funds the Taliban, therefore it would seem to be morally right to destroy the poppy fields. However, doing that will cut off the livelihood of many poor farmers, for whom the poppy is their only crop. Hence there is a dilemma – unless you want to create further suffering, you need to make it possible for alternative crops to sustain the local economy. However, that cannot be done until the opium poppy and the drug trade based on it is removed. But that cannot happen until ... and so on.

Leave it to charities?

Many charities operate internationally. They respond to need and provide a means for people who feel that they have a moral responsibility to help to give practical expression to their moral convictions. But, typically, charities depend on:

- political co-operation from the country within which they wish to operate
- cessation of military action – or at least the agreement of the warring factions that the charities can operate.

So charitable help depends on agreements that concern national sovereignty and the terms and conditions under which wars are fought. When we look at ethics from a global perspective we therefore have to address these issues because, however much people wish to respond charitably, the help that can be given is limited or short term, without political stability and peace.

Fair trade

If those who live in the developing world are to be allowed to help themselves, they need to receive a fair price for the goods they produce or the food they grow. Apart from ensuring a long-term solution to the problem of poverty, this promotion of fair trade overcomes the stereotype of the charity as being an organization for doling out money to those it deems worthy to receive it. Fairtrade labels now appear on clothing, food, jewellery, flowers and cosmetics. By choosing to buy Fairtrade products, the customer at least knows that he or she is not exploiting those who have produced them.

Who is responsible?

Sometimes an individual – perhaps a head of state – is portrayed as being personally responsible for an issue that has international moral repercussions (e.g. Colonel Gaddafi of Libya is sometimes presented as personally responsible for decisions about the support of 'terrorists'; similarly, Saddam Hussein was presented as the embodiment of the threat posed by Iraq; President Bush was equally presented as responsible for the war against Iraq or the failure to capture Bin Laden). Although the media find this convenient, it may mask a more complex set of power relations, both within the countries concerned and internationally. International ethics is more often concerned with the relationships between institutions rather than individuals. And institutions are controlled by charters, and are required to operate within legally enforceable rules. It is not therefore immediately obvious who is morally responsible for the actions of an institution.

For reflection

If you are in charge of an institution you might act as its figurehead, and thus be seen as an appropriate person to blame if things go wrong. But:

- Should a minister of state be the person to resign if there is a scandal within his or her ministry?
- Is the chief executive of a charity responsible for individual decisions taken by his or her staff?

- Are you morally responsible for all those things that are done in your name (or in the name of an institution you represent)?
- If you knew something was wrong, but took no action, you made a moral choice. You are responsible – not for the original wrong, but for your own inaction.
- If you were not told that anything was wrong could you be blamed for not knowing, and therefore not acting? Surely, your responsibility in this case is to be well informed, and if you have not done everything within reason to find out what is happening you might be guilty of negligence. But does your negligence mean that you are guilty of whatever has gone wrong?

War and peace

War is the most destructive of all human activities – not just in terms of the loss of life and the damage done to the infrastructure of a country, but in the broader sense that war takes away the basic security that enables civilization to continue, for civilization depends on security and peace. Ethical issues arise whenever peace is threatened by an act of aggression, and, in general, actions are deemed 'just' or 'right' if they aim to re-establish peace and justice. But if a just peace can only be secured by the use or threat of violence, does that make it right?

It is not surprising then that there is an ongoing debate about the ethics of war, and this section will try to outline just a few of the key issues. The debate centres on a number of questions:

- When, if at all, is it right to go to war?
- Who has the right to declare war? A single nation? The United Nations?
- How should wars be fought, if they cannot be avoided?
- Is any one form of weapon inherently morally better than another?
- Is the use (or even the possession) of weapons of mass destruction ever justified ethically?
- How do you distinguish terrorism from warfare?
- Is it possible to guard against terrorism and warfare without eroding either civil liberties or the right of nations to self-determination?

And behind these questions are others relating to the relationship between individuals, minority groups and nations, where these give rise to conflicting loyalties. There is also the question of religion, and how that relates to the divisions between or within nations.

The 'Just War' theory

The starting point here is whether, and in what circumstances, a war can be considered just. There are two categories of issues here:

1 Those concerned with the right to go to war (*jus ad bellum*).
2 Those concerned with the way in which a war should be fought (*jus in bello*).

The principles for this were set out by Thomas Aquinas in the thirteenth century, but with later developments. A just war approach would argue that:

It may be just to go to war if:

1 it is done by proper authority (e.g. by a nation, not by an individual. Can a terrorist group be a 'proper authority'? And what of 'State-sponsored' terrorism – if the group has the backing or one or more sovereign states, would that make the act a valid act of war?)
2 there is a good reason to go to war (e.g. in self-defence. But does that give a nation the right to a pre-emptive strike against another, for example on the basis of intelligence that suggests the other is in possession of weapons of mass destruction?)
3 the intention of going to war is to establish peace and justice (in other words, war should not become an end in itself, but only a means of restoring justice).

The conduct of war is considered right only if:

1 it is waged against military personnel, not against civilians. (But is it ever possible to wage war without civilian casualties, either directly or indirectly? Can 'smart weapons', which claim to minimize 'collateral' damage, be seen as more acceptable morally? What about the economic harm and further suffering that civilians face even when the war is over?)
2 the force used is proportional. (In other words, the harm likely to be caused by an action should not outweigh what that

action sets out to gain. It is very difficult to judge this, but an example of its failure might be the huge loss of life in some of the battles of the First World War, for a negligible gain.)

3 minimum force is used in order to achieve one's end (which would preclude the use of all weapons of mass destruction, or excessive conventional force against a lightly defended target).

Those who go against the accepted norms of warfare may be accused of crimes against humanity if, for example, they deliberately set out to kill civilians. Here the issue is intention; was that killing the accidental consequence of military action or its deliberate aim? In other words, if civilians are killed because a bomb fails to hit its intended military target, does this have the same moral force as the deliberate disregard for civilian life? In weighing up such things, we need to ask if sufficient care was taken by those planning the attack, and so on.

Suicide of war criminal

Milan Babic, a former Croation Serb leader, was found dead in his cell in the detention unit in The Hague in March 2006; apparently he had hanged himself. He had admitted war crimes from the early 1990s. During his trial in 2004, he admitted that he had taken part in 'the worst kind of persecution of people simply because they were Croats and not Serbs' and added:

'Even when I learnt what had happened, I kept silent. Even worse, I continued in my office, and I became personally responsible for the inhumane treatment of innocent people.

These crimes and my participation therein can never be justified. I'm speechless when I have to express the depth of my remorse for what I have done and the effect that my sins have had on the others.'

Perhaps the most terrible point of moral choice was when he remained silent, and thus became drawn into accepting responsibility for what was going on. Responsibility here is quite different from that of a military commander who, within established conventions, makes decisions as a result of which many are killed. Here it is action outside the conventions of the 'just war'.

In terms of the ethical principles that underlie the conduct of war, there are two basic lines of argument. One is conformity to agreed statements about rights and responsibilities in the conduct of war. An example of this would be the Geneva Conventions about the treatment of those military personnel who are captured in war, prohibiting torture and so on. The other approach is to use a utilitarian assessment – whether it is the overall aim of a war, or the use of a particular weapon, there is a balance between what it is hoped to gain (e.g. ending the war sooner, restoring justice, saving the lives of other military or civilians) against the destruction and loss of life involved.

Terrorism

In general, acts of terrorism are condemned on a 'just war' theory, even if those carrying them out claim that their cause is just, because:

- they are not backed by legitimate authority. (But should a nation state constitute that authority, or the United Nations? Can a religion constitute valid authority?)
- they are generally (but not always) aimed at causing civilian casualties as a means of influencing public and political opinion.

In a war situation, the invading nation has a responsibility to restore peace to the country it invades. Failure to take proper steps to manage the aftermath of war detracts from any moral validity in conducting that war in the first place. With terrorism, this is simply not possible. The terrorist causes destruction as a political gesture, as an act of anger or defiance. He or she is not in a position to restore the situation to normality after the damage has been done. Hence the normal rules of war are set aside, and it cannot be argued, for example, that minimum force has been used to achieve an aim.

There is a fundamental problem with historical perspectives on this. Yesterday's terrorist may, in retrospect, be seen as a freedom fighter and become an ally. This is particularly significant where terrorism has been limited (or has attempted to limit itself) to attacks on military personnel or other representatives of the state, rather than on the civilian population. Hence, the terrorist of today may see his or her action as an expression of a struggle that will one day vindicate the acts of terror – seeing them as the only option in a situation where injustice cannot be opposed by legitimate means. The standard counter to such an argument is that all other methods to restore justice should be exhausted first, which is seldom the case.

From bombs to ballots: Is Hammas fit to govern?

This is the headline in the *Independent* on Friday 27 January 2006, as the Palestinian group Hammas, who had waged a terrorist war against Israel, killing 427 over the previous six years, celebrated winning a majority of seats in the Palestinian parliament.

- Is it possible for a group to change fundamentally once it is given a democratic mandate to rule?
- If democracy (particularly in the Middle East) is seen by the West as the ideal political vehicle with which to move forward, can the democratic choice of the Palestinian people not be respected?

If the initial answer to either or both of those questions in 'no', how is it ever possible to produce reconciliation and progress when one faction or political group has resorted to terrorism in order to seek what it perceives to be justice? Does an act of terrorism effectively close off the possibility of a negotiated agreement in the future?

But this raises questions about how you produce a utilitarian assessment of the long-term results of any action. The terrorist might claim that his or her action will, in the long run, contribute to an overall justice and will therefore be justified. Others will argue that the intended end result, however just in itself, cannot be used to justify acts that deliberately cause suffering to the innocent.

Weaponry

All weapons which by their nature and method of use are likely to cause civilian casualties, or are not a proportionate response to a threat, or which do not represent minimum necessary force, may be deemed wrong. In the extreme case, the use of weapons of mass destruction (i.e. nuclear, chemical and biological weapons), which by their nature cause widespread damage and loss of life, cannot be justified. The only justification for holding such weapons is deterrence. On the other hand, conventional weapons, used inappropriately (e.g. the systematic bombing of cities) can have the same devastating effect as weapons of mass destruction, and can therefore be condemned on the same basis.

Smart weapons are designed to destroy their pre-selected targets and minimize collateral damage. The sight of a cruise missile flying along a street in Baghdad, before turning right to seek out a particular basement of a government building, is awesome in its use of technology for warfare. The aim is that, with smart weapons, a country might be subdued with minimum loss of life. Although, in spite of the huge increase in the use of such weapons (e.g. between the First and the Second Gulf War), civilians continue to be killed, since no war can be exclusively 'smart'. But is a weapon with such a specific aim therefore more moral than one that kills in a less well targeted way, or that causes more civilian casualties?

Religion and warfare

Historically, many wars have been fought between nations or groups that are from different religions, or different branches of a single religion. Are such religious differences the cause of war, or are they used as a proxy for deeper social and economic divisions? Modern examples might include the conflicts and tensions in the Middle East between Jews and Muslims, in Kashmir between Muslims and Hindus, in Nigeria between Christians and Muslims, in Iraq between Sunni and Shi'a Muslims and until recently in Northern Ireland between the Catholic and Protestant communities. Looking further back in history, there were the Crusades and later the Wars of Religion in Europe, following the Reformation.

The just war arguments presented above came from a Western tradition that was largely influenced by Christianity. But Judaism and Islam also have clearly defined principles of self-defence, regulating when it is appropriate, or even necessary, to take up arms.

According to the Talmud, both Jews and non-Jews may kill a pursuer in order to save their own life. It is also permissible to kill an attacker who is threatening the life of another person. But it is obligatory for a Jew to attempt to stop, and if necessary to kill, a person who is trying to kill another Jew. These come from the scriptural principle of the right to self-defence. But it is wrong to kill a person after he or she has committed the act and is allowed only as a way of preventing them from doing so. So, according to Jewish principles here, killing should not be for the purpose of punishment only – it is only permitted in order to seek to prevent further harm.

When it comes to warfare itself, the principle again is one of self-defence. In general the interpretation of the Talmud does not permit warfare for the purpose of territorial expansion and aggression. Warfare should also be restrained. So, for example, in laying siege to a city, one should do so on three sides only, never completely, so that civilians and those who do not wish to fight should be given some means of escape. On the other hand, it is clear that, if Israel or a Jewish population is under threat, there is an obligation to go to war against the aggressor.

In Islam, there is the principle of *jihad*, which may be translated as 'struggle'. It takes two forms: the 'greater jihad' is the spiritual struggle of every Muslim to overcome personal faults, but the 'lesser jihad' is obligation to struggle against external threats to Islam or the community of Muslims.

Valid reasons for performing the lesser *jihad*:

• to defend the Ummah (the Community of the Islam) against external threat. (e.g. if a Muslim country, or the Muslim population within a country, is threatened, Jihad against the aggressor becomes an obligation)

• to fight on behalf of the oppressed against injustice (whether or not the victims of that injustice are Muslim).

However, there are rules about how *jihad* should be put into practice. It should be used only as a last resort, when peaceful means fail to defend the community, it should be carried out with compassion, causing minimum suffering to achieve its aim, and it should seek to establish justice.

A Muslim is therefore obliged to protect both himself or herself and other people against injustice, but not to initiate violence. The key text for this in the Qur'an is Sura 2: 190–191. 'Fight in the way of God against those who fight against you, but begin not hostilities. Lo! God loves not the aggressor.'

Within both Hinduism and Sikhism there is a tradition of self-defence, although within Hinduism there is an ancient principle of *ahimsa*, refraining from taking life of any sort. This same principle is found in Buddhism, and particularly in Jainism. Hence, for these religions, the consequences (karma) of taking life are very serious, and warfare is to be avoided by all means possible. Passive resistance has been a key feature of the *ahimsa* approach to perceived injustice.

Feminist issues

It may be argued that much traditional thinking has been biased against women, since most ethical thinkers have been male, and their values and arguments have been influenced by their gender. Feminist thinkers are therefore quick to point out that many views are not reached as a result of rational argument, but are the unquestioned norms of a particular society and culture, norms that frequently disregarded the views, needs and abilities of women.

Feminism arose out of this perceived injustice, and to appreciate feminist ethics it is therefore useful to reflect on the historical relationship between the sexes and its influences on women's consciousness and moral concerns.

The feminist movement generally traces its origins to the eighteenth century. With the coming of the Industrial Revolution, more men took paid employment away from home, while the women remained at home to bring up the children and became dependent on male earnings. For the previous two centuries men had started to demand more religious freedom and civil rights, but had done so in a way that largely excluded women.

From that period, stimulated by Mary Wollstonecraft's *A Vindication of the Rights of Women* (1792), 'feminists' (to use the term in a broad sense of those concerned with women's rights) campaigned for education, for equality in work, and for a place in civil and political life. They argued against what they saw as domestic tyranny and unfair treatment, in a world in which the laws, the economic system and socially accepted ways of behaving, were devised for the benefit of men.

By the second half of the twentieth century the issues had broadened considerably. It was no longer a matter of women working unequally within the existing male-dominated structures, but an overall critique of the language and culture that reflected those structures, along with a new awareness of the value and significance of womanhood and of female sexuality.

One particular criticism of existing moral systems from a feminist perspective was that they were based on arguments formulated by male philosophers and emphasizing the place of reason rather than intuition or emotional commitment, and therefore biased against women (the earlier view, held by Wollstonecraft and others, was that reason was 'gender neutral'). The 1950s saw the development of virtue ethics (see

Chapter 06) as one way to get away from 'masculine' discussion of rights and duties, towards a consideration of the qualities that make a person 'good'.

Headteacher decapitated by Taliban

In January 2006, armed men dragged a secondary school headteacher into a courtyard and forced his family to watch as they cut off his head. This took place in Qalat, Afghanistan. And the reason? The school offered education to girls. In the previous months, threatening notices had been pinned to walls in the town, calling for an end to the education of girls. The previous month a teacher in another province had been pulled out of his classroom and shot. Many schools are closed, and only 8 per cent of the pupils in those that remain open are girls.

This followed a series of attacks on schools and colleges, of which 165 had been burnt down or forced to close.

Clearly, there is a fundamental difference in the perception of the place of women in society, between the Taliban militants on the one hand and the Afghan government and the agencies that are there attempting to assist it on the other. Those campaigning for the right of women to be treated equally, whatever society they live in, could argue that the very brutality of the attacks illustrates the problem of a male-dominated political and religious ideology.

Although Islamic society tends to treat women rather differently from men, it is essential to distance the actions of a radical minority from the fundamental views of Islam as a religion and way of life. In any case, it is difficult in all such situations to decide where religion ends and politics begins – for deeply held social and political attitudes tend to become associated with the religion with which they are associated.

A key question for feminist ethics (as for virtue ethics) concerns essentialism: is there a particular, fixed 'essence' of womanhood? In other words, are there particular features of being a woman that influence her emotions, aspirations and sexuality, or are these things simply created by society and therefore able to be changed by common consent? The overall aim of much feminist thinking was to find structures that would enable women to fulfil themselves as women. Hence feminist ethics has, to some extent, taken the 'personal development' approach, along with an appreciation of distinctively feminine virtues.

Feminist views impinge on many areas of ethics, including **business ethics** (e.g. the 'glass ceiling' above which few women manage to rise; the inequality of opportunity in the workplace), environmental ethics and sexual ethics. But there are also issues that are of particular concern because they are intimately connected with the experience of womanhood within situations dominated by men. An extreme among such situations is rape.

Rape

The sexual urge is probably the strongest of all human inclinations, and it is 'natural' – both in the sense that it fits in with what people would do in a natural state, unchecked by laws, and because (through its functions of continuing the species) it has a place within the 'natural law' scheme of morality.

Although social customs and laws vary from one country to another, heterosexual intercourse is generally legal, provided that:

- the partners are over the age of consent
- consent is freely given
- it does not cause public nuisance (e.g. it should be done in private).

Rape is the term used for an act of sexual intercourse where consent is not given, or where a partner is below the age at which valid consent can be given (statutory rape). It is the violation of one person by another, as opposed to legal sexual intercourse, which is enjoyed (hopefully) by mutual agreement. But once we start to ask about what is natural, there are many issues to be considered.

- According to natural law, every act of intercourse should be open to the possibility of conception, and should (on a strict interpretation) have that as its 'end'. Does this mean that the forcible act of intercourse imposed by a husband upon a wife in order to conceive a child (assuming that the wife does not want to conceive) is therefore right?
- Is marital rape possible, or does marriage imply acceptance of sexual intercourse under all conditions? Is there a point at which it is 'natural' for one or other partner to refuse to have sex?
- In the case of the rape of a stranger, it is assumed that the person committing the rape finds the victim sexually

attractive. If the person raped actually dresses in a way that is sexually provocative, or behaves in a provocative manner, can he or she be considered to have contributed to that act of rape, by deliberately behaving in a way that invites sexual attention? Is it 'natural' to want to look sexy? If so, can one then argue that it is wrong for a person to respond to that implied sexual invitation?

Date rape

Two students attend a dance and both become drunk. They return at the end of the evening to the girl's room and sexual intercourse takes place. The following day, realizing what has happened, the girl claims that she has been raped.

In defence, her partner argues that they were both drunk at the time, and that the girl was a willing partner in the sexual act, and was not subject in any way to force.

- If there are no strict social rules (e.g. if it is believed that other students in a similar situation would willingly take part in sex), does acceptance of a situation (returning to her room) imply consent?
- Can rape be retrospectively applied to an unwise sexual act?
- How specific does consent have to be? Does it have to include verbal agreement, or can it be intuited?
- 'Date rape' is a feature of social ambiguity. Two people go out together, each expecting something different of the other. Is it reasonable to separate out the act of intercourse (which gives rise to the claim that rape has taken place) from the rest of the social situation?
- Does it make any moral sense, in the case of date rape, to ask about what is 'natural' as opposed to what is agreed by written, verbal or implied contract?

This issue of date rape highlights the difference between 'natural law', what is 'natural' and what is socially acceptable. It is an area where legislation seems most difficult to frame, simply because it is such a 'natural' situation, open to the personal interpretation of the parties involved.

From a traditional feminist perspective, a critical emphasis may be placed on the assumption made by men in cases of date rape that women will, unless they make it clear to the contrary, be sexually available.

Other women would not wish to place such an emphasis, and whilst asserting the absolute right to veto sexual activity where it is unwanted, would see men and women as more equal participants in the ambiguities of selecting sexual partners.

There can be a backlash within feminism (or post-feminism) against over-emphasis of the vulnerability of women in cases of rape, or the treatment of rape as a unique form of crime against the person. In a television interview in 1998, Camille Paglia – an American academic and social critic, who describes herself as a feminist – was quoted as saying: 'If rape is a totally devastating psychological experience for a woman then she doesn't have a proper attitude towards sex.' She has been critical of some feminists, suggesting that they encourage women to think of themselves as victims.

There is also the argument that traditional notions of rape are based on the idea of women being man's property, and rape therefore rendering her valueless. Quite apart from the violence, both physical and emotional, shown to the person raped, this highlights the wider issue of the perception of gender differences, and of women as being valued primarily in terms of their value for men.

Protection for rape victims?

In Libya, women and girls who have been raped are placed in centres for what may be described as 'social rehabilitation.' Accused of 'brainwashing' by a human rights report, the Libyan government responded by arguing that the report ignored Islamic values and the protection of women who might be in danger of 'honour' killings by their family.

(Reported by Anne Penketh, *The Independent*, 28 February 2006, p. 26.)

- One issue to consider here is how you balance an international standard by which human rights might be judged against the expectations of a particular society or religion. When does protection become punishment?

Sexual issues

It is a caricature of medieval society to say that the sexual act was often one expressing power and property rather than love, or even straightforward lust. Nevertheless, it is true that for many societies and for much of history the legitimate expression of sexuality has been controlled by social norms, including the stability of family life (requiring sex to be confined to marriage partners) the prohibition of homosexuality, and the use of marriage as a means of forging political, financial or social links between families or even nations. Clearly, in such situations the moral dilemmas are more to do with power and control, with treating other people as ends rather than means, and of the relative importance of society and the individual.

By contrast, there have been other societies where the norms of sexual behaviour have been quite different from those of Western countries in the twenty-first century. The liberal approach to bisexuality in Ancient Greece, for example, was not something to be challenged by philosophers, but was accepted as the norm.

Sexual morality is a topic in which relativism and existentialism have considerable influence – for the quest for meaning in life generally involves understanding one's own sexuality, and when it comes to sex, proclivities and expectations vary enormously, and what seems natural and right to one person may disgust another.

The history of sexuality need not concern us here, except to point out that, in modern debates about sexuality, there are at least three different ethical approaches.

The 'natural law' approach

This approach, exemplified by the views of the Catholic Church, tends to separate the sexual act itself from general issues of sexuality and sexual orientation, and to regard it as objectively either right or wrong, depending on whether or not it includes the possibility of fulfilling its natural function, the procreation of children. As we argued previously (see page 48), such an approach tends to regard masturbation, homosexuality, oral and anal sex as wrong, simply because they cannot lead to conception.

Sexual orientation, if it does not lead to specific sexual acts, is a different matter. Commenting (in July 1993) on discussions about whether the age of consent for homosexual sex should be lowered, the late Cardinal Hume is reported to have said that, while homosexual acts are 'objectively wrong', they (homosexuals) should not feel guilty about their sexual orientation. The Vatican speaks of homosexuality as a 'disorder', but that should not imply a sinful situation or even a sickness.

Notice an implication of this distinction. A homosexual relationship – in the sense of an emotional attachment between two people of the same sex – is not itself sinful. This means that, if you take personal development and fulfilment as a criterion of morality, then there is nothing wrong with homosexuality. The only debate is between those of the 'natural law' view, who see specific acts of homosexual sex as wrong, and those who, examining mainly the relationship and its implications, judge it as they would a heterosexual one – the actual nature of the sexual acts being considered less important than the emotional commitment and affection that they express.

Utilitarianism

When it comes to the problems of sexual relationship, the agony columns of magazines are full of utilitarian advice, which generally takes the form 'if you do X, the likely consequence will be Y.' Hence, for example, contraception is recommended in order to avoid unwanted pregnancy, which in turn is presented as a situation likely to lead to unhappiness, either because it ends up with an abortion or through motherhood for someone not ready or able to take on that commitment.

On that basis, wearing condoms is advised, to avoid pregnancy and HIV infection. The fact that it frustrates the natural 'end' of sex in the conception of children is of less consequence. Indeed, for the person asking for advice about their situation, conceiving a child was most unlikely to have been their intended 'end'. Sex may have been all to do with lust, or self-esteem, or not wanting to be considered prudish, of seeking to please, or not wanting to be left out. Hence the issue of whether sex is 'right' or 'wrong' depends, for a utilitarian, on a whole range of 'preferences' for those involved.

A typical utilitarian view might be expressed as:

'It's not hurting anyone, and it's what we want, so why shouldn't we?'

Let us assume that this view is taken by a teenager, confronted by a parent who realizes that he or she is in a sexual relationship. The parent might argue:

1 'It's wrong unless you're married.'
2 'It will lead to unhappiness because ...'
3 'Well, if you're going to have sex anyway, just make sure you use contraception.'

The first of these is based on an absolute rule, which could be backed up either in terms of a religious or social tradition. Marriage is a contractual and social phenomenon, not a biological one, so it is no good trying to argue the case for sex being restricted to marriage by some form of natural law argument. It can be countered only by opposing the authority on which it is based.

The second is clearly utilitarian, and will probably become the fall-back argument if the first is challenged. The third is equally utilitarian, and illustrates the way in which a utilitarian argument can shift with changing circumstances. While there is a possibility that the young person may be dissuaded from having sex, the utilitarian argument sets out the possible hazards, but once it becomes clear that the option in favour of sex is inevitable, then the next best moral outcome is one that attempts to minimize harm.

It is interesting to note that, although the arguments presented by the parent and the young person may sound very different – the one authoritarian and the other libertarian – they may actually be using very similar utilitarian methods of assessment.

So, for example, in advertising about contraception and the risks of HIV infection, the arguments in favour of taking a 'responsible' approach to sex are utilitarian. The same utilitarian approach surrounds issues of adultery and the break-up of marriages. Very often the crucial factor in the discussion is not the fact of the sexual desire of a married person for someone other than their marriage partner, but on the potential harm this might do to others, and particularly to children of the marriage.

And the utilitarian assessment spreads outwards from the adulterous relationship – to take both the particular people involved, and the more general point about the number of single parent families in society, their dependence upon the State for welfare help and so on. In these arguments, the sexual act is not considered from a traditional 'rule-based' point of view, but from one that includes the emotional, social and economic consequences.

I am not arguing here that the utilitarian approach is necessarily the right one in dealing with sexual ethics, merely that it is very commonly used in such debates.

Personal growth

Increasingly, people claim that they embark on a sexual relationship as part of the quest for personal fulfilment. The ideal relationship is portrayed as one that enables both partners to grow as individuals through their contact with one another. Sex is seen in that context – as a pleasure in itself, but also as a way of becoming intimate with the partner, sharing in a way that has an effect on the relationship as a whole. Unlike those motivated by lust, this approach sees sex as a means to an end, not necessarily an end in itself. If the sex helps to cultivate a good, fulfilling relationship, then it is good.

This approach is increasingly used to justify the establishment or break-up of a relationship. The image of the bored and depressed housewife, whose life is stunted through a relationship that offers her no personal fulfilment, has been the starting point of books and films. Equally, the middle-aged man, sexually attracted to a younger woman, finds that he starts to take new interest in his appearance. By falling helplessly in love, he discards conventional values by which he has lived for years. He also discovers things about himself.

These vignettes are not in themselves the subject matter of ethical debate – although, fleshed out with details, they can become so – but they illustrate the fact that in many spheres of modern Western society, the criterion used for the assessment of sexuality and marriage is that of personal development, and of self-discovery, renewed energy and self-confidence through a fulfilling relationship.

The fact that personal development, particularly for women, can become an important touchstone of sexuality illustrates changes in society. Sexual behaviour can become intertwined with sexism – the belief that one sex is superior to the other. There have been (and still are) societies in which a wife is regarded as the property of her husband. In Britain, until 1882 women had no control over their own property or money once they were married. What does this sort of control and power do to the physical side of sexual relationships? Power, independence, and women's control over their fertility have made sexuality a much more balanced thing, and have allowed personal development to be viewed as a realistic expectation of the sexual relationship.

Divorce

When divorce was introduced into English law in 1670, it was available to men (not women) by an Act of Parliament, and only on the grounds of adultery or life-threatening cruelty. Prior to that divorce was granted only by the Church courts, and on the basis of non-consummation, impotence or insanity. The present UK divorce rules were set down in the 1969 Divorce Reform Act, which introduced the idea of a 'no fault' divorce, on the basis of mutual consent and two years' separation. However, adultery is still cited as grounds for divorce in 27 per cent of cases. With the changing grounds for divorce and the huge increase in the numbers of people divorcing, there has come a very different view of the nature and expectation of marriage.

Where there is a fixed view of the nature of marriage and of family life, the break-up of marriages is generally seen as morally wrong, and as going against the fundamental purpose of marriage. In the eyes of the Catholic church, for example, a marriage can be ended only if it can be shown never to have been a valid marriage in the first place. In other words, its validity is based on something deeper than the legal formality of marriage.

For others, the relationship is what counts, and the formalizing of that in terms of marriage is a secondary matter – and one that is determined entirely by social convention. In such arguments, it is the quality of the relationship that counts, and if that relationship has broken down, then divorce is simply the legal acknowledgement of what has happened. The acceptance of divorce on the grounds of 'the irretrievable breakdown of the marriage', rather than because of some particular 'fault' on the part of one or other of the partners, implies that it is the future (or lack of it) for this particular relationship that constitutes the basis for divorce.

When it comes to the practicalities of divorce – division of property, the proper care of any children of the marriage and provision for the welfare of all concerned – the criteria used shift towards the utilitarian; seeking to minimize pain, if not actually to promote happiness.

Some issues in medical ethics

Medical ethics is concerned with the moral principles by which doctors and other therapists decide how they should treat patients, and with the way in which medical technology as a whole should be used within society.

Medical ethics is seldom based on utilitarian principles alone, for there are serious questions about the meaning of 'health' and general principles of the value of human life to be taken into consideration. There are also questions about when life starts and when it ends. Medicine may be practised by those who see it as an expression of their own religious commitment, and their particular religious values.

Nevertheless, some of the most topical questions for medicine today are often considered in a way that reflects a utilitarian approach to ethics.

Research

In 1964, the World Medical Association set out principles that were intended to guide doctors who were to be involved with medical research. Two of these principles are definitely utilitarian. They are:

- That the objectives of the research should be in proportion to the inherent risk to the subject (in other words, the probable results should justify what is being done).
- Before starting any clinical trial, the risks involved should be assessed in terms of the foreseeable benefits to the subject. In other words, the person taking part in the medical trial should be expected to benefit personally. It would not be acceptable to expect a person to accept a risk just for the sake of some future unspecified gain in medical knowledge, however important that might be held to be.

Example

During the Second World War medical experiments were forcibly carried out, under the Nazi regime, on inmates of concentration camps. These were regarded as crimes, because there was no intention to offer the subjects any benefit – they were harmed simply for the sake of gaining medical knowledge.

Organ transplants

There are two ways in which utilitarian arguments are used in this issue. Let us consider the situation with kidney transplants. Many thousands of people suffer kidney failure in Britain each year, but there are not sufficient medical facilities to treat them all and some die as a result. A significant number are waiting for a kidney transplant at any one time. If doctors were allowed to take the kidneys from any healthy person who was killed in an accident, more patients would benefit. This might suggest that there should be an 'opt out' clause for the transplantation of organs, so that doctors could be free to operate on anyone who had died unless he or she carried some identification deliberately forbidding such an operation. (At the moment, permission has to be obtained from next of kin, often in very difficult circumstances.)

Issues here include:

- Freedom of the individual (to allow or forbid transplantation of organs).
- Whether or not a dead person has rights.
- Whether a relative of a recently deceased person is morally justified in refusing to allow transplantation of their organs, given the benefit that can be gained by doing so.
- Whether the scale of human medical need should be allowed to overrule other considerations – allowing automatic removal of suitable organs, including those of brain-dead but artificially sustained patients.

A second moral issue regarding transplantation is quite different. It examines the cost of transplant operations, and compares it with the benefit to the health of people through routine screening and other less costly forms of treatment. A utilitarian might then ask if it is right to give one person a heart transplant, if the money for that operation could have been used to benefit a greater number of people with less dramatic illnesses. This is not the same as the choice between forms of treatment (e.g. between a kidney transplant or maintaining a person on dialysis), but whether the cost of either is justified, given the state of human health globally, following a strictly utilitarian moral line.

Sometimes transplantation involves a living donor, for example, with bone-marrow transplants, the donor is often a close relative. In the case of a relative, or a volunteer discovered as a result of the search for a compatible donor, there is little by way of a moral problem. A person is free to give something for the benefit of another. On the other hand, should you create a person in order for them to become a donor? This rare moral dilemma is a real one.

Example

It was reported in *The Independent* in April 1990 that a woman in the USA had decided to have a second child, in order that the baby might provide bone marrow suitable for transplanting into her 17-year-old daughter, who suffered from leukaemia.

This step was taken because a nationwide search had failed to find any compatible donors.

Tests on the mother showed that the then unborn child was a girl, and that she had a 99 per cent chance of being a compatible donor.

- Is it right to bring a child into the world with the specific intention of using that life to save another, even that of a close relative?

A strictly utilitarian argument would say that it is, provided that the newly born child did not risk death as a result of giving life. Those whose ethics are closer to the 'natural law' approach might argue that it is a misuse of the process of giving birth to do so only for the secondary reason of saving someone else. On the other hand, you might want to argue that many children are conceived as a result of a failure of contraception – is that more moral than to conceive for a specific purpose? What of the person who conceives a child in order to have an heir to inherit a personal fortune? Is that any more or less manipulative than to conceive in order to use the child for a more immediate life-saving medical process?

There are general questions to be asked about the morally acceptable limits of medical and scientific procedures. Are such procedures to be evaluated in terms of potential benefits? If so, it is very difficult to specify exactly how much is to be gained, or from what particular experiments. One of the main areas here is the use of 'spare' embryos – collections of cells that could, in suitable circumstances, develop into a human being – for experimentation. The argument against such experimentation is based largely on when human life is considered to begin – and therefore on whether the use of these early embryos is the equivalent of killing human beings. The argument in favour is based on a utilitarian assessment of the potential benefit to be gained from such experimental work.

Example

In July 1998, the British government announced new guidelines to minimize the risk to the public of the use of 'humanized' animal organs in transplantation (xenotransplantation). Living pig tissue had already been used in clinical trials. The benefit of having a supply of tissue is to be balanced against the dangers that animal diseases may be transmitted to humans, with unpredictable consequences.

Here, the arguments are generally utilitarian, evaluating the situation with respect to humans rather than pigs.

In many of these debates, we see that two different forms of ethical argument are set against one another: 'natural law' (or at least a general view of the nature and rights of a human being) against 'utilitarianism', representing the results that are anticipated.

Clearly, there is a general moral duty on doctors and other health service employees to treat the sick to the best of their ability. However, when it comes to allocating limited resources, it is a matter of assessing how benefit should be spread across the range of deserving cases. The basis of decisions then becomes a utilitarian one – as competing claims are weighted against each other.

Why rationing looms for the NHS

Under this headline, an article by Jeremy Laurence in *The Independent*, 2 March 2006, examined the choices facing the British health service as it appeared to be heading for a deficit of £790 million by the end of the financial year. It was pointed out that, in spite of pressure to do so, NHS trusts and health authority chief executives had failed to implement sufficient cuts to come into line with the required budget.

With the cost of modern treatment, the expectations of patients, and the need to upgrade hospital facilities and equipment, there is almost no limit to what could be spent on a health service. In spite of introducing a market-based system in the NHS, with primary care trusts purchasing treatment from the hospital trusts who provide it, the system has not managed to control spending. Hence the prospect of rationing – 'It is a word, and a prospect, that health ministers dread.'

- How do you decide between pay rises for medical staff, the provision of new equipment and buildings, and the on-going cost of drugs and basic care? How do you evaluate – if it came to that choice – between one very expensive operation that stands only a modest chance of success for a seriously ill patient and the provision of more straightforward procedures that can enhance the quality of life for many people? Would a straight utilitarian assessment suffice here?

Ovarian grafts

In 1999, in New York Methodist Hospital, a surgeon succeeded in grafting ovarian tissue back into a patient from whom it had originally been removed and frozen. This aims to allow women to regain their fertility after undergoing treatment that renders them sterile by destroying their ovaries. The tissue is simply removed before the treatment and replaced afterwards.

Such a technique could have the additional consequence of allowing women to have children later in life by returning their own younger ovarian tissue to them. A representative of the Royal College of Obstetricians and Gynaecologists in London commented: 'We decided that in the light of recent scientific progress it was time to consider the ethical issues and develop a voluntary code of best practice.'

The beginning and end of life

If ethics is concerned to examine moral issues that relate to the rights and responsibilities of individuals and to the value of human life that are implied by them, it is understandable that all matters related to choosing when life should begin and when it should end, are going to be of particular importance. Ethics is most sharply focused when it is a matter of life or death, whether that is at the beginning or end of the human life-span.

Artificial methods of conception

Statistics vary, but around 10 per cent of heterosexual partnerships are naturally infertile. Of these, the infertility is due to the woman in about 85 per cent of cases.

The possibilities for overcoming this are:

1 If it is not possible for the couple to conceive through copulation, the male partner's semen may be used for artificial insemination – called AIH (Artificial Insemination – Husband).

2 If the male partner is infertile, the couple could use semen from a donor – called AID (Artificial Insemination – Donor).

3 If the woman cannot produce a viable ovum, this can be supplied by a donor, fertilized using the partner's semen, and then implanted in the womb.

4 Where neither ovum nor semen are viable, both can be donated, brought together and fertilized artificially, and then implanted in the womb. In this case the whole embryo has been donated, with no genetic link with either partner.

5 If either or both sperm and ovum are viable, but the woman cannot go through pregnancy and childbirth, it is possible to arrange surrogacy (womb leasing). Sperm and ovum are brought together – either being donated – and artificially implanted in the womb of the surrogate mother.

Some issues raised by this:

1 The last three of these methods have been made possible by in-vitro fertilization (i.e. the natural process of fertilization takes place in an artificial environment, literally 'in glass'). Is the development of this medical technique moral, immoral or amoral in itself?

• Most technical developments are amoral. For example, a fast car is not immoral in itself, but may become the occasion of immoral activity if it is driven in a way that endangers life. A first ethical point to decide is whether there should be limits to technology, or a point at which the development and availability of a technology is in itself immoral. Here, of course, everything depends on the basis of your ethical argument – natural law, utilitarianism, personal development, etc. A utilitarian argument (see

Chapter 04) will justify a technology if it offers overall benefit to those involved – and on this basis, any medical technique that people believe will improve their life is acceptable (except, of course, if the cost of such techniques means that other people are deprived of basic medical care). If the criterion used to assess this is the personal development of the individuals concerned, then any technique that improves personal mental or physical performance is justified.

In setting your limits (if any) to what medical technology should be allowed to offer, you might want to consider:

- Would you like (e.g. through genetic engineering) to be able to choose the sex and all the physical characteristics of your child? If so, would you like to live in a world where everyone's characteristics had been selected in this way?

- If it were possible, would you be prepared to authorize a brain transplant for someone close to you – enabling life to continue, but with a totally different set of mental characteristics and memories? Who would the 'new' person be?

- Would you authorize the development and use of a medical technique that could save lives but would be so expensive that it would starve other medical services of funds? (This is a realistic and serious moral issue within any health service whose funds are limited.)

- You might argue that, in a world where there are quite enough unwanted children, it is immoral to develop expensive techniques to conceive more. Infertile couples should be encouraged to adopt children instead.

2 Where either semen or ovum (or both) has been provided by a donor, should the resulting child ever be given information about that donor or donors?

- What is the basis of human individuality? Is it the genetic link with parents as providers of semen and ovum or with parents as those who care for a child and bring it up? Is the donor really a parent? You might want to contemplate the difference between a child who is adopted, and who claims the right to find out details of his or her natural parents, and the child who is actually born from the womb of his or her 'mother', but who finds that genetically he or she is linked with one (or two) unknown donors.

- If the donor could be traced, should the child be able to inherit from that donor, or make any other claim? Alternatively, should a donor be able to make any claim on a child born as a result of that donation?

3 With surrogacy, this problem has an added complication because the 'natural' mother and the 'parents' are in touch with one another, and the situation is reversed – in that it is the donor (or donors) who find themselves bringing up 'their' child.

- In Britain, following the 1990 Human Fertilization and Embryology Bill, the 'mother' in such cases is defined as the woman who gives birth, and the 'father' is her husband, provided that he has agreed to the procedure (i.e. the person who donated the semen is not considered to be the legal father of the child, whether that person was an unknown donor or the person commissioning the surrogacy). This means that the couple who want to use a surrogate mother place themselves in the position of donors – once the child is fertilized, the legal 'mother' is the person in whose womb that embryo is lodged. The commissioning couple then have to adopt the child once it is born, although this adoption is not legally enforceable. It is possible for the surrogate mother to change her mind and refuse to hand over the child.

- The surrogate mother may be a close relative of the donor couple, or she may be previously unknown to them. She may give her services free, claim only her expenses, or (illegally in Britain) receive payment.

- The British Medical Association (BMA) published a report on surrogacy in 1990, offering guidelines to doctors. The ethical basis of the recommendations was that all decisions should be made in the best interests of the child. It also advised that surrogacy should be considered only after the failure of all other methods of fertility treatment.

4 The conception of a child is a biological process, part of which may be carried out in an artificially constructed environment. But the birth is also a matter of personal relationships and the emotions associated with them. In a 'natural' context, these two features of human reproduction come together in an act of sex that leads to pregnancy and birth.

- The BMA guidelines mentioned above take the basis of ethical decisions as the welfare of the child to be conceived – this is a utilitarian argument, based on expected results. A natural law argument would want to consider the welfare of the child that is to be born, but would do so in the context of whether or not the actual process of conceiving that child was in accordance with an understanding of what is the natural place of sex and childbirth in human life. In doing this, it would separate out the actual technical acts involved with the conception, and assess each of these rationally.

- You might argue, on the basis of natural law, that, because the sexual act is the natural way in which fertilization takes place, the attempt to replicate that process in a clinical environment detracts from the unique and personal context of natural fertilization. If you take this line of argument, you might need to accept that many other medical techniques – from life-saving surgery to the use of antibiotics – could also be challenged. The whole basis of medicine is to change the natural course of disease or to make good a disability. A natural law basis for ethics could equally claim that this is the product of human reason, and that the development of medicine is therefore a natural human function, given the desire to relieve suffering.

- A further ethical line to be considered here might be the right of the individuals concerned to have certain experiences in order to further their own personal development. You might wish to ask at this point whether 'motherhood' or 'fatherhood' is a right that people can claim on the grounds that they will not be fulfilled as a person unless they experience it.

- In the UK, 90 per cent of all treatments for infertility are undertaken privately, and are quite expensive. Should infertility be considered an illness, for which there should be free treatment?

Is infertility a 'disease'?

Commenting on the issues of funding for the National Health Service, Lord Winston suggested that realism was needed about the costs or treatment and who should pay, arguing that patients must eventually be required to contribute to the cost of their treatment. But he also commented on the lack of funding for fertility treatment, arguing that childlessness should be considered a 'disease', and was not presently given the priority it deserved.

(As reported in *The Independent*, 6 January 2006, page 24f)

- If childlessness is a disease, is there a 'norm' to which all people may expect to conform?
- Should having small breasts or large feet be considered a disease worthy of treatment?
- Should embryo selection be a suitable treatment for those who are 'diseased' by having too many children of one gender when they would have preferred to have a child of the other?

These may be extreme examples, but it does raise the ethical issue about what is normal and what is 'disease' and therefore deserving of treatment.

5 In the course of in-vitro fertilization, several eggs may be fertilized successfully. If more than one of these is implanted successfully the result is a multiple birth. There is therefore a limit to the number of fertilized embryos that can be used immediately. The remainder could be frozen to be used later, discarded, or used for research.

- The embryo has the potential to become a person – indeed, it already has the genetic information that will determine all the characteristics of that human being into which (given the right conditions) it will grow. Should it therefore be treated as a person? Is it right to discard a 'person', or to use him or her for research?
- In the normal course of events only about 60 per cent of embryos actually succeed in establishing themselves in the womb and growing into babies, and in the case of in-vitro fertilization the success rate is much lower. In depriving a 'spare' embryo of implantation, we are not depriving it of a certainty of development, but only of a possibility.
- If the embryo does not become a human being at the point at which it is fertilized (and therefore genetically defined), at what point does this humanization come about? This point is debated especially in the context of abortion, but it applies equally to all issues of fertility and the very early stages of life.

Choosing the sex of a baby

When conception takes place 'in vitro', embryos of both sexes may be produced, and since a selection is taken from these for implantation in the womb, it is possible to select either male or female embryos, or a mixture. It would therefore be possible to choose the sex of the child to be brought to birth.

There is a valid medical reason for selecting embryos by sex (e.g. to prevent the continuation of genetically transmitted diseases – muscular dystrophy, for example, affects only boys). More controversial would be selection in order to fit the social requirements of the parents, perhaps as a result of cultural pressure to produce male offspring.

The fundamental issue here is whether, at the point at which a child is conceived, that child is to be an end in itself or a means to an end (to use the important distinction set out in Kant's second version of the Categorical Imperative). Clearly, to choose a child of a particular sex for social reasons would be to put the preferences of the parents ahead of the naturally random selection of male and female in the natural process of conception and birth. Any child born for some already determined purpose – e.g. to be a male heir – is to treat that child as a means to an end. Only if that child is free to develop equally as male or as female is it treated as an end in itself.

Of course, it could be objected that this is not limited to situations of artificial conception. How many children are born without being subject to some degree to their parents' hopes for the future? It is extremely difficult for any parent to stand back and let their offspring be absolutely autonomous human agents.

Abortion

Of all the ethical issues people face today, abortion is probably the one that most clearly illustrates the contrasting bases upon which moral judgements are made. The facts are not in doubt, the arguments have been presented time and again, and yet there is no consensus view.

The issue of abortion can be approached logically, pragmatically, or from the standpoint of the personal, physical and emotional needs of the woman who seeks the abortion. It can be seen as an intensely personal issue, or one that is a touchstone for the protection of human rights throughout society. Abortion may be seen on one side as a woman's right, and on the other as the first step towards compulsory euthanasia, selective breeding and wholesale denial of the uniqueness and rights of each human person.

Abortion has frequently been presented, from a feminist standpoint, as an issue of personal choice and freedom. As the growing foetus is essentially still physically part of her, should a pregnant woman not be free to make decisions as to its future? Both abortion and contraception are close to the original agenda of feminism, because childbearing lay at the heart of the imposed domesticity of women. Taking charge of one's own fertility was seen as a major step in the direction of freedom and equality.

British law requires that the agreement of two doctors be given for a pregnancy to be terminated. Abortion can be legally permitted if the foetus is seriously defective, if the risk to the health of the mother from having the child is considered greater than the risk of the termination, and if the birth of the child would have a seriously damaging effect on the mother, taking into account the psychological and social situation of the mother and other members of the family.

Abortions can take place (according to British law) up to 24 weeks after conception. However, they can be performed after that if there is a risk that the mother will be permanently injured by continuing with the pregnancy, or if the child is seriously handicapped.

An anti-abortion argument
Both the ancient Greeks and Romans killed weak or deformed babies by exposing them to the elements. This was justified ethically by both Plato and Aristotle, on the grounds that death was to be preferred to a stunted life.

Christianity opposed this, on the grounds that each person had an eternal soul, and was made in the image of God. The decision about when a person should die was to be left to God alone. The crucial question: When does human life start? If the foetus has a 'soul' then it should be protected.

St Augustine thought that the foetus was 'animated' (received its soul) 60 or 80 days after conception. English law originally followed this principle, and distinguished between abortions before and after 'quickening' – the time when a mother might feel the movement of the child within her.

At the moment of conception, when the ovum is fertilized, a unique genetic code is fixed, which will determine the characteristics of the individual. Does this mean that a 'person' should be considered to exist – and therefore protected and given rights – from that moment?

A problem – twins

There are three stages at which the tiny bundle of cells that can become a human being may divide and produce two or more individuals:

1 It can happen on about the fourth or fifth day after conception – this is at about the eighth cell division. In this case, each twin will go on to develop its own placenta.

2 It can happen around the time when the bundle of cells becomes implanted in the womb. In this case, the twins will have the same placenta, and may be identical.

3 It may happen at about the twelfth or fourteenth day, by which time the resulting twins will have to share the same amniotic sac, and may be joined ('Siamese twins').

The genetic code is established at conception. But at any stage through until about the fourteenth day, one could not say whether that genetic code was going to result in a single or multiple birth. Is it therefore reasonable to say that there is a unique human person before the possibility of twins forming?

There are cases of cells dividing to form twins and then, during this early stage, coming together again to result in a single birth. If each is an individual with rights from the moment of conception, does this mean that the surviving foetus is guilty of murder? Of cannibalism, even, if it has absorbed another human individual into itself?

This situation highlights the problem of taking genetic identity as the unquestioned basis of human individuality.

The problem over the separation of twins does not preclude the idea that from the time of conception there should be respect for (or even human rights given to) an embryo, but it does raise questions about exactly when human identity is established.

In Britain (following the 1990 Human Fertilization and Embryology Act) the age limit for abortions was lowered to 24 weeks (except in exceptional circumstances, where the health of the mother is seriously threatened). In the USA the Supreme Court decision of 1973 set the time limit for abortions at six months. The general recognition here is that it is wrong to kill a foetus if it is capable of surviving independently. At this point, it receives the right of protection as a separate human being. The point made by the anti-abortionists is that such right of protection should be extended back to the earliest stages of conception.

It could be argued that many pregnancies are terminated naturally, which might make an abortion an 'elected miscarriage', and that therefore there is no reason why an individual foetus should be protected. But this argument is not logical. Human beings are being killed naturally all the time. If I stab someone through the heart, I cannot plead in my defence that many people suffer sudden cardiac arrest, and that I am simply electing that the person should die in that particular way. To induce a cardiac arrest is an action for which I would be morally responsible. To terminate the life of a foetus is also an action for which moral responsibility should be taken, irrespective of whether or not nature might have done the same thing.

Those who oppose abortion also point out that, once life is devalued at one particular point, then all life is under threat. They may present abortion as a touchstone for assessing issues like involuntary euthanasia, or even eugenics (selective breeding). Once the principle is established that it is legally and morally acceptable to destroy life in one particular, then life in general is threatened.

The pro-freedom argument
This argument is not presented as pro-abortion, because very few people would actually choose to have an abortion. It is not regarded as a 'good' to be sought, but rather as the lesser of two evils. The argument is about who should decide whether an abortion is to be carried out.

Those who say that a woman should be free to decide whether or not to have an abortion generally do so on two grounds:

1 That the foetus is essentially part of a woman's body until it is capable of independent life, and that the potential mother therefore has total moral right to do what she wishes with her potential offspring, simply because, at this stage, the life is seen as potential, rather than actual.
2 That giving birth to children should be seen in terms of the overall situation in which a woman finds herself. She should be free to decide that her own personal development will be stunted by continuing with the pregnancy, or that the financial and social circumstances into which the child would be born would be such that perhaps the whole family might suffer as a result.

In part, this argument is utilitarian – weighing the loss of the potential life now against the benefits to the mother and others.

In utilitarian terms, those who justify abortion generally use an act utilitarian approach, whereas the anti-abortionists use a rule utilitarian approach. Even where benefits in this particular situation appear to go in favour of abortion, a rule-utilitarian view might be that the right to destroy life in one situation threatens life everywhere, and that the greater good is achieved by giving all life a chance to develop.

Arguments about abortion may therefore involve all the forms of ethical justification so far outlined. 'Natural law' is used to protect the unborn child; utilitarianism in both forms is used to assess the result of the abortion, personal development and the freedom of an individual in a 'right to choose' argument.

Because women are so intimately involved with the process of conception, pregnancy, birth and child-rearing, the ethical discussion of abortion tends to highlight other issues in terms of women's rights and their role in society.

Euthanasia

The word euthanasia means literally 'good death', and it is used in situations when death is deliberately chosen. Euthanasia is not a term that applies to situations where death happens by accident (a person with a painful illness might be killed in a motor accident), nor where death occurs as the secondary effect of, for example, failed medical treatment.

Euthanasia may be divided into four categories for purposes of ethics:

1 **Suicide.** This is self-administered euthanasia. Suicide is not illegal (although it may be considered morally wrong), but helping someone to commit suicide is illegal.
2 **Voluntary euthanasia.** This is carried out at the request of the person who wishes to die but is not able to commit suicide, or for a person who is no longer able to ask to die but has left instructions that he or she wishes to be helped to die in certain circumstances.
3 **Involuntary euthanasia.** This is when someone is killed in order to save him or her additional suffering, and when, in spite of being able to ask to die, the person has not actually done so. Like a child's visit to the dentist, it is imposed 'for his or her own good' but possibly against his or her wishes.
4 **Non-voluntary euthanasia.** This is the killing of someone who is not in a position to ask to live or die (e.g. a person in a long-term coma following severe brain damage).

In practice, you can divide euthanasia into 'active' and 'passive'. **Active euthanasia** involves an action taken to end life, e.g. the giving of a lethal injection. However good the motive, it is 'killing'. **Passive euthanasia** is 'allowing someone to die' by withholding treatment and letting nature take its course.

- Under British law, a person has the right to refuse treatment as long as he or she is fully competent to make that decision.
- If a patient is not in a position to ask for or refuse treatment (e.g. if unconscious) then a doctor can decide to withhold treatment. He or she is not required to consult with the patient's relatives about this, although it is considered good medical practice to do so.
- If a person dies as the result of treatment being stopped, relatives could be in a position to sue the doctor concerned. Because of this, a doctor can apply to a court of law to ask for a ruling on whether or not to discontinue treatment. The legal decision is a safeguard for the doctor.

It is often assumed that passive euthanasia, in the sense of simply 'allowing to die' by withholding treatment, is a less contentious issue than actively taking steps to end a person's life. However, some (e.g. James Rachels, in his book *Can Ethics Provide Answers?*) have argued that ethically they are not so far apart, and that if the first is permitted there is a good case for the second to be permitted as well. There is another important element (presented by Rachels), namely that the process of natural death once treatment or life support has been removed might well be long drawn-out business, whereas a simple administration of a lethal drug is more likely to be the quick and painless alternative. Accepting only passive euthanasia does not therefore represent an 'easy way out' in moral terms.

- In the Netherlands euthanasia is available, although it is not strictly legal. Under guidelines drawn up by the Royal Dutch Medical Association, two doctors have to be involved and, having helped someone to die, they must inform the Dutch equivalent of the Director of Public Prosecutions that they have done so. It is accepted that no charges will be brought against them.
- In Australia's Northern Territory, 22 carefully worded questions, published in 1996 and designed to protect against subsequent civil, criminal or disciplinary action, take doctor and patient through to the decision about voluntary euthanasia. For example, the person requesting euthanasia must be of sound mind and must have thought about the implications for his or her family.

- In 1967 in the USA, a lawyer called Luis Kutner coined the term 'living will' for a document that sets out the conditions under which a person wishes to be allowed to die. Since then many millions of Americans have drawn up such a will, and most states have passed laws that protect the rights of someone who is dying to have his or her wishes followed. The suggested wording for this was:

> *If I should have an incurable or irreversible condition that will cause my death within a relatively short time, and am no longer able to make decisions regarding my medical treatment, I direct my attending physician ... to withhold or withdraw treatment that only prolongs the process of dying and is not necessary to my comfort or to alleviate pain.*

Any justification of suicide and voluntary euthanasia is generally made on the grounds that death is preferable to the suffering that would be involved if the person continued to live – in other words, it is based on expected results (relief from anticipated pain). This may be related to the pain – physical or emotional – that the individual suicide may be experiencing, or it might be the suffering of other people that the suicide seeks to avoid. For example, a person may sacrifice his or her life in order to give others a better chance of survival in a situation where the means of supporting life are limited. Equally, a person may be prepared to die in a suicide mission in order to support a political cause. In these cases, too, the basis in ethics is the expected results of the action.

Notice, however, that the suicide bomber or other person who gives his or her life in order to achieve some political goal, is in a very different situation from anyone contemplating suicide or seeking euthanasia in the face of a serious illness. The one is motivated by religious or political ideology – an ideology that takes precedence over the life of that individual. The other depends on the assumption that the individual life must be respected, even if that life becomes intolerable. And such respect can be shown on both sides of the euthanasia argument, either by allowing a person to die sooner with dignity, or in offering better palliative care to allow the final stage of life to be a positive experience.

Gladiators ...

An examination of the remains of 67 Roman gladiators, found in a cemetery in Turkey, showed that wounded men were carried from the arena and their sufferings ended quickly with a hammer blow to the head.

A traditional Catholic and natural law approach would argue that suicide goes against the idea of humanity as the 'faithful steward' of a life given by God. In other words, by seeking death one is avoiding the natural course of one's life, and the potential for making creative use of whatever happens, even if that involves suffering or personal distress. An exception to this might be the case of a religious person who is prepared to become a martyr rather than renounce his or her faith. In this case, the law of double effect comes in again – the person does not choose to die but to maintain his or her integrity. The death penalty is a secondary result, not the intended end of that act of defiance.

The Oath of Hippocrates, originating from the fifth century BCE and taken (in one of a number of modern forms) by doctors, requires them to promise 'to give no deadly medicine to anyone if asked, nor suggest any such counsel'. The problem here is that many medical treatments and drugs are 'deadly' if given in sufficient quantity, and there is a balance to be struck, especially in the case of those suffering from terminal illnesses, between giving sufficient drugs to keep them pain free, and actually shortening their lives by doing so. In this case, the ethical principle used is 'the law of double effect' – you are responsible only for the intended result of your action, not for any secondary or unforeseen results. In this case, a doctor may feel justified in increasing the dose of a painkilling drug to the point at which the drug becomes lethal, simply because the alternative is to allow the patient to remain in intolerable pain. The intention is not to kill, simply to remove pain.

In the case of non-voluntary euthanasia, you need to decide when a life begins and when it ends. Is a person who has been in a coma for a number of years actually alive? He or she may have natural functions – breathe, have a heartbeat and some residual brain activity – but is that really what we mean by human life?

Right-to-life boy 'has intolerable existence'

Under that headline, an article in *The Independent*, 7 March 2006, described an application made in the High Court by doctors who argued that the 17-month-old boy in question was being kept alive by a ventilator, was in 'a wealth of discomfort and pain', and that the machine should therefore be turned off. He is suffering from an incurable degenerative muscle-wasting condition, is almost completely paralysed, but does not appear to be mentally impaired. The parents, however, argued that the boy enjoyed their visits, and that steps should be taken to prolong his life.

This is thought to be the first time that doctors have asked to turn a machine off in the case of someone who is not in a 'persistent vegetative state'. The problem is that nobody knows just how much the child is aware of, since he cannot respond.

- Does the fact that the child is mentally sound make any difference to the ethical validity of what the doctors or parents want?
- Legally, the Court will decide. But who morally should take ultimate responsibility for what happens – parents, doctors or the Court?

Judgement in the case was given on 15 March. Against the arguments of the doctors, it was ruled that the machinery supporting the child's life should not be switched off. The judge said that, since the child was conscious, and since it had been argued that he could feel pain, it was equally possible that he might feel pleasure, and that he might understand the sights and sounds that his senses were picking up, as any other child of that age. At the time of writing, it is likely that this landmark ruling will go to appeal.

'Pro-life' campaigns, although generally focused on the issue of abortion, are relevant here. If you argue that human life begins at the moment of conception and ends at the moment of death, and that the person should be treated as a full human individual between those two moments then, whether you are dealing with an unborn child or an unconscious adult, that individual should be protected in exactly the same way as a conscious adult. In this respect abortion and euthanasia are often linked, and the ethical basis for this position is 'natural law' – it is not that the unborn child is going to be happier by being born, nor that the unconscious patient is going to experience benefit by being kept alive: it is simply that, by virtue of being a human individual, one should be allowed to fulfil one's natural life.

Voluntary euthanasia societies generally argue that euthanasia should be allowed if:

1 a person is diagnosed by two doctors as suffering from an incurable illness, likely to cause pain, distress, etc., and

2 a person has made a written request for euthanasia if the situation above should occur, at least 30 days beforehand.

The moral basis for this position is respect for the human individual and the right of the individual to have his or her wishes followed.

Euthanasia illustrates the ethical division between 'natural law' arguments and those based on 'situation ethics'. In the latter, a person should do whatever love requires in a particular situation – and that may allow euthanasia, both voluntary and non-voluntary.

Underlying almost all of the points that have been made above is the basic question of whether human life has an intrinsic value and, if so, how that value is defined. Quantity of life? Quality of life? Integrity of the individual? Contribution of the individual to society?

Example

On 24 January 2006, Anne Turner, a retired doctor, ended her life with the help of Dignitas, a Swiss clinic that specializes in assisted suicide. She had been suffering from a progressive degenerative disease, and was determined that she did not want to continue living through its final stages, the implications of which she understood and found intolerable. With her three grown-up children to support her, she went to Zurich, and celebrated the final days with a concert, a meal together and champagne. Then she drank a mixture of barbiturates, prepared for her by the clinic, fell asleep within five minutes and was dead half an hour later. Her son, coming out from the flat where the suicide took place, shortly after her death, said:

'She was ready to go and that makes it all the easier for us. We will respect her choice and we will miss her very much. We are very thankful that her suffering is over.'

From an article by Jeremy Laurence in *The Independent*, 25 January 2006, p. 11

Genetics

We shall focus here on two advances in genetics that raise ethical issues: the identification of the function of particular genes, leading to the draft publication of the human genome in 1999, and the cloning of Dolly the sheep in 1997.

Genetic privacy

Genes are essentially a code that describes the way in which our bodies are put together, their characteristics and their susceptibility to disease. The vast amount of information given on the human genome – the sequence of 70,000 working genes in human DNA – provides a resource that could transform medicine, both by predicting disease and by producing genetic modifications to counter it. In theory, the DNA taken from any cell in the body can describe the present and future health of that individual.

A key ethical question here concerns the right of an individual to his or her own genetic information, and the right to keep that information private. Let us take two examples of the possible abuse of such information by a third party:

- Insurance companies work on the basis that the future is unknown. Although loading premiums against smokers, drug abusers and those with dangerous occupations or who take part in dangerous sports, insurance is based on the average life expectancy of a male or female of a particular age. But what if an insurance company insisted that everyone applying for life insurance should submit to a DNA test to reveal their probable future health and length of life? Would not that be an infringement of privacy?

- Employers like healthy employees; those who develop chronic illnesses are a drain on company resources. What if an employer insisted on a DNA test as a condition of employment? Might that render some people unemployable, simply on the basis that they might at some future date develop a disease? If the individual knows this information, should he or she be forced to reveal it?

In any case, would you want to know your likelihood of developing disease? What consequences might that have for your relationships with family and friends? Would you go ahead and marry someone if you knew that they had a genetic predisposition to a particularly unpleasant disease?

The potential of genetics for aiding the treatment and prevention of cancer and other diseases is enormous. But what is becoming increasingly clear is that these advances will bring with them ethical problems in terms of how the increased information that technology provides is to be handled.

Choosing the future

Another issue related to genetic information is the possibility of predicting, and possibly manipulating, the future of a yet unborn child. We have already considered the issue of choosing the gender of a child through the selection of embryos fertilized 'in-vitro' for implantation. With genetics, the range of selection extends to particular physical features. Would it be right to select the appearance of a child, or to terminate those that did not fit our requirements?

The key issue here is related to the second of Kant's general ethical principles, that people should be treated as ends in themselves, never as means. Following Kant, it would be wrong to choose to have a child produced exactly to fit our requirements, for this would take away the child's autonomy – it would be a mere extension of ourselves. Of course, it should be recognized that this happens anyway, in terms of training and education and the aspiration that a child will hold particular values or follow a particular career. But genetics could add a whole new dimension to such 'designer children'.

Example

In 1999, the Human Fertilization and Embryology Authority published a consultation paper on 'pre-implantation genetic diagnosis'. Where an embryo is the result of artificial fertilization, it can be checked and will be implanted in the womb only if it has no genetic abnormalities. This technique has been used to screen out serious conditions such as cystic fibrosis and muscular dystrophy. But it could equally be used to select embryos by sex or intelligence or susceptibility to illnesses later in life. In effect, the debate is about which conditions are sufficiently serious to warrant the destruction of that embryo.

Clones

The immediate reaction of the media to the successful cloning of Dolly the sheep in 1997 was a flurry of speculation that human cloning was just round the corner, raising a whole raft of ethical problems.

Identical twins are effectively clones, in that they are genetically the same; the artificial process of cloning produces identical twins who are not the same age. Just as identical twins above a certain age develop their own characteristics and identity, so clones would not grow up to be the same in all respects. Nevertheless, there are some fundamental problems with human cloning:

- Dolly the sheep was created by cell fusion, in which the nucleus of an already differentiated adult cell was fused with an unfertilized egg from a donor animal. Of the 430 attempts to do this, 277 reconstructed embryos were produced, 23 of which developed sufficiently to be introduced into 13 foster mothers, and only one (Dolly) was successfully taken through to term. There were many severe genetic abnormalities, leading to miscarriage. Imagine the scale of emotional suffering involved if this process, in its present form, were used on humans.

- The decision to produce a child that is a clone of oneself, or of one's partner, in itself produces moral dilemmas. Can such a child be an autonomous individual? This is a more extreme version of the selection or manipulation of particular genetic characteristics in the unborn, mentioned above. Imagine a family in which a son is the clone of his father, a daughter of her mother. The middle-aged father would see in his daughter the exact image of the woman he married 20 years earlier; the mother would bring up a younger version of the man with whom she fell in love. Is this likely to be an emotionally healthy family situation?

- Hitler had a particular view of the ideal Aryan family. Those who did not fit that image were considered to be a disease, infecting the pure Aryan stock. The results of that view are well known: the holocaust, selective breeding, and kidnapping of children with the right characteristics. Now, one would not suggest that cloning would follow the horrors of Nazi eugenics, but it does reduce the variety of the human genetic pool. Sexual reproduction is constantly throwing up new genetic variations, some good, some bad. That's how evolution works. Without variations a species cannot progress.

Although there may be scope for cloning techniques to be used as a way of overcoming infertility, allowing a child to be born with the genetic characteristics of the infertile partner, the overall complexity and failure rate of the process, the diminishment of the human genetic pool by reducing human variety, and the threat to the autonomy of individuals would suggest that, with our present state of knowledge, cloning remains both ethically and practically inferior to sexual reproduction – and less fun!

Cloned animals 'safe to eat'

In April 2005, Professor Jerry Yang of the University of Connecticut, following a study into proteins and nutrients in meat and milk from cloned cattle, found no significant differences between the cloned and natural products, and therefore considered the former to be equally safe for human consumption.

Does this justify cloning? How does it relate to animal rights? Does it suggest that cloned animals might, in the future, become an economically viable option to allowing cattle and sheep to reproduce naturally before being fattened up and eaten?

Creating spare tissue

One of the most exciting possibilities raised by developments in genetics is the ability to use adult DNA to create stem cells, which are able to differentiate and grow into any form of cell needed by a body. This enables the production of new and healthy tissue that could replace diseased or damaged tissue. Such techniques could replace transplants, with none of the associated problems of rejection.

This presents relatively few ethical dilemmas if the medium within which the new cells are grown is human. On the other hand, genetically modifying the bodies of animals so that they can grow spare parts for humans raises the possibility of disease being transmitted between species. In such cases, the benefit to an individual of such a technique would need to be balanced against the general threat to the human species posed by animal diseases. It also raises the possibility (patents for which are already filed in the US Patent and Trademark Office in Washington) of genetic manipulation to create creatures that could be up to 50 per cent human, used for menial tasks, drug experiments or the growth of spare parts for human beings. What would be the status of such a creature? Should it have rights?

The final question

By manipulating genes we may be able to eradicate genetically transmitted diseases, promote particular physical qualities and detect and eliminate features we do not like. Genetics already provides a vast source of information about the great variety to be found within humankind.

- The final question is, who decides (and how do we decide) what is a good gene and what a bad one?

Which is preferable for humanity, variety or perfection? Do we shape human life to fit a preconceived ideal? If so, whose ideal should it be? We have an unprecedented amount of information; that is a scientific fact: what we do with it is an ethical question.

Media issues

It is difficult to live in a developed country and not be influenced by the media, whether newspapers, journals, books, radio, television or the Internet. Both the content and style of what is presented have a profound effect on attitudes and assumptions and influence lifestyle. If it were not so, politicians would be less concerned about their media image and businesses less willing to pay for advertising.

We can do little more than list the many ethical issues that are raised here under broad headings.

Content

Facts are seldom allowed to speak for themselves: both in the selection of information put out by the media and in the language chosen and style of presentation used, there is an element of interpretation. Sometimes the particular viewpoint expressed in the evaluation and significance of what is described is obvious – in a party political broadcast, for example. Sometimes both sides of an argument are presented, in an attempt to maintain objectivity and fairness, but more often the particular bias of a report has to be inferred.

Ethical issues here include the rights and responsibilities of the media in reporting events. The right to individual privacy, for example, needs to be balanced against the public interest in disclosure. Objectivity and balance in presentation is one ideal, but so is the need to give a genuine and freely admitted interpretation and evaluation of what is described. There is also the possibility of a genuine conflict of interest between government, the public and those who own or control the media.

Freedom and censorship

Freedom from political control is regarded as essential if the media are to play a positive role within a democratic system.

If those who control the media are to take as their priority the overall interest of society, then they cannot unquestioningly accept the particular interpretation of events presented by any government, pressure group or individual. On the other hand, there is a danger that commercial media simply reflect the interests of those who own them but who are unaccountable to either government or public.

Censorship and propaganda have always been used as tools of government. Sometimes this has been done for what is perceived as the overall benefit of society (e.g. withholding information that might be of use to an enemy or terrorist group) or to boost morale. At other times it may be imposed in order to frustrate the critical evaluation of government or to silence the voice of opposition. The ethical issue here is to assess the overall public good, and this generally is done on a utilitarian basis.

Needs self-criticism?

In China, all newspapers are controlled by the government, and political criticism is therefore limited. In January 2006, a weekly supplement of the *China Youth Daily* was shut down and it editor was required to write a self-criticism (an admission of faults, commonly required by those condemned during the Cultural Revolution in China) and was told that the supplement would not be able to continue to be published until its ideology had been corrected.

Could censorship be justified in a 'rule utilitarian' argument, on the basis that social cohesion and benefits spring from a positive view of the political order? This would be the case, if it were shown that those publishing the 'offending' material represented only themselves, and did not represent a larger constituency.

It is often pointed out that those who investigate stories in the public interest, or who receive information in confidence, should be free from any compulsion to reveal their sources. Two reasons are generally given for this: that the source might be harmed if his or her identity were revealed, and that future investigations would be hampered if potential informants knew that their identity might become known.

Censorship also applies to material that is regarded as unsuitable for public consumption on the grounds that its sexual or violent nature may tend to corrupt. There are two ways of approaching this ethically. One is to ask if there are certain things that should be opposed because they are inherently wrong (e.g. pornography showing violent or sexual abuse of children) and cannot be justified on the basis of individual preference. The other is to attempt a utilitarian assessment of the extent to which it is either desirable or possible for the State to police material of a pornographic nature, and whether its prohibition simply drives it underground.

Example

On 27 October 1999, at the High Court in Belfast, the Lord Chief Justice of Northern Ireland ruled that notes taken by Ed Maloney, the northern editor of the Dublin-based *Sunday Tribune*, of an interview nine years earlier with a man now being investigated need not be handed over to police. He said: 'Police have to show something more than a possibility that the material will be of some use. They must establish that there are reasonable grounds for believing that the material is likely to be of substantial value to the investigations.'

- In this case, the notes were not essential to the murder investigation. But the point is made here that, had they been so, they would have had to have been passed on to the police.
- Does this imply that, if proved relevant, all such notes can be used in a prosecution? If so, to what extent is a journalist free to interview someone without being regarded as potentially an information-gathering service for the courts?

Has a state any right to impose moral standards on its citizens? If so, on what grounds?

Impact

Individuals are influenced by the images with which they are presented. If something is shown in a way that makes it appear quite ordinary (e.g. a television drama showing the taking of illicit drugs), there is a temptation to regard such behaviour as normal, even if it is known to be illegal. The content of what is shown in the media may therefore influence the attitudes of society as a whole. It could be argued that the media can trivialize important topics, and encourage unthinking acceptance of behaviour that should be a matter of ethical scrutiny.

A visual medium such as video or television requires less imagination than reading a book: what may be hinted at with words may be shown in graphic detail on the screen. It may be argued that this desensitizes people to the true significance of what they witness. On the other hand, it is widely believed that, since the Vietnam War, television has had a significant impact on the public perception of the gruesome reality of warfare.

In other words, quite apart from the content, ownership and censorship of the media, the impact of the media on individuals is also ethically significant. They are influenced by it, and that influence should be part of a utilitarian assessment of the good or bad effects of the media.

Business ethics

Although, since the time of Plato, there has been discussion of the different roles of people within society, and although concepts of justice and equality have economic implications, business ethics is a fairly recent addition to the range of topics covered in ethical debate.

There are various approaches to business ethics:

- From the perspective of the individual you can explore what constitutes a fair exchange. For example, is a person paid a fair wage for the work he or she is employed to do? Are goods being sold of a quality that the customer expects? Are the terms of a contract just? Is a business arrangement to the benefit of all concerned or does it reflect a fundamental injustice? What are my obligations to my employer? What, as an employer, are my obligations to my employees?

- At the next level of organization you can explore the ethical behaviour of corporations. What responsibilities should a company have towards those it employs? How are decisions made within the company, and on what basis? Is the maximizing of profits the sole duty of a company, or should it be balanced by other factors?

- Then you can ask about the role of business within society as a whole. What are its obligations in terms of the environment, for example? Does a company have a responsibility to the society within which it is set (e.g. the role of multi-national businesses)? What effect on choices and values does free-market capitalism have? Should businesses be controlled by the state or limited in what they can do (e.g. should companies be allowed to achieve a monopoly position, thus controlling their own market)?

- Finally, there are the most general ethical questions about business and the markets, looking at how the production and distribution of goods, the making and sharing of profits, and the world of market manipulation actually shapes the general lifestyle and ethical outlook of society. It is one thing to supply something that people need, but what is the morality of deliberately using advertising to persuade people that they want something that they really don't need? This leads to questions about the ethics of advertising – is it legal, decent and honest? Does it attempt to mislead in any way?

At one extreme, a free-market view might say that the only responsibility of a company is to make profits for its stockholders. If that company performs some social benefit (e.g. sponsoring a charitable event) it should do so only in order to enhance its public profile or in some other way improve its standing and performance. The social action is not an end in itself, but only a means to an end.

From a newspaper advertisement ...

WEALTH WARNING

Join the only bank with an ethical policy

Your money will never be used to finance the supply of arms to oppressive regimes

... illustrated with an image of a grenade.

Although a good indication of ethical intent, this does leave open the definition of what constitutes an 'oppressive' regime. It reflects a growing desire to put one's money where one's ethical heart is.

Recently, however, there has been an increasing sense that corporations have wider responsibilities to those who own them, are employed by them, consume what they produce, live near them, or are polluted by them. This wider circle of interest – sometimes referred to as the 'stakeholders' – reflects all who are affected in one way or another by what a company does and is reinforced by litigation. It is becoming increasingly common for those who have bought faulty products or whose environment has been adversely affected by a company to take that company to court, seeking damages.

Example

Under American law, employers are liable for sexual harassment in the workplace. In one notable case, a multi-million dollar award was made against a law firm in San Francisco when a secretary who had been taken out to lunch by a senior lawyer accused him of brushing her breast on the pretence of dropping some sweets into the pocket of her blouse!

Where such litigation is possible, companies have a special interest in maintaining good relationships between staff! One Los Angeles law firm specializing in labour law provides 'love contracts' for companies to use if members of their office staff embark on affairs with one another, to the effect that the relationship is fully consensual. Thus prevents either party from taking subsequent legal action.

The ethical arguments are sometimes utilitarian, weighing up who wins and who loses from a particular line of action; at other times they relate to rights and obligations, particularly in terms of employment law. But underlying many of the issues in business ethics is the second of Kant's ethical principles – that people should be treated as ends in themselves, never as means to some other end. Clearly it is very easy to see employees or customers simply as means to making a greater profit, which, according to Kant's principle, would be wrong. On the other hand, an organization that makes a profit for its stockholders but at the same time sees its role as providing a service or commodity that is needed may claim that general welfare is its end, and that the making of profits is the necessary means to bring this end about.

Example

In 1995, Anita Roddick, whose 'Body Shop' chain of stores had already done much to promote the idea of 'green economics', set up the New Academy of Business, to focus on four areas:

- developing international trade in ways that enhances social justice and human rights
- the need to protect the environment and pursue sustainable development
- the responsibilities of business to its local and national communities
- the development of enlightened and creative workplaces.

Advertising

The Advertising Standards Authority receives complaints from members of the public who consider that an advertisement is not honest, or if it offends in some way. The ethical issues concern whether the advertisement defrauds in some way, by promising something that the product cannot deliver, or whether it is sexist, racist or in some other way contravenes accepted norms.

Of course, those who devise adverts try to catch people's attention by the images they use, and these images suggest more than can be said about the product in words – but are the images relevant to the product? One magnificent image was of a bronzed man lounging back in the stern of a sleek powerboat, slicing through blue water; everything to suggest a desirable life (or man, depending on your gender or proclivity). On closer inspection he is seen to be holding a bottle of water, label turned towards the camera. That label is reproduced in the corner of the photograph, with the words 'Serving suggestion'! Nothing illegal in that advert – but it suggests rather more than water is likely to offer you! But when does a hint or a suggested advantage become a deception? Perhaps it is all a matter of taste, of irony and of humour.

> ### Fashion chain's TV fight takes a battering
>
> An article on 25 February 2006 by Susie Mesure, Retail Correspondent for *The Independent*, outlines recent complaints made to the Advertising Standards Authority about the French Connection retail chain's television advertising campaign, which features two women fighting, getting soaked with water, and finally kissing. The sexual content of the advert is obvious, as is the violence. The fight is meant to symbolize a quote from the designer Yves Saint Laurent, who said 'Fashion fades, style is eternal' – so fashion and style, in the form of two women, battle it out. The subtlety is probably missed on most viewers, who – recalling French Connection UK's earlier, debatably dyslexic campaign – think, FCUK that!

Copyright

It is increasingly recognized that business is not just about physical goods and services. Intellectual property is equally important, whether it is the value in a song that is written, a computer game that is devised, a film, book, magazine or design. The value of these things goes beyond the physical object that you can buy. Hence copyright.

If things that are expensive to create in the first place are copied and shared for nothing, then the whole economic base that allowed them to be created will gradually be eroded. Things only get produced if someone pays for them, or if there is money to be made from them subsequently in some way. Selling books, CDs, software and so on is a way of paying back the cost of production and making a profit on the business.

Dan Brown stars in High Court tale of treachery and intrigue

A report by Cahah Milmo in *The Independent*, 28 February 2006, outlines the case of Dan Brown, author of the best-selling *The Da Vinci Code*, who was being sued by the authors of *The Holy Blood and the Hold Grail*, published in 1982, for allegedly using the theory set out in their book as the basis for his novel.

Facts themselves are not copyright, so you can always quote a fact, no matter where you have first come across it. But a narrative, a coherent piece of research, and particularly the actual words used, belong to the original author. Where they are used by someone else, permission needs to be obtained, and the original source of that material should be made clear.

Today, it is all too easy to make illegal copies of copyright material, and because it is easy, people assume that it does not matter. However, a basic utilitarian assessment of the ethics of copyright piracy shows that it cannot be in anyone's long-term interest. Arguments about theft, from whichever ethical perspective, apply equally to copyright theft.

The counter offensive on behalf of copyright owners takes three different forms:

1 Taking legal action against copyright theft.
2 Devising technical means of preventing illegal copying.
3 Creating licensing schemes to allow people, for a reasonable payment, to make a copies, where that is preferred to buying the physical goods themselves.

Following this last route, it is recognized that schools and colleges, for example, will need to make copies of printed material for students to use for their courses, or to put texts up on a college intranet or 'virtual learning environment'. Through getting a licence, such copying becomes legal, and a small payment goes to the publisher and author for each copy that is made. This present book is often copied under licence, and although the author receives rather less than if every student bought their own copy, it provides some compensation for this very convenient way of sharing information.

One of the major battlegrounds in the field of copyright at the moment concerns the illegal downloading and sharing of music through file swapping on the Internet.

Illegal file-sharers fined for the first time in Britain

In the first judgement of its kind in Britain, the High Court found two men guilty of illegally swapping music over the Internet. One was fined £5,000 with costs estimated at £13,500 and the other, who pleaded that he was unaware that he was doing anything wrong, was fined £1,500 plus costs, on the grounds that 'ignorance is not a defence'.

some conclusions

This book has attempted to present a general introduction to some of the major ethical arguments, showing some of the strengths and weaknesses of each in turn. Now, by way of conclusion, I want to draw together some of the themes and to give my own comments and evaluation.

The opening chapter was called 'The Art of Living'. This was intended to emphasize that the process of making moral choices, and the task of reflecting on the possible justification for them, is a creative and personal activity. Sometimes, when immersed in the details of a utilitarian argument, trying to assess consequences in a detached way, one can lose sight of this feature of moral choice. No matter how clearly the predicted results of an action are presented, people make their own decisions, often in what appears to be an irrational manner. They are responding to things that they value, memories of past actions, past hurts perhaps. They feel compelled by impulses, both conscious and unconscious, to do what they feel they must do. They are sometimes prepared to accept painful consequences, even admit that they are foolish – and yet the choice is made. The actual process of moral choice is by no means simple, and ethics (if it is to be not only a comment on how moral choices are actually made but also a guide to how moral choices should be made, which is the implication of most ethical arguments) needs to reflect this.

Ethics – moral philosophy – is a rational activity. It studies moral choices, explores their implications and looks at how they may be justified. And therein lies its inherent weakness. Ethics tends to assume, just because it is a rational discipline, that a single theory may be found to explain the nature of moral thinking and give an overall view of life, by which the results of moral thinking may be assessed. Its ideal is to find a definition of good and bad that will transcend individual preferences, and command universal acceptance. That is fine in theory, and yet it does not do justice to the human complexity of moral choice.

The problem was made more complicated by the narrow definition of meaning that dominated philosophy in the earlier part of the twentieth century. If a meaning of a statement is given only with reference to what can be empirically verified, or to the definitions of words, then there is little scope for the sort of creativity that is found in moral language. We saw in Chapter 02 how ethical thinkers have met this challenge and have come to recognize the variety of uses to which moral language is put – giving commands, registering preferences, expressing emotions. Ethics is too fluid and complex an activity to be confined to a language appropriate to science rather than art.

In the chapter on 'natural law' we saw how rational consideration of the final end and purpose of an object or an activity could be used as a touchstone for whether it was being used or abused: it is designed and intended for one 'right' purpose, and anything else is deemed to be wrong. **Natural law is clear cut, straightforward. It is a 'clean' theory, attempting to cut through the messiness of human experience. But it is also abstract, cerebral and linked to a philosophy that no longer commands universal acceptance.**

When we moved on to utilitarianism, the argument was very different, but the impulse to systematize and quantify remained. The same drive that sought a rational explanation of final causes within the world now struggled with a definitive balance of happiness offered to the maximum number of people. But, again, this rational approach became more complicated because it needed to ask about what constituted happiness, and whether the gains should be immediate or long term, confined to the act or the general rule or the preferences to those involved. It became a quest for results – a quest which, as one event leads on to another, can never be completed.

Common sense tends to go along with utilitarianism: avoiding suffering and giving happiness are, after all, (on an emotional as well as a rational level) deeply embedded in human experience. And yet utilitarianism, in itself, does not seem to be enough. There are so many situations in the world – from the horrors of civil war, to the tragedy of drug abuse – for which, from a logical and utilitarian point of view, there can be no possible justification. Why do those involved not see it? Why do they not stop their spiral of violence and death? Why cannot they accept a utilitarian judgement on their actions, when all the evidence about the consequences of what they do is plain for all to see?

The answer to these questions is that choices are not always rational, and that sometimes they are made in the face of known consequences. The expected results of an action inform, but cannot define, a moral choice – they form part of a moral quandary; factors need to be weighed, and yet the weighing is not the whole of the experience of choice. To describe someone as 'cold and calculating' or 'hard headed' implies a narrow view of human choices and moral responsibility. Such a person could probably give a very definite utilitarian justification of his or her action, **and yet the feeling remains that there is more to the art of living than simply assessing results and acting accordingly.**

But what is this elusive 'more' that transforms an action based on calculated results into an act of creative living, of self-affirmation, of agonizing importance for the individual concerned? Kant approached this 'more' by seeing it as a categorical imperative – as something absolute, not depending on results. We might appear to be conditioned, but we experience ourselves as free. We might not know what the results of our action will be, yet we feel compelled to do it anyway.

Yet Kant offers the most generalized and theoretical of all frameworks for moral choice: that I should will that the maxim of my action become a universal law. Wanting everyone else to be free to make their decision according to the same principles that I choose to apply, makes perfect sense. If I want to do something, I should allow everyone else to have that same choice. I should also make my decision as though I were legislating for a kingdom within which everyone is a free and autonomous agent. **Yet I know that my choice is not, in actual fact, going to be enacted as a universal law, and that I am not legislating for others – and this remains in the back of my mind, even if I try to consider the implications of making it so.** At the end of the day, I go ahead and make my choice as a unique individual. **Universalizing every moral principle, and acting only on those that can be universalized, is likely to produce a lowest common denominator of moral thinking – giving form but not content to what is considered right or wrong. It is hardly the stuff of which 'the art of living' is made.**

Yet alongside this, Kant's second form of the categorical imperative – that everyone should be treated as ends and not only as means – touches another deeply held sense of what is right. Like the presupposition of utilitarianism, that we want to share benefit with all concerned, it touches the common sense bedrock of moral discussion.

We looked at morality from the standpoint of personal development. And here there came a perspective that was closest to the idea of 'the art of living', for here was moral choice being used and justified in terms of its function of creating and expressing the human will. But that perspective alone was not enough – **a world full of egocentric individuals, each determined to pursue his or her own development, is not a welcome prospect.** We therefore explored the social and legal perspective on morality, and then on the global or universal issues and the special problems they raised.

Then we looked at the ways in which the world religions formulated their values and moral principles. Without being able to explore exactly what each religion would say about each moral issue, it was at least clear that some worked on the basis of detailed legislation, others on general rules, flexible social requirements, or on whether an action was skilful in leading to spiritual development. The religions provide a wide measure of consensus on the general values that enhance human life, and each provided its own form of 'the art of living'.

And, in the light of all these ethical theories, we looked at two challenges to moral debate – scepticism and relativism – and noted how these have tended to undermine traditional ethical arguments, whilst recognizing in a multi-cultural, multi-faith world which includes such a wide range of philosophical and political views, consensus in ethics is unlikely.

Finally, we looked at a small selection of the many areas today for which there is an obvious need for ethical exploration and guidance.

Moral progress: illusion or necessary hope?

We live in a world of change; everything evolves, nothing is fixed. Whether we look at the evolution of species or the changes happening in society, we try to make sense of change as though it were a story, and ask about the ending. Faced with change or development we tend to ask 'Where is it going?' Progress – as opposed to random or circular change – implies a direction and an end point.

History is always a story told from a particular perspective; facts in themselves do not make history. In the same way, descriptive ethics – the catalogue of who does what in what society and during what era – does not touch on the fundamental issues of normative ethics. It does not ask if society is 'better' now than in Greek, Roman or Medieval times. We may not burn witches, but do we still torture? Is the freedom to be openly homosexual a return to the enlightened times of the Greek city state, recovering from a temporary period of unfair repression? Is there a new world order emerging, or is universal communication merely giving the opportunity for people to exploit more widely?

If facts alone cannot make a normative moral argument, then facts alone cannot prove that there is moral progress.

Hence, any attempt to prove moral progress will hit the same problem that utilitarianism finds – that there is no end point at which all the evidence is in and we can make a definitive judgement. At that level, moral progress remains an illusion, never unambiguously proved or demonstrated.

And yet ... If there were no sense of progress, of trying to improve a situation or cultivate a virtue, would the sense of right and wrong continue? Is having a conscience compatible with an absence of hope or any sense of what a better life could be? The art of living as a human being involves thinking, creating, hoping, willing; it is always oriented towards the future. **We may look back, but we live forwards**. Without any hope that morality makes sense, the very experience of morality becomes nonsense. In this sense, moral progress is a necessary hope – for without it, the rest of moral discussion loses its significance. There may be no evidence whatsoever that things are improving. But in the face of that bleakness, the moral impulse is to want to make it so – to construct a life according to our intuitions of what is right.

Progress is therefore a bit like freedom; analyse it empirically and it vanishes. I am utterly determined by events beyond my control, and yet I sense that I am free to choose what to do. **In the same way, I have no evidence of progress, but the experience of morality is of constructing a better situation and therefore of willing progress.**

So where does this leave us?

The moral choices people make are based on many things, but they are rooted in an understanding of the nature of the world, and the values that arise from that understanding. For some people this is well thought out and rational; for others it is provided by a religion and accepted ready made; others act instinctively, their understanding and valuation of the world working through their unconscious.

In the broadest sense, this is metaphysics: the quest to understand the meaning and value of the world as a whole. This is the process that lay behind the 'natural law' arguments, but it can be broader than the world view of Aristotle on which that theory was based.

The moment of moral choice is therefore informed by the way in which we generally understand and value life. Iris Murdoch expressed it in this way:

> We act rightly 'When the time comes' not out of strength of will but out of a quality of our usual attachments and with the kind of energy and discernment which we have available. And to this the whole activity of our consciousness is relevant.

> (Iris Murdoch, *The Sovereignty of Good*, 1970, p. 53)

To ask 'What should I do?' implies the question 'What is life for?' Life is constantly changing; nothing, not even our galaxy, remains fixed. We can try to run from this truth – craving absolutes that will justify our decisions for all time – but it is an illusion. Constant change is a reality, and it affects not just the world around us, but ourselves. We are not fixed as individuals, our minds shape the future; the choices we make today define the sort of people we become tomorrow.

We also have to accept that life, however much we shape it to suit our own ends, involves suffering and death. We can work to minimize suffering and promote happiness, but we cannot remove the fact that humans are limited and fragile creatures. Fallibility and failure are not just accidental features of life that should be quickly removed and forgotten; they are a feature of living in this sort of world, in which human aspirations outstrip human abilities.

Every choice we make is informed by many things – hopes, fears, the things we value and the understanding of life that we have gathered through education, the influence of others and personal experience. Whether we recognize this consciously or not, the act of making a moral choice sums up all that we have become.

The relationship between ethics and the moral life is rather like that between literary theory and the creative writer, or between musical theory and the act of composition. Writer and composer use all their feelings, intuitions, values and insights to produce a work of art that is unique. Later, the theorists and critics may analyse it, place it in within categories or the development of a particular style, show influences.

Ethics is rather like that. It analyses moral choices and devises theories to show how they may be justified. It is a valuable process, a useful guide for future action, but it can never fully explain the process of creative living.

taking it further

Further reading

Written particularly for students, the following titles in the *Access to Philosophy* series (Hodder & Stoughton) give a broad introduction to aspects of Ethics:

An Introduction to Philosophy and Ethics	Mel Thompson 2003
Environmental Ethics	Joe Walker 2000
Ethical Theory (2nd edition)	Mel Thompson 2005
Issues of Life and Death	Michael Wilcockson 1999
Sex and Relationships	Michael Wilcockson 2000

Many of the classical texts mentioned in this book are available in paperback (see particularly the *Penguin Classics* series, but several other versions are available of the more popular). See for example:

Plato, *The Republic*

Aristotle, *The Nicomachean Ethics*

Machiavelli, *The Prince*

Hobbes, *Leviathan*

Hume, *A Treatise on Human Nature*

Bentham, *An Introduction to the Principles of Morals and Legislation*

Kant, *Fundamental Principles in the Metaphysics of Morals* and *The Critique of Practical Reason*

Mill, *Utilitarianism*

Nietzsche, *Thus Spoke Zarathustra*, *Beyond Good and Evil*

Moore, *Principia Ethica*

There are also a number of anthologies, including

Johnson, O. A., *Ethics: Selections from Classical and Contemporary Writers*, 7th edition, Harcourt Brace, 1994

For a useful historical perspective on ethics

MacIntyre, A., *A Short History of Ethics*, 2nd edition, Routledge and Kegan Paul, 1997

For an Eastern perspective on ethics

Thompson, Mel, *Eastern Philosophy (Teach Yourself)*, Hodder Headline, 2003

Thompson, Mel and Appelbaum, D. (eds), World Philosophy, Vega, 2002

And for those seeking a clear outline of the moral principles that inform the major world religions

Holm, Jean with John Bowker (eds), *Making Moral Decisions*, Pinter (a Cassell Imprint), 1994

Other useful books include

Mackie, J. L., *Ethics: inventing right and wrong*, Penguin, 1990

Murdoch, Iris, *Metaphysics as a Guide to Morals*, OUP, 1992

Singer, Peter (ed.), *A Companion to Ethics*, Blackwell, 1991

Singer, Peter, *Practical Ethics*, Cambridge, 1996

Sterba, J. P. (ed.), *Ethics: the big questions*, Blackwell, 1998

Rachels, James, *Can Ethics Provide Answers? and other Essays in Moral Philosophy*, Rowan and Littlefield, 1997

Warnock, Mary, *An Intelligent Person's Guide to Ethics*, Duckworth, 1998

For general reference, covering all aspects of philosophy

Honderich, Ted (ed.), *The Oxford Companion to Philosophy*, OUP, 1995

Concise Routledge Encyclopedia of Philosophy, Routledge, 2000

Alternatively, key 'Ethics' in the Amazon website and browse the 24,392 results. Interesting, within the top 20 titles listed there are classic texts by Machiavelli, Plato, Mill and Nietzsche, a new book by A. C. Grayling on the allied bombing of German cities in World War II, a book on choosing children and the ethics of genetic intervention, one on medical ethics, one on counselling, one on nursing, and another on the causing death and saving lives, along with a book on the ethics of the Japanese samurai. Amazon in the USA yields 15,755 results for 'ethics', including three books on business ethics within the top 10, and one classic text – Aristotle. There is no doubt that publications on ethical issues, like the issues themselves, are alive and kicking!

Websites

There are a huge number of sites covering all aspects of ethics – from academic departments offering notes on ethical theories, to single-issue campaign groups. Keying 'ethics' into Google is likely to produce literally millions of sites, but the search can easily by narrowed by specifying particular issues, terms or theories.

The web is constantly changing, but – at the time of writing – the following are just a few of the sites you might find useful in following up issues discussed in this book:

www.bbc.co.uk/religion/ethics/index.shtml gives a summary of a whole range of issues and arguments, and is very clearly set out. This is a useful resource for students wanting a concise summary on a topic.

As with any subject, there is a huge amount of material available in Wikipedia. Just go to the ethics page and start following links: **en.wikipedia.org/wiki/Ethics**

For a huge, authoritative encyclopedia of philosophy: **plato.stanford.edu/contents.html**. But be aware that keying 'ethics' alone into the search engine on this site is going to produce an absolutely vast collection of references. Home in on what you want and be aware of alternative terms – e.g. for 'utilitarianism' the direct reference in the index may be 'consequentialism'.

Easier to use is **www.iep.utm.edu/** the website for the Internet Encyclopedia of Philosophy. Hit 'E', and then 'Ethics' and you are at a good point to start.

Although with a Canadian slant to some issues, **www.ethicsweb.ca** has some interesting and accessible resources, including relevant material on applied ethics for international visitors to the site.

users.ox.ac.uk/~worc0337 is a resource for many aspects of philosophy, maintained by Dr Peter King of Pembroke College, Oxford. Either go to the 'Philosophy around the Web' section, or start with the Simplified Index and go from there.

For those who want information on utilitarianism and its application to a range of issues, see **www.utilitarianism.com**

And finally, a handy way into information on a range of ethical, philosophical and religious topics is **www.rsweb.org.uk/ethics/**, which provides links to a range of other sites, including the Internet Encyclopedia of Ethics, mentioned above. Clink on a basic index entry to be taken to a list of related topics and sites.

If you want to check out my other books on philosophy and ethics, to see additional material of interest to students and teachers, or to contact me with your views, suggestions or questions, log on to: **www.mel-thompson.co.uk**

glossary

a posteriori Used of an argument that depends on sense experience.

a priori Used of an argument that arises prior to, or is not based on, a consideration of evidence from sense experience.

absolutist Used of moral arguments that suggest that it is possible, in theory, to find moral principles that can be applied universally.

agapeism Moral theory based on the application of love to each situation.

ahimsa The principle of non-violence; used in Jain, Buddhist and Hindu philosophy.

altruism The unselfish consideration of others.

amoral An action that, with respect to the person who performs it, is done without reference to any moral system.

axiological ethics The study of the values that give rise to moral choices, and upon which those choices are based.

cardinal virtues Prudence, justice, fortitude and temperance; Stoic principles of the moral life, found in Plato and Aristotle and used also by Aquinas.

categorical imperative Used particularly by Kant, this refers to a sense of absolute moral obligation (c.p. 'hypothetical imperative'). In Kant, it takes two particular forms: that an action is right only if it is possible for the person acting to be prepared to accept the basis of that action as a universal law; that persons should be treated as ends, and not simply as means.

consequentialist ethics Ethical theories based on results (e.g. utilitarianism).

deontological questions Questions about a person's rights and duties.

descriptive ethics This term refers to the description of the social behaviour that may raise ethical issues.

determinism Philosophical view to the effect that every act is totally conditional and therefore that agents are not free.

Dharma This is a Sanskrit word used for 'reality' or 'truth', in the sense of the way in which the world is organized. It is used in both Hindu and Buddhist ethics. For Hindus it means right or appropriate action or duty (i.e. duty that is in line with fundamental reality); for Buddhists it refers to the teaching of the Buddha.

double effect, the law of The principle that an action may be considered right, even if a secondary effect of that action is harmful, or could be considered wrong.

egoism Theories that place the human ego as of primary concern.

emotivism The ethical theory that moral assertions are in fact the expression of emotions, i.e. to say something is wrong means that you dislike it.

hedonism The view that the quest for happiness is fundamental to morality.

humanism A cultural movement stemming from the rediscovery of the classical works of Greek philosophy. Humanist ethics emphasizes the dignity of humankind and the centrality of human reason as opposed to the unquestioning acceptance of tradition.

intuitionism The view that 'good' cannot be further defined (in other words, it cannot be explained by more basic concepts) but only known through intuition.

karma 'Action' in Sanskrit; used of the idea that actions (good or bad) have an effect on the person who performs them. It is found in slightly different forms in Hinduism, Buddhism and Jainism.

logical positivism A philosophical view that accepted as meaningful only those statements that could be verified with reference to sense experience (and therefore argued that most ethical statements were meaningless).

logos The Greek term for 'word', used by the Stoics for the fundamental rationality in the universe and therefore the basis of a 'natural law' approach to ethics.

meta-ethics Second-order statements, explaining the nature and function of ethical language.

metaphysical ethics An approach that relates morality to an overall view of the nature of reality.

natural law The ethical theory based on the idea of the 'final cause' or purpose of things, which defines their proper use.

naturalistic fallacy The common error (pointed out by Hume and G. E. Moore) of trying to derive an 'ought' from an 'is'.

non-cognitive Used of a view that moral claims are related to the emotions and preferences of people who use them, rather than to any objective fact.

normative ethics A study of the moral norms or principles.

preference utilitarianism The utilitarian theory based on the satisfaction of the preferences of the individuals concerned.

prescriptivism The theory that ethical assertions prescribe courses of action, i.e. to say something is 'good' is to recommend that you should do it.

relativism, ethical The view that there are no absolutes, but that right and wrong are relative to each social, historical or cultural context.

situation ethics The theory argued by Fletcher in the 1960s that Christian morality should be based on doing whatever is most loving, even at the expense of traditional moral rules.

teleological ethics Used of any ethical theory based on the expected end or purpose (telos) of an action.

utilitarianism A theory that evaluates morality according to its aim of achieving 'the greatest good for the greatest number'.

virtue ethics A moral theory based on the development and promotion of qualities and virtues that embody the good life.

index